BEYOND DIAGNOSIS

The Wiley Series in

CLINICAL PSYCHOLOGY

J. Mark G. Williams *School of Psychology, University*
(Series Editor) *of Wales, Bangor, UK*

Further titles in preparation: *A list of earlier titles in the series follows the index*

BEYOND DIAGNOSIS

Case Formulation Approaches in CBT

Edited by
Michael Bruch and Frank W. Bond
University College London Medical School, London, UK

Foreword by Ira Turkat

WITHDRAWN

JOHN WILEY & SONS

Chichester · New York · Weinheim · Brisbane · Singapore · Toronto

Other Wiley Editorial Offices

John Wiley & Sons Inc., 111 River Street, Hoboken, NJ 07030, USA

Jossey-Bass, 989 Market Street, San Francisco, CA 94103-1741, USA

Wiley-VCH Verlag GmbH, Boschstr. 12, D-69469 Weinheim, Germany

John Wiley & Sons Australia Ltd, 33 Park Road, Milton, Queensland 4064, Australia

John Wiley & Sons (Asia) Pte Ltd, 2 Clementi Loop #02-01, Jin Xing Distripark, Singapore 129809

John Wiley & Sons Canada Ltd, 22 Worcester Road, Etobicoke, Ontario, Canada M9W 1L1

British Library Cataloguing in Publication Data

A catalogue record for this book is available from the British Library

ISBN 0-471 97525-7 (cased)
       0-471-98222-9 (paper)

Typeset in 10 / 12pt Palatino by Dorwyn Ltd, Rowlands Castle, Hants.
Printed and bound by Antony Rowe Ltd, Eastbourne
This book is printed on acid-free paper responsibly manufactured from sustainable forestry in which at least two trees are planted for each one used for paper production.

For VIC MEYER and TED CHESSER

CONTENTS

ABOUT THE EDITORS

Michael Bruch is a Senior Lecturer in Psychology and Consultant Cognitive–Behavioural Psychotherapist in the Department of Psychiatry and Behavioural Sciences, University College London. His main research interests involve conceptualisation of complex disorders, psychotherapy training and supervision, and case formulation. He is also joint course director in the University College London CBT unit and provides teaching, supervision and consultation to universities and psychotherapeutic institutions.

Frank W. Bond, BA, Diploma, MSc, PhD, is a Research Fellow in the Department of Psychology, Goldsmiths College, University of London. His main research interests include (1) examining the validity of various behavioural and cognitive–behavioural psychotherapy theories. In addition, Dr Bond (2) investigates how different organisation-directed and individual-directed worksite stress management interventions affect worker well-being and organisational effectiveness. Dr Bond also conducts psychotherapy and is a consultant to organisations.

LIST OF CONTRIBUTORS

Peter G. AuBuchon   *The Agoraphobia and Anxiety Treatment Center, 112 Bala Avenue, Bala Cynwyd, PA, 19004, USA*

Frank W. Bond   *Department of Psychology, Goldsmiths College, University of London, New Cross, London SE14 6NW, UK*

Michael H. Bruch   *Department of Psychiatry and Behavioural Sciences, University College London Medical School, Wolfson Building, Riding House Street, London W1N 8AA, UK*

Gerald C. Davison, PhD   *Department of Psychology, SGM 501, University of Southern California, Los Angeles, CA 90089-1061, USA*

Windy Dryden   *Department of Psychology, Goldsmiths College, University of London, New Cross, London SE14 6NW, UK*

Michael K. Gann   *Department of Psychology, SGM 501, University of Southern California, Los Angeles, CA 90089-1061, USA*

David Lane   *Professional Development Foundation, Studio 21, Limehouse Cut, Morris Road, London E14 6NQ*

Victor Malatesta   *The University of Pennsylvania School of Medicine, 111 North 49th Street, Philadelphia, PA 19139-2797, USA*

Hans Reinecker, PhD   *Institut für Psychologie, Universität Bamberg, Markusplatz 3, 96 045 Bamberg, Germany*

Ira D. Turkat, PhD   *Florida Institute of Psychology & University of Florida College of Medicine, 1111 Avenida Del Circo, Venice, FL 34285, USA*

FOREWORD

The clinician who endeavors to help a person change problematic behavior, sooner or later will have the think about the task to be undertaken. Such "thinking" is the cornerstone of the present text.

When I was a graduate student in the 1970s, I was struck by the lack of useful manuscripts available on how clinicians conceptualize clinical phenomena. I became determined to change that. With the help of individuals such as Henry Adams, Victor Meyer, Monte Shapiro, and Joseph Wolpe, I expended a good deal of energy attempting to develop a literature devoted to this topic. Today, as we approach the new millennium, I am deeply gratified by the contents of the current volume.

The clinician who reads this book will be grateful for the very practical information offered. The researcher who seeks a novel area to investigate will find the present text replete with interesting hypotheses, ripe for exploration. The practitioner who aims to participate in the scientific process but lacks the resources to conduct well-controlled group research, will find exemplary models for contributing to the psychological literature.

The ultimate goal of clinical psychology should be to prevent psychopathology from occurring. To do so, we will need to understand what causes these disorders in the first place and why they continue to be exhibited. This understanding presently eludes us. By focusing on how to "think" about clinical phenomena, the following pages guide us down the right path.

Ira Daniel Turkat
Venice, Florida

SERIES PREFACE

The aim of the Wiley Series in Clinical Psychology is to provide a comprehensive collection of texts which together illustrate the range of ways in which the science of psychology may be applied to problems in mental health. Some years ago, when the Wiley Series was in its infancy, I carried out an informal survey among those responsible for training in clinical psychology, asking them what books were most lacking for helping them in their teaching on postgraduate courses and programmes. "Books to help trainees understand how to do a proper formulation" was the most consistent reply. The reason for this perceived need was not just the lack of good texts. It also arose from the uncomfortable feeling that although a case formulation approach remained one of the most distinctive things that a clinical psychologist did, the skills were in danger of withering on the vine unless re-newed, re-taught, and passed on. As the quote from Professor Rachman in the Editors' Preface notes: "the omission of a case formulation can leave the clinician, and the patient, with an amorphous blur". This volume, edited by Michael Bruch and Frank Bond, draws together several international experts in the field of case formulation. Making clear the debt they owe to the early seminal work by Meyer and Chesser, the chapters trace the development of the field, bringing the reader up to date with the latest evidence to support their view that moving beyond diagnosis in the treatment of clinical problems is essential. The chapters provide numerous clinical examples to illustrate the points being made. This is a book for practitioners, and trainee practitioners. It will be welcomed by those responsible for training the next generation of psychologists since it so clearly and compellingly makes the case for conducting hypothesis-driven interventions that are constantly monitored for their effectiveness. Responding to the knowledge that no two people who seek help are the same, even if they present with similar symptoms, the chapters in this book show how best to analyse and respond to such differences, how to elicit the different causal pathways, and how to clarify the different ways in which problems are maintained, in both adults and children, in straightforward as well as extremely difficult cases.. The book will also be welcomed by undergraduates wondering about a career in clinical psychology. It will be used by many other mental health professionals who see, in this methodology, a way of working with their clients that is truly collaborative, honouring individual's experiences yet asserting the importance of bringing about demonstrable change.

PREFACE

The case formulation process imposes a necessary discipline on the clinician's reasoning and actions, and generally leads to the construction of specific goals and thereby to specific outcome criteria. By contrast, the omission of a case formulation can leave the clinician, and the patient, with an amorphous blur that has no direction and can have no clean conclusion.

S. Rachman

Formulating cases on the basis of individualised assessment was originally proposed by Victor Meyer, the pioneer of individualised behaviour therapy. Over the past 30 years, this approach has been revised several times, and it is now most commonly referred to as *cognitive–behavioural case formulation*. In comparison to many other behaviour therapy developments, this idiographic approach to assessment and treatment originated and developed from the psychiatric setting, not from the laboratory. In the hospital, standardised techniques, or "cookbook" approaches to treatment, appeared largely ineffective in helping people who suffered from very severe psychological problems. From work with these patients, it appeared that an individual-based, case formulation approach achieved better results than did the more ubiquitous approach of "symptom-technique matching", which involves using specific techniques for particular symptoms.

The relative success of case formulations over symptom–technique matching may have occurred for two reasons. Firstly, people often presented with similar complaints (e.g., avoiding social situations). Upon further analysis, however, these individuals often showed tremendous variation regarding the development, manifestation, and maintaining mechanisms of their problems. Secondly, earlier versions of diagnostic manuals did not help the behavioural clinician conceptualise and treat people who had severe, complex, and multiple disorders. These two reasons for the success of the case formulation approach are considered throughout this book.

This text also highlights the significant progress that clinicians have made in developing and improving case formulation strategies. These advances, made by people such as Ira Turkat, David Lane, Michael Bruch, and Victor Malatesta, are detailed and evaluated in this book. By considering these advances, we hope that the reader will see that the case formulation approach is ever evolving but always faithful to its primary philosophy: conducting hypothesis-driven interventions that are constantly monitored for effectiveness.

One aim of this book is to disseminate the many developments and applications of cognitive–behavioural case formulation approaches. In so doing, we hope to provide a helpful response to many requests that we have had from practising clinicians. These queries, whilst diverse, have all expressed frustration with the therapeutic impotence of the many "cookbook" solutions that have been offered for a myriad of psychological problems. We certainly hope that, in in this text, clinicians can discover how their colleagues have developed and improved the case formulation approach to cognitive–behaviour therapy. Hopefully, by being aware of these therapeutic strides, clinicians will be better able to understand and treat their clients.

It is for these reasons (i.e. recent developments and clinicians' enquiries) that we think that it is timely to offer a comprehensive update on cognitive–behavioural case formulation approaches. To ensure that we remain relevant to the clinician's world (as oppossed to the researcher's), all contributors to this volune have placed particular emphasis on clinical examples. Hopefully, these will demonstrate how practitioners can employ the assessment and treatment strategies that authors recommend. Also, by emphasising case examples, we trust that this book will be relevant and informative to people who are training to become cognitive–behavioural therapists. In addition, we believe that this text will also interest any mental health practitioner who is interested in the application of cognitive-behavioural methods to psychological and psychiatric disorders.

The case formulation approach began at University College London about thirty years ago. We do not wish, however, for this book merely to be an account of how the model has evolved at our institution. Rather we wish for this volume to show how different, eminent clinicians have shaped this idiographic approach to cognitive–behavioural psychotherapy. To this end, the contents of this book are as follows.

In Chapter 1, Michael Bruch discusses the development of individualised approaches in behaviour therapy, which are now labelled case formulations. This chapter purpose three, related reasons for the development of these approaches. They centre around: (1) the complex disorders that are found in psychiatric settings; (2) the purpose and limitations of the diagnostic model; and, (3) the relative inadequacy of standardised, behaviour therapy techniques. This chapter also addresses the issue of divergence and similarity in case formulation models.

In Chapter 2, Michael Bruch considers "how to" issues in case formulation by describing the approach and clinical procedures that are practised at University College London. In particular, Bruch discusses the role of the initial interview; how to generate appropriate hypotheses; developing and using the problem formulation; clinical measurement and evaluation procedures; the self-schema model for complex problems; and the role of the therapeutic relationship.

Chapters 3–9 present various cognitive–behavioural case formulation approaches that different clinicians employ. In each chapter, a practitioner details how he conceptualises behavioural disorders. In particular, the specialist discusses how his assessment leads to an individualised case formulation, and to help illustrate his approach, he presents a case example. In describing his formulation process, the author shows how he handles issues concerning: (1) the development of the clinical problem(s); (2) the conceptualisation and implications of multiple problems, if applicable to the case example; and, (3) the conceptualisation of phenomena such as cognitions, emotions, and behaviour. After detailing the problem formulation, each author discusses how it guides a treatment strategy, including the selection and/or development of therapeutic techniques. Finally, authors indicate how they verify the case formulation during the course of therapy.

In order to demonstrate the variety of problems to which case formulations are relevant, we ensured that the chapters in this text cover a diverse range of psychological disorders. Furthermore, several contributors to this book discuss rather difficult clinical examples, in order to show how case formulations can help clinicians conceptualise and treat people with complex problems. We would now like to identify the authors that have contributed to this book and mention, briefly, the types of problems that they discuss.

Windy Dryden, in Chapter 3, is very much concerned with acknowledging and respecting the individual client. To this end, in fact, he rejects the phrase "case formulation", as it indicates to him the "objectification" of the individual. Instead, he prefers the term, "understanding the person in the context of his/her problems" (or UPCP). In his chapter, Dryden emphasises how clinicians cam employ rational emotive behaviour therapy (REBT) to understand and treat people's problems. For he is, as ever, keen to rectify what he perceives as the "continuing marginalisation of REBT" in the cognitive–behavioural therapy establishment. In his case example, Dryden discusses a person who is experiencing problems with anxiety and depression.

Gerald Davison and Michael Gann, in Chapter 4, illustrate very precisely and effectively how a clinician can use a case formulation to understand and treat successfully a person's problem. They demonstrate clearly how their approach is rooted in developing and testing hypotheses about the client's difficulties. Usefully, they show how clinicians often have to work with other health-care professionals when treating a client, and they demonstrate how potential problems inherent in this process can be handled adeptly. The case example that they employ concerns a person who is suffering from social evaluative anxiety.

Frank Bond, in Chapter 5, first details the case formulation approach that is employed at University College London. He then demonstrates its use in conceptualising and treating a person who has generalised anxiety disorder. In his case example, Bond asks his client to examine the unhelpful consequences that result from trying to control negative thoughts, feelings, and sensations. Through this examination, which is integrated into a thorough case formulation, Bond develops an intervention strategy that addresses the hypothesised mechanism that underlies his client's presenting problems.

David Lane, in Chapter 6, provides a very detailed account of the complexities that are involved in treating difficult children and adolescents. His approach is labelled "context focused analysis", and it advocates the need to consider environmental agents such as parents, schoolteachers and social workers, when treating young people. In his chapter, Lane argues strongly for an idiographic approach, when working with troubled adolescents, and he maintains that diagnostic labels do not greatly facilitate effective treatment with this group of people.

Peter AuBuchon and Victor Malatesta, in Chapter 7, discuss the controversial issue of the therapeutic relationship. After a review of this topic, they propose that there is no "correct" type of clinician–client interaction. Rather, they argue that a therapist's "style" should be based upon the client's case formulation. Through two case examples, they demonstrate the benefits of devising an interactive style that is based upon an idiographic analysis of a person. In one of their case examples, they discuss a person who is suffering from obsessive–compulsive problems, and in another one, they present an adolescent whose conduct is a problem.

Hans Reinecker, in Chapter 8, presents a cognitive–behaviour therapy model that emphasises self-regulation and self-management. He demonstrates the usefulness of this model in a detailed case example of a woman who is overly fearful of acquiring AIDS. Reinecker carefully shows how his treatment plan stems from an idiographic formulation of his client and her problem. In addition, he demonstrates the importance of employing constant measures of change, in order to ensure that his treatment interventions are having their desired effect.

Frank Bond, in Chapter 9, addresses the issue of manual-based treatments and case formulation. Specifically, he maintains that any nomothetic treatment protocol needs to be tailored to an individual and that the most efficacious way to conduct this accommodation process is by employing a case formulation approach. Such an approach is recommended, because it necessitates a thorough assessment procedure that promotes hypothesis generation and testing. Bond employs a detailed case example to illustrate his arguements. Finally, he discusses how advocates of a case formulation approach can use nomothetic treatment procedures to enrich their clinical work.

In our judgement, texts on cognitive–behavioural psychotherapy typically detail interventions that address specific symptoms or diagnoses. They fail, therefore, to provide adequate advice on how to identify and treat factors that may actually maintain people's problems. This book attempts to fill this lacuna by providing advice on (and examples of) how to accomplish these critical, therapeutic tasks. In this book, we are not suggesting that diagnosis-determined interventions are unhelpful. (Indeed, Chapter 9 discusses how clinicians can use them effectively.) Rather, we are maintaining that any therapeutic intervention needs to be selected and implemented on the basis of a thorough, idiographic case formulation.

We are grateful to our contributors who have provided excellent examples of cognitive–behavioural case formulation approaches. In a book such as this, we believe that Victor Meyer and Edward Chesser deserve special tribute, for they are surely the "spiritual fathers" of the case formulation philosophy. The senior editor acknowledges the stimulation and support that these men have provided him, and he thanks them for their invaluable contributions to his professional identity. The junior editor would also like to thank these men for their influence, guidance, and support. In addition, he would like to acknowledge the impact and help of the following people in his professional (and personal) development: Aidan Conway, Gerald Davison, Windy Dryden, and Gary Emery. Our thanks also go to Michael Coombs, the senior editor at John Wiley & Sons, who showed great interest in our work and has provided constructive support throughout the whole publishing process. We would also like to thank Lesley Valerio at John Wiley & Sons, for all of her help.

Michael Bruch
Frank Bond
London, November 1997

CHAPTER 1   The development of case formulation approaches

Michael Bruch

> There is nothing as practical as a good theory
> Kurt Lewin

INTRODUCTION

Why beyond diagnosis? Are there limitations with the psychiatric model? How can we define a relationship between psychiatric diagnosis (PD) and case formulation (CF)? To answer these questions it seems appropriate to contemplate reasons and developmental conditions for CF as a clinical approach. This is done with particular reference to the University College London (UCL) model.

Traditionally, clinicians dealing with behavioural disorders, especially in the psychiatric setting, were mostly expected to define and organise their clinical work in terms of nosological categorisation. Prescription for therapy would be decided accordingly. When, in the 1950s, behaviour therapy (BT) arrived on the scene, there seemed little willingness on the part of the medical establishment to change this tradition. However, this attitude caused growing irritation and dissatisfaction amongst (especially non-medical) behaviour therapists as hardly any instrumental value could be found in a classification system that mainly aims at "scientific" order and communication (at times with dubious validity and reliability), but appears less helpful in or even intent on explaining mechanism and directing treatment of respective disorders.

Beyond Diagnosis: Case Formulation Approaches in CBT.
Edited by Michael Bruch and Frank W. Bond.
© 1998 John Wiley & Sons Ltd.

What are the problems with psychiatric diagnosis?

Apart from being merely descriptive, there can be considerable overlap between categories. Despite considerable improvements and refinements over the last two decades (American Psychiatric Association, 1994), this is largely true to this day, as Turkat (1990) has pointed out for the case of personality disorders. For example, when clinicians were asked to sort the criteria for all disorders to the matching categories, they were only able to assign 66% of these correctly, indicating lack of validity and diagnostic overlap (Blashfield & Breen, 1989). Thus, it is hardly surprising that there is a tendency to assign a cluster of categories to presented problems (6–8 in the case of personality disorders).

Perhaps more serious, from a learning perspective, is the lack of interest in understanding in a learning mechanism of disorders. Grouping problems into categories cannot advance this case as learning biographies get blurred. Thus, PD will not enable us to explain onset, development and maintenance of a disorder. Such information, however, is considered to be vital for a learning-based approach.

Another problem with psychiatric classification is the notorious concepts of *mental illness* and *normality* which are essentially value judgements, at least as statistical deviations from a mean. These concepts inevitably imply labelling (e.g. Szasz, 1961) which in itself is counterproductive for learning oriented therapeutic efforts. Despite great efforts towards operationally defined categories in diagnosis, the issue remains contentious, especially for non-medical psychotherapists.

Despite these shortcomings, psychiatrists expressed some interest in BT (Eysenck, 1990), possibly in the hope of finding a symptom-focused technique which could be prescribed in line with medical model thinking. In those days, clinical psychologists were working under psychiatrists and were given limited scope to conduct BT under medical supervision.

However, given this background, it is not surprising that most efforts to develop treatment methods resulted in standardised treatment technologies, usually designed to match a diagnosis for psychotherapy outcome studies, rather than addressing real needs of individual patients. More recently, advances in "operationalised" diagnosis (e.g. DSM IV, 1994) have facilitated the development of more comprehensive disorder-focused treatment manuals. These tend to be more sophisticated as most are developed in clinical settings (see Wilson, 1996, 1997 for discussion). Despite substantial improvements there remain strong doubts as to whether or not treatment manuals will ever be able to address the complexity of individual problems fully, which as yet remain largely untried and untested (Malatesta, 1995a, b; Hickling & Blanchard, 1997). That is not to say that manuals, given of their technical expertise, may not be useful in clinical work (e.g. acquisition of technical skills by trainees) providing adjustments to individual cases can be made (see discussion later in this text).

To conclude, it seems to us that PD was not exactly a fertile breeding ground for clinical BT.

Turkat, rather known for his preference to formulate cases, has nevertheless given two main reasons why behaviour therapists should not reject well-established classification systems, despite their obvious problems (Turkat, 1990).

First, precise communication using operational terms is required if knowledge is going to be advanced in a scientific manner. Second, a taxonomic system whose validity is based on genuine clinical observations may be useful in assisting the process of hypothesis generation and may thus complement the initial interview meaningfully. For these reasons Turkat (1990) proposes that diagnosis and formulation should coexist. This is argued as follows:

> It is important to realise that the formulation of the case refers to the nature in which the presenting phenomena appear (in the clinician's eye) to organise, develop, and most unlikely unfold in the future. Diagnosis, on the other hand, particularly with our present state of knowledge, does not accomplish what a formulation does. Rather, the diagnosis is merely a shorthand description of various behaviours that often coexist in the same individual. In this sense, the diagnosis is merely descriptive, utilised for communication and classification purposes (Adams, 1981). As noted elsewhere (Turkat & Maisto, 1983), the diagnosis and formulation complement each other. They are not the same, nor should they be construed as being the same. It is particularly problematic when one uses a diagnosis as his or her "formulation". I find the term *diagnostic formulation* to be a confusing one. (p.17)

Given the diverse natures of CF and PD, it may seem surprising that early attempts of learning theory experiments took place in psychiatric settings.

Individualised BT using experimental methodology goes back to the very roots of BT itself. Indeed, most pioneers (e.g. Wolpe, 1960; Lazarus, 1960; Meyer, 1960) started out by applying learning principles to the assessment and treatment of clinical cases. It is this body of work which can be considered as the foundations of case formulation.

However, the current label arrived much later. Turkat (1985) introduced the term "case formulation" which is now fairly consistently applied for this concept and practice in the field of behavioural and cognitive therapies (e.g. Persons, 1989, Malatesta & AuBuchon, 1992). For some, however, the term is regarded as controversial (e.g. Dryden, this volume), for allegedly "objectifying" human beings as cases. Nothing could be further from the nature and intentions of CF. Given today's sensitivity regarding politically correct terms, this may not be the most fitting label, however, it is the substance which matters most. In earlier days no distinctive label, other than "individualised" was used, nor did it appear necessary or fashionable in those days. The remainder of this chapter is addressing the origins of this unique clinical development.

THE CONTRIBUTION OF THE MAUDSLEY GROUP

The foundations for clinical–experimental work on the basis of learning principles, both for assessment and treatment, were laid by Hans Eysenck (1990) and his team in the early 50s at the Maudsley Hospital in London. Eysenck's critical account and now famous paper on the effects on psychotherapy and spontaneous remission (Eysenck, 1952) had inspired new psychotherapeutic thinking, mainly guided by experimental and learning psychology. This approach to psychotherapy was subsequently labelled "behaviour therapy". It was timely that this therapeutic innovation coincided with the establishment of clinical psychology in England, also led by Eysenck: Both developments, the "new profession" compatible with a "new approach", formed the basis for strong synergistic effects for years to come.

In the early days, Eysenck strongly encouraged experimental investigation of single cases on the basis of learning principles. This task was taken up by Monte Shapiro (1955, 1957; Shapiro & Nelson, 1955) who pioneered a suitable methodology which allowed assessment and conceptualisation of psychiatric disorders in their clinical context. Its main assumption was that each patient constitutes a scientific problem of his or her own and that the skills of the clinical psychologist were used to solve this unique problem by applying general methods of experimental psychology in a special framework of learning theory.

To elaborate, Shapiro proceeded as follows: patients were interviewed to achieve a precise description of their problem behaviour. Next, it was attempted to quantify these subjective reports with suitable valid measures. Further, learning models were employed to explain the problem under investigation, or new models were formulated on the basis of individual data and learning principles. From here predictions were made which were subsequently tested in clinical experiments, in order to eliminate false hypotheses. Having conducted such a rigorous procedure Shapiro expected to arrive at a valid model of explanation in learning terms which could be subjected to further verification procedures. It is notable that the clinician operates like a researcher in the clinical field, which necessitates a considerable amount of time and resources.

There can be no doubt that Shapiro's experimental method has enabled extensive accumulation of learning-based knowledge in clinical settings. Thus, it can be regarded as the pioneering version of the scientist–practitioner model, which is now universally proposed as the most suitable procedure for CBT. It was appropriate and necessary to carry out such detailed and meticulous work to further the fledgling BT in applied settings.

On the other hand, a number of problems became increasingly obvious with Shapiro's approach. Shapiro himself was of the opinion that his method should be universally applied in clinical practice; however, such views proved misguided as it soon turned out that his aspirations were unrealistic for the clinical practice. Only a small number of clinicians (i.e. the Maudsley group) working in specialised research settings were able or interested to follow his recommendations and protocol. Clinicians working in routine practice, even given strong interest, did not have the expertise, time, and necessary resources to develop models of explanation and individually tailored treatment programmes according to his complicated experimental procedure.

Other problems concerned appropriate operationalisation and measurement of problem behaviours. It turned out that clinicians, if not specially trained, found it difficult to select or even develop suitable instruments for psychotherapeutic evaluation. Instead, there was a tendency to resort to old style psychometry, which is rather designed for assessment of personality traits, diagnostic labelling and statistical comparisons.

Or, therapists were not prepared to subject their interview style or preferred treatment techniques to empirical scrutiny and would continue with procedures which were perceived as effective according to their own experience and convictions. Finally, patients' suffering acutely, were looking for quick results and did not want to participate as guinea pigs in long-winded experimental investigations.

To conclude, despite its creative inventiveness, high scientific standards and potential usefulness, especially for complex problems, Shapiro's method was never fully established as a clinical tool in the field of psychotherapy. Typical examples of early experimental work were published in two separate volumes (Eysenck, 1960, 1964) which still provide

fascinating reading for the student of cognitive–behavioural psychotherapy, as they give good insight into the clinical work of pioneering
behaviour therapists.

THE CONTRIBUTION OF VICTOR MEYER

Victor Meyer, who was one of Eysenck's early students, started practising
as a clinical psychologist in 1955 and dedicated his work to *clinical* BT. He
soon began to realise that BT, with all its scientific ambitions, was moving
away from single case work and was no longer addressing itself to genuine clinical problems any longer. Describing this dilemma he later stated
(Meyer, 1975):

> The emphasis in the literature is on the experimental approach to various
> problems in the field, and the majority of textbooks on BT have been written
> by authors who have little or no experience in the clinical application of the
> principles of BT. As a result, the current literature deals mainly with various
> problems and issues for pure and applied research and prepares the reader
> only to become a research worker in the field. Clinical practice and training,
> and the problems involved in these aspects of BT, are relatively ignored . . .
> thus, would be behaviour therapists find very little help from the literature
> concerning the nature of their duties and the problems pertaining to their
> role as clinicians. (p.11).

To halt this growing trend, Meyer suggested that the following questions
ought to be answered if one was concerned with best clinical practice and
clinical research strategy: *What treatment, by whom, is most effective for this
individual, with that specific problem, under which set of circumstances, and
how does it come about?* Obviously, this was to promote the "scientist–
practitioner" who investigates scientifically but adapts to the clinical setting fully.

Despite Meyer's concerns, research endeavours became increasingly obsessed with developing standardised techniques required and produced
by controlled research trials that were flourishing. It became obvious that
BT was moved further and further away from its supposed clinical base,
in fact researchers started preferring analogue settings, typically investigating students with small animal phobias who were easily accessible in
university research departments. This practice culminated in so-called
"symptom–technique matching", the idea being to select standard
methods to match diagnostic categories, which greatly facilitated research
but was otherwise providing poor clinical outcomes, especially with more
complex disorders. For the clinician, if he was at all able to follow such
academic aspirations, this process provided little guidance in dealing

with the complexities of real clinical problems and raised more questions than it answered.

Meyer (1975) sums up the problems from the clinician's point of view:

> . . . most of the writings on behaviour therapy by "experts" are experimentally oriented and advocate a technological approach to treatment by giving "scientific respectability" to the techniques that have been derived from learning principles and intensively investigated. This no doubt has an influence on the practice of behaviour therapy. It is not surprising, therefore, that many practising behaviour therapists apply certain prescribed techniques to certain psychiatric conditions. Also, psychologists and psychiatrists seeking training in behaviour therapy expect to be grilled in techniques and the range of their applicability. Originally, I did subscribe to this approach, but, after gaining wide clinical experience, I was struck by its considerable limitations and its inappropriateness in many cases (Meyer & Chesser, 1970). The problems of technology are twofold. First, not all patients sharing the same complaint respond to the procedural requirements of techniques. For example, in the case of systematic desensitisation, some patients find it difficult to relax, some fail to conjure up clear images of phobic scenes in relevant modalities, some do not report anxiety to clearly imagined phobic stimuli, and a proportion fail to generalise adequately to real-life situations.
>
> Second, and more important, one seldom finds cases with isolated complaints in psychiatric clinics. It is more likely that one is confronted with a number of complaints and problems that may or may not be directly related to the main complaint presented by the patient; or the main complaint may turn out, according to the therapist's assessment, to be other than what the patient himself believes it to be. (p.16)

Typically, the research oriented behaviour therapist tends to ignore individual differences and is rather concerned about matching group designs to allow, for example, comparison and evaluation of treatment techniques.

Meyer, on the other hand, was rooted firmly as a clinician in the psychiatric setting, where he attempted to apply the fledgling BT to more severe and chronic problems, for example, existential problems, personality disorders and obsessive–compulsive disorders. It was also seen as important to complement clinical work with research and training based in the same setting. In other words, research and training ought to be adjusted to clinical requirements and not the other way round. Meyer (1975) expands on this as follows (Meyer, 1975):

> Thus, as a therapist, I attempt to guide all my activities in terms of learning principles, no matter whether the goal of treatment is to modify motor, autonomic, or cognitive aspects of disordered behaviour. For myself, behaviour therapy is an ongoing process during which observations are collected, hypotheses put forward to account for them, tests of hypotheses

carried out, adjustments to new observations made, and so on . . . the advantage of the approach advocated here is that the clinician would be able to formulate treatment programmes for every patient that would be flexible enough to meet the myriad problems and practical obstacles found when treating patients and would not be obliged to put technical strait-jackets on his patients. It is not the technological approach but the application of the principles that has enabled behaviour therapy to be extended to virtually every type of psychiatric picture. In my opinion, learning principles offer a distinct contribution in the attempt to understand aetiology and to design treatment for psychiatric disorders . . . attempt to structure my approach explicitly and systematically in terms of learning principles. (p.21)

Further, Meyer (1975), pointed to the crucial role of initial interviewing in this approach. He was critical of standardised or over-comprehensive schemes (e.g. Kanfer and Saslow, 1969) which he thought were too distant or cumbersome. Instead of rigid adherence to a one scheme, therapists should be encouraged to develop hypotheses about the nature of the complaint. Such an approach shapes the interview and makes it fluent and will also be helpful in establishing rapport with the patient. Sources for hypotheses can be contextual, knowledge of learning principles, and personal experience, as Meyer (1975) explains:

The importance of this is obvious, since decisions about the goal and choice of treatment depend on the kind of information elicited from the patient . . . The main sources of information are the patient's verbal report, nonverbal behaviour during the interview, and response to psychological tests. In addition, the therapist has at his disposal other means of gathering information, such as seeing the relatives of the patient, observing the patient in his own environment, or getting the patient to observe and record his own behaviour. (p.22)

On the basis of such information a so-called "problem formulation" is established which attempts to integrate all relevant data into a meaningful picture. This is then discussed with the patient.

The patient is then given the formulation in simple terms, and the objective of treatment is discussed with him. The subject should give his consent concerning the goal of treatment. Close relatives should also be consulted about it, particularly when the target behaviour is social behaviour. The therapist should consider the patient's wishes within the context of his own formulation, and it should be his duty to attempt to adjust the patient to the environment to which he wishes to be discharged, if possible.

Following this, the patient is given a simple general outline of possible treatment procedures and the rationale underlying them. The therapist emphasises the tentative nature of his formulation, but he also indicates that the patient's responses early in treatment may demonstrate any necessary modifications. While motivating the patient to undertake treatment, the therapist at the same time attempts to give him a realistic expectation for outcome. In addition, the patient is told that he is expected to be an active participant in the treatment, and that as soon as possible he will be required to become his own therapist and to exert self-control. Understanding of every step undertaken in therapy is essential and will enable him to cooperate and participate actively (Meyer, 1975, p.23).

In other words, great emphasis is placed on understanding the patient's problem, explaining the rationale, seeking cooperation and thus building resolve and motivation for the treatment programme.

Another important aspect of Meyer's approach was the development of the therapeutic relationship. At the time, this was more or less ignored in BT, partly as a (over)reaction to psychodynamic therapies, in which relationship issues were seen as being to prominent and thus distractive regarding treatment goals. Meyer & Liddell, 1975) present their rationale by noting:

> The relationship between the behaviour therapist and his patient is conceptualised in terms of learning principles from the start of the behavioural analysis. The patient's life style will give some idea of what type of behaviour the therapist must show to become a potent reinforcer. For the behaviour therapist there should be almost as many types of relationships as he sees patients. This adaptability is more important in cases of interpersonal problems than with isolated phobias. The behaviour therapist aims at something approaching an instructor/trainee relationship; he tries to avoid to hide behind the therapeutic veil. In the ideal situation he hopes that the patient will gradually become his own therapist and their interaction should reflect this. (p.237)

According to Meyer, in most cases the therapist should structure his behaviour so it serves as an effective social reinforcer. The type of relationship to be developed should precisely meet the needs of the individual patient. This is illustrated as follows:

> If, for instance, the basic problem presented is fear of authority, then the therapist will behave in such a way as to make it easier for his patient to learn skills appropriate when dealing with people in authority. On the other hand, the therapist who treats an isolated phobia will attempt to inspire confidence and to make his patients relax in his presence. (Meyer & Liddell, 1975, p.226)

Obviously, there must be limits in accommodating patients needs as this may lead to overinvolvement ("pathological relationship") or unwanted shaping of patient's behaviour by means of verbal conditioning etc.

FURTHER DEVELOPMENTS

Further developments on Meyer's CF approach were carried out by his students, who, for the first time, attempted to apply CF in other settings, e.g. outpatient services, behavioural medicine. In particular, Turkat's important contributions enabled the model to take roots in the US where the field was rather dominated by academic research interests at the time. Luckily, this coincided with a growing interest in clinical issues and more complex problems, like personality disorders. This new emphasis was reflected in several meetings of the proceedings of the American Association for the Advancement of BT in the early 80s. Critical analyses and recommendations regarding the nature and direction of BT were put forward by a number of distinguished behaviour therapists (e.g. Wilson, 1982).

Ira Turkat, a clinical psychologist from the US, who had done his clinical internship with Victor Meyer in the late 70s, tried to make the model more refined and accessible. In his work, Turkat was also greatly influenced by Henry Adams, Monte Shapiro, and Joseph Wolpe, all of whom had also collaborated with Meyer at one time.

In contrast to Meyer, who was a rather reluctant publicist, Turkat's great achievement was to define and operationalise the "Middlesex approach" in numerous publications, thus "putting it on the map". Most relevant in this respect were his two textbooks entitled *Behavioural Case Formulation* (Turkat, 1985) and *The Personality Disorders* (Turkat, 1990). Initially, Turkat proposed the label "behaviour-analytic approach" (Meyer & Turkat, 1979) to emphasise the individual analysis of behaviour, but later he argued against this "poor choice of a label" as he feared that it implied synthesis of behavioural and psychoanalytic approaches (Turkat, 1986). Eventually, the term "case formulation" was adopted, making it more consistent with Meyer's original wordings, which were "behavioural formulation" or "problem formulation". However, there still appears to be some confusion about the concept as was recently documented in a debate in the "behaviour therapist". Adams (1996) has clarified this by pointing out that . . .

> *case formulation* is not a treatment procedure. It is a method for understanding the patient and their problems that allows for the selection and design of treatment procedures based on the knowledge of their case. (p.78)

To elaborate, Turkat emphasised the "tripartite nature" of CF, consisting of the *initial interview, clinical experimentation*, and the *modification methodology*. Continuous hypothesis generation and testing was proposed as a logical link between these components, and it also allows for corrective feedback when hypotheses cannot be verified. Apart from these rules, the process should be adjusted to the individual case in a flexible manner.

The main function of the initial interview is to achieve a *problem formulation*, as opposed to a diagnosis, which Turkat also advocates obtaining as

a tool for communication. According to Turkat, diagnoses and formulations should complement each other (as discussed above), but he admits
that a diagnosis has no immediate use in achieving a valid problem
formulation.

The problem formulation itself comprises three elements:

> (1) A hypothesis about the relationship among various problems of the
> individual; (2) Hypotheses about the aetiology of the aforementioned diffi-
> culties; (3) Predictions about the patient's future behaviour. (Turkat, 1990,
> p.17)

In other words, the formulation assumes the status of a personalised
clinical theory to explain the nature and mechanism of the patient's problem. Although an experimental approach is adopted, Turkat (1990) points
out that a clinical assessment can hardly have the rigour of a controlled
research experiment. The main focus, in consideration on current limited
knowledge on psychopathology, has to be on reasoned hypotheses and
clinical data.

In conducting the initial interview, Turkat (e.g. 1990) makes a number of
recommendations:

- The *initial interaction* should be closely monitored, as it can provide
  non-verbal cues regarding, for example, the appearance, mannerisms,
  and motivations of the patient. However, Turkat cautions that hypotheses may be wrong and the temptation to seek consistent data should
  be resisted.
- Next, he recommends to attempt a precise *problem specification* on the
  basis of information offered by the patient. This may involve a number
  of problems which are not always presented in order of priority by the
  patient or possibly not mentioned at all. To guide more detailed specification, Turkat has proposed the behaviour analysis matrix (Turkat,
  1979) which investigates components of behaviour in more detail, including antecedent and consequent conditions. This procedure will be
  addressed in the next chapter.

The gathering of relevant data helps to generate hypotheses which in turn
open the path for further information. Of great importance is what Turkat
labels "aetiology inquiries" which are directed at identifying predisposing, precipitating, and maintaining factors. Aetiology inquiries are in es-
sence a combination of assessment of individual learning history and
functional analysis. Investigation into predisposing factors aims at identifying vulnerability factors arising from genetic, social, cultural, professional, religious backgrounds etc., in interaction with learning processes.

In contrast, precipitating factors refer to the immediate trigger and maintaining factors to reinforcing conditions of the problem behaviour.

The precise examination all of these variables, continuously guided by hypotheses, is seen as critical for the development of the formulation, which is discussed in great detail with the patient. For further verification of this *clinical theory*, Turkat proposes "clinical experimentation", a quasi-experimental procedure. This serves two main functions: (1) to validate the formulation by making predictions which are subsequently evaluated, and (2) to specify further relationships between independent and dependent variables. The design and measurements should fit individual requirements, that is, simple and obvious problems may not require extensive testing whereas complex problem formulations may have to be examined in a more rigorous manner. Turkat (1990) notes:

> Given the tremendous range of variables that could be generated from the diverse nature of psychopathology presented by personality disorder cases as well as the infinite possibilities involved in formulation of those problems, it is impossible at present to articulate very specific step-by step guidelines for engaging in clinical experimentation. The notion is in its infancy and at present time its success in everyday clinical practice depends on the ingenuity and skill of the particular clinician involved. (p.28)

Once this process has resulted in a acceptable formulation, the "modification methodology" is developed accordingly. In the first instance agreement is sought with the patient both regarding the formulation and intervention hypotheses. The "ideal plan" emerging from this is not always acceptable or practical, but any compromise must be supported by the formulation. On the other hand, a valid formulation should also enable the clinician to make predictions about obstacles that are likely to occur during the course of treatment. Another important aspect in the design of treatment is described as "intervention sequencing" which is a formulation-based prioritising of treatment targets, especially with complex cases comprising several complaints which may be interdependent. As Turkat (1990) points out, this is in stark contrast to "technical" BT (symptom focused) where only the most obvious presenting complaint receives attention. Finally, the style of relationship is also developed on the basis of the formulation, thus rejecting standard enhancement techniques as, for example, applied in the Rogerian approach.

These points will be elaborated further in the next chapter.

Jacqueline Persons proposes a CF model from a cognitive perspective (Persons, 1989). It is noteworthy that Persons makes no reference to the pioneering experimental work of Shapiro and Meyer. Although Persons admits to having been strongly influenced by Ira Turkat's work, she does not incorporate what one may describe as the backbone of most CF models, namely the clinical–experimental procedure. However, this is perhaps of little surprise as cognitive therapists are somewhat reluctant in employing basic experimental methodology (Persons, 1991).

It is to Persons' credit that she realises as a cognitive therapist that the CF approach offers appropriate guidance in understanding difficult cases, especially with deeply seated problems and clients lacking compliance. This has been acknowledged by other cognitive therapists too (e.g. Beck *et al.*, 1990).

However, on close inspection, her elaborations, apart from providing a plethora of interesting clinical anecdotes, cannot add anything new to the advance of the CF model, as she readily admits herself, ". . . the model presented here is not particular original" (p.11).

From the UCL vantage point it is probably more contentious that Persons appears predominantly interested in enriching the scope of her cognitive approach with elements of the CF model as she understands it. She fails to grasp the potentials of CF in offering a unique experimentally based scientist–practitioner approach which goes beyond particular therapeutic schools, even outside the cognitive–behavioural framework, when supported by a rationale.

These shortcomings can be demonstrated with her apparent lack of understanding of Lang's triple response analysis which facilitates experimental analysis of cognitive–behavioural components greatly and has thus become one of the most important aspects of CF investigations. It may be questioned whether Person is interested in this type of assessment of behaviour: for example, according to Lang's proposals concepts like mood ought to be understood and investigated in terms of response system interactions and not as singular independent concepts.

Further, Persons' conceptualisation of underlying mechanisms (almost always irrational or dysfunctional beliefs!) in support of "overt difficulties" appears rather narrow. Clearly, CF is rarely reliant on one singular belief (be it dysfunctional or irrational) and tends to be much more complex, as will be outlined in the next chapter. For example, no reference is made to the issue of cognitive processing and reciprocal interactions of response systems.

Persons' attempt to distinguish and separate CF from "biological, diagnostic and traditional behavioural models" is dubious (one cannot compare apples with pears) and misleading as it does not acknowledge the integrating and unifying intentions and potentials of CF; in other words

CF was not designed to enhance one particular therapeutic approach, rather one attempts to utilise all established principles and knowledge to formulate cases.

Other inconsistencies with our understanding of the CF model become apparent when diagnostic assumptions are associated with "underlying psychological mechanism", for example the assertion that certain thinking styles are typical for certain personality disorders.

Persons makes much of the so-called problem list which indeed can be a useful strategy for identifying problems and priorities, but is hardly a *sine qua non* condition. On the contrary, the whole point of CF is that it is not a mechanistic exercise, in fact it is one (of several) options to enable generation of hypotheses about the structure and primacy of problem behaviours. For these reasons, it is hardly acceptable that the therapist makes additions to the problem list if and when he or she sees fit. This is judgmental and interpretative in the psychodynamic tradition.

The case for quantitative measures is also argued inappropriately. Such measures should always be subordinate to the CF procedure, i.e. devices to generate and verify hypotheses, enable clinical experimentation and evaluate change. Ideally, these would be "tailor made" according to requirements (see next chapter).

To summarise, it is felt that Persons' understanding of CF is somewhat at variance with all major model variants. According to UCL philosophy, CF is not designed to enhance a preferred model (i.e. cognitive); instead, it is an approach which may draw on more than one model if so required. Also, CF is not merely a synonym for "underlying cause" which seems to imply some psychodynamic analogy, rather it is the attempt to formulate a valid *clinical theory*.

This is not to say that Persons conceptualisation is without merits: it clearly serves the specific purpose to address some of the clinical shortcomings of the cognitive model (e.g. Turkat, 1982; Bruch, 1988), particularly with difficult, complex patients, which she aptly describes.

THE CONTRIBUTION OF DAVID LANE

We conclude this chapter with a brief introduction and evaluation of the work of David Lane, also a former Vic Meyer student, who has gone furthest in refining and operationalising the CF approach. As his approach was predominantly developed in school settings working with children and adolescents, the label "context–focused analysis" is proposed (Lane, 1990). A chapter illustrating this highly specialised work in a typical setting is included in this volume.

Lane has been developing his model over a span of two decades. It provides a particular challenge as it focuses on a particularly difficult to treat group of clients. The most comprehensive update can be found in his text entitled *The Impossible Child* (Lane, 1990).

In more detail, Lane proposes five phases for the complete individualised intervention programme. This is labelled DEFINE:

> Define the problem or objective, Explore the factors of influence, Formulate an explanation of factors of influence, Intervene using an action plan based on the formulation, and Evaluate the outcome of the plan based on the formulation. (p.116)

In the *definition* phase information is sought from those who are involved with a problem as help is not always requested by the sufferer (especially important in the context of children and adolescents). The goal is to identify a target problem: "The process is one of growing awareness" (p.118).

In the *exploration* phase, expert-led gathering of relevant data proceeds to determine influencing factors for the presented problem according to principles of learning: "The process is one of observation" (p.118).

In the *formulation* phase observations are evaluated and integrated to achieve a model of explanation. Behavioural experiments are carried out to test the validity of explanations: "the process is one of hypothesis testing (the pragmatic scientist)" (p.118).

In the *intervention* phase a treatment strategy and plan is developed which builds logically on the formulation: "It will ideally specify the 'what, how, who and when' necessary for behaviour change. The process is one of structured practice" (p.119).

Finally, in the *evaluation* phase problem and goal-oriented measures are employed to assess gains and failures and determine new objectives, if necessary. Reinforcing feedback is provided throughout: "The process is one of monitored achievement" (p.119).

Because of its influence, details of Lane's model will be addressed in Chapter 2 of this text.

The scope of this text does not allow for a discussion of the significant contributions of several other clinicians. However, Victor Malatesta and Peter AuBuchon (who also contribute to this text) deserve a prominent mention. Both were involved in the development of formulation-based inpatient programmes (Malatesta & AuBuchon, 1992) building in the main on Turkat's work. Their contributions seem especially important as they are clinically based and provide strong evidence for successful outcomes, despite the restrictions and limitations in a routine service provision. More recently, Malatesta contributed to the ongoing debate on formulation-guided versus manual-based treatment strategies (e.g. Malatesta, 1995a, b) which will also be addressed later in this text.

In the main it was Turkat's and Lane's elaborations which had strong impact on the further refinement of the UCL case formulation model as it evolved in parallel. Continuous dialogue helped to achieve further conceptual clearness and optimise clinical operationalisations. This will be outlined in the next chapter.

REFERENCES

Adams, H.E. (1981). *Abnormal Psychology*. Dubuque: Brown.

Adams, H.E. (1996) Further clarification on case formulation. *The Behaviour Therapist*, **19**(5), 78.

American Psychiatric Association (1994) Diagnostic and statistical manual of mental disorders (IVth edition. Washington, DC: American Psychiatric Association.

Blashfield, R.K. & Breen, N.J. (1989) Face validity of the DSM III R personality disorders. *American Journal of Psychiatry*, **146**, 1575–1579

Beck, A.T. *et al.* (1990) *Cognitive-Therapy of Personality Disorders*. New York: Guilford.

Bruch, M.H. (1988) *The Self-Schema Model of Complex Disorders*. Regensberg: S. Roederer.

Eysenck, H.I. (1952) The effects of psychotherapy: an evaluation. *Journal of Consulting and Clinical Psychology*, **16**, 319–324.

Eysenck, H.J. (1960) *Behaviour Therapy and the Neuroses*. Oxford: Pergamon.

Eysenck, H.J. (1964) *Experiments in Behaviour Therapy*. Oxford: Pergamon.

Eysenck, H.J. (1990) *Rebel with a Cause*. The autobiography of Hans Eysenck. London: W.H. Allen.

Hayes, S.C., Strosahl, K. & Wilson, K.G. (in press). *Acceptance and Commitment Therapy: Understanding and Treating Human Suffering*. New York: Guilford Press.

Hickling, E.J. & Blanchard, E.B. (1997) The private practice psychologist and manual based treatments: Post-traumatic stress disorder secondary to motor vehicle accidents. *Behaviour, Research and Therapy*, **33**(3), 191–203.

Kanfer, F.H. and Saslow, G. (1969) Behavioural diagnosis. In C.M. Franks (ed.) *Beharioural Therapy: Appraisal and Status*. New York: McGraw-Hill.

Land, D. (1990) *The Impossible Child*. Stoke on Trent: Trentham.

Lazarus, A.A. (1960) The elimination of children's phobias by deconditioning. In H.J. Eysenck (ed.) *Behaviour Therapy and the Neuroses*. Oxford: Pergamon.

Malatesta, V.J. (1995a) "Technological" behaviour therapy for obsessive compulsive disorder: The need for adequate case formulation. *The Behaviour Therapist*, **18**, 88–89.

Malatesta, V.J. (1995b) Case formulation enhances treatment effectiveness. *The Behaviour Therapist*, **18**, 201–203.

Malatesta, V.J. & AuBuchon, P.G. (1992) Behaviour therapy in the private psychiatric hospital: Our experiences and a model of inpatient consultation. *The Behaviour Therapist*, **15**, 43–46.

Meyer, V. (1960) The treatment of two phobic patients on the basis of learning principles. In H.J. Eysenck (ed.) *Behaviour Therapy and the Neuroses*. Oxford: Pergamon.

Meyer, V. & Chesser, E.S. (1970) *Behaviour Therapy in Clinical Psychiatry*, London: Penguin Books.

Meyer, V. & Liddell, A. (1975) Behaviour therapy. In D. Bannister (ed.) *Issues and Trends in Psychological Therapies*. London: Wiley.

Meyer, V. & Turkat, I.D. (1979) Behavioural analysis of clinical cases. *Journal of Behavioural Assessment*, **1**, 259–69.

Persons, J. (1989) *Cognitive Therapy in Practice. A Case Formulation Approach*. New York: Norton.

Persons, J. (1991) Personal Communication. New York City.

Shapiro, M.B. (1955) Training of clinical psychologists at the Institute of Psychiatry. *Bulletin of the British Psychological Society*, **8**, 1–6.

Shapiro, M.B. (1957) Experimental methods in the psychological description of the individual psychiatric patient. *International Journal of Social Psychiatry*, **111**, 89–102.

Shapiro, M.B. & Nelson, E.H. (1955) An investigation of an abnormality of cognitive function in a cooperative young psychotic: An example of the application of the experimental method to the single case. *Journal of Clinical Psychology*, **11**, 344–351.

Szasz, T.S. (1961) *The myth of mental illness*. New York: Hoeber.

Turkat, I.D. (1979) The behaviour analysis matrix. *Scandinavian Journal of Behaviour Therapy*, **8**, 187–189.

Turkat, I.D. (1985) *Behavioural Case Formulation*. New York, Plenum.

Turkat, I.D. (1986) The behavioural interview. In A.R. Ciminero, K.S. Calhoun & H.E. Adams (eds) *Handbook of Behavioural Assessment* (2nd edn), New York: Wiley-Interscience.

Turkat, I.D. (1982) Behaviour-analytic considerations of alternative clinical approaches. In P.L. Wachtel (ed.) *Resistance: Psychodynamic and Behavioural Approaches*. New York: Plenum.

Turkat, I.D. (1990) *The Personality Disorders. A psychological approach to clinical management*. New York: Pergamon.

Turkat, I.D. & Maisto, S.A. (1983) Functions of and differences between psychiatric diagnosis and case formulation. *The Behaviour Therapist*, **6**, 184–185.

Wilson, G.T. (1982) Psychotherapy process and procedure: The behavioural mandate. *Behaviour Therapy*, **13**, 291–312.

Wilson, G.T. (1996) Manual based treatments: The clinical application of research findings. *Behaviour, Research, and Therapy*, **34**(4), 295–314.

Wilson, G.T. (1997) Treatment manuals in clinical practice. *Behaviour, Research, and Therapy*, **34**(4), 295–314.

Wolpe, J. (1960) Reciprocal inhibition as the main basis of psychotherapeutic effects. In H.J. Eysenck (ed.) *Behaviour Therapy and the Neuroses*. Oxford: Pergamon.

CHAPTER 2   The UCL case formulation model: clinical applications and procedures

Michael Bruch

> I have no data yet.
> It is a capital mistake to theorize before one has data.
> Insensibly one begins to twist facts to suit theories,
> instead of theories to suit facts.
>
> Sherlock Holmes

This chapter aims to provide a description of the case formulation approach as developed and practised at University College London (UCL). As mentioned already in the last chapter, this presentation will make particular reference to the work of Ira Turkat and David Lane, both of whom were associated with the Cognitive–Behavioural Psychotherapy (CBT) unit at UCL and have made strong contributions to the model in recent years.

As the initial interview is of central importance in this procedure, special attention will be devoted to this aspect.

Unlike in psychiatry, where the interview is mainly guided by a categorical classification system (e.g. DSM), case formulation is an experimental, hypothesis-driven procedure in pursuit of a "clinical theory" (the problem formulation) which subsequently assumes a guiding role for the ongoing therapeutic process. In addition to explaining acquisition and maintenance of a presented disorder, this model is designed to facilitate

Beyond Diagnosis: Case Formulation Approaches in CBT.
Edited by Michael Bruch and Frank W. Bond.
© 1998 John Wiley & Sons Ltd.

consistent intervention hypotheses, leading to individually tailored treatment programmes.

THE CLINICAL PURPOSE

Case Formulation is about developing a "clinical theory" of the individual problem under investigation. This is done within the cognitive–behavioural framework. To achieve this, relevant information has to be obtained, suitable hypotheses developed and tested. This extensive process appears justified, as important decisions and interventions are to be made that involve long-term consequences for the client. Furthermore, it is expected that quality and outcome of the interview will be crucial for building the motivation and problem insight of the patient as well as being instrumental in establishing the beginnings of a constructive therapeutic relationship. Let us consider this model in some more detail.

The case formulation procedure is applied in a dynamic and deterministic manner. It rests on the assumption that disordered behaviours can be understood according to established cognitive–behavioural knowledge assisted by experimental principles of investigation. In this approach the initial interview is of pre-eminent importance as we set out to achieve a plausible framework, the problem formulation, to account for the behaviour in question in terms of its causal history and maintaining factors. This is also expected to enable us to make predictions about future behaviours, thus guiding the design of treatment interventions.

Another important assumption are *individual differences* in problem behaviours. Approaches developed in a clinical setting have always acknowledged this fact. Meyer's (e.g. 1957) original pioneering work focused on the *individualised analysis* of complex cases in the psychiatric setting as it was felt that psychiatric labelling was not instrumental for the treatment of patients at the time. On the level of *psychiatric diagnosis* presenting complaints might appear identical; however, ideographic analysis might suggest discrepancies in terms of their causal histories and mechanism of the disorder, thus suggesting different problem formulations.

The case of social phobia may serve as an example: The underlying mechanism may relate, for example, to lack of social skills or fear of negative evaluation, which subsequently would recommend different treatment priorities and/or sequencing of treatment strategies.

Finally, the narrowness of classical and operant conditioning models merely focusing on functional analysis of presenting complaints has proved insufficient for complex clinical cases. We consider it useful to keep an open mind concerning additional, suitable knowledge, both from within and outside the learning framework. Employing innovating and creative practice we are keen to extend our scope and to improve our model for understanding, in order to match the complexity of human behaviour, abnormal behaviour in particular. In case formulation we attempt to utilise any relevant knowledge from any discipline which can further the application of operationalised methods to effect behavioural changes. Hereby, the only limitation is that such knowledge can be understood and applied according to the learning frame of reference involving experimental methodology. This is necessary to avoid conceptual confusion which in our opinion would undermine constructive integration of "new" methods. As clinicians we consequently intend to do this with reference to clinical applications to the individual case. For example, Meyer (1970) has suggested such diverse fields as *social and cognitive experimental psychology, physiology, anatomy, neurophysiology, sociology, pharmacology,* and even *electronics* as suitable sources to broaden our methodology.

FOUNDATIONS AND ASSUMPTIONS

The UCL case formulation approach was originally pioneered by Meyer (1957). This has already been outlined in the last chapter. In distinction to other behavioural developments Meyer applied learning principles directly to the clinical settings with psychiatric inpatients.

To facilitate this, the distinction between learning *principles* and learning *theories* seemed important: principles in this sense refer to observable phenomena which were experimentally verified, but were not indicative of any theoretical explanation. Theories, on the other hand, were considered as highly speculative (especially in the 1950s) and thus neither valid nor useful for experimental assessments and development of individually tailored treatment programmes. Problems and limitations of learning principles have been critically discussed elsewhere (Meyer, 1975).

More recently, Turkat & Maisto (1985) have proposed case formulation as a "scientific approach to the clinical case". They emphasise both process and outcome of science, the former referring to the experimental method requiring hypothesis generation and testing, the latter producing a method to modify the problem behaviour under investigation. This dual aspect approach seems important, as it emphasises the practical implications of a problem formulation, unlike psychiatric diagnosis which has rather limited relevance in guiding the therapeutic process.

The outcome of such clinical work justifies the assertion that successful application of learning principles to clinical phenomena has been demonstrated without any doubt. The fact that this approach was started as a clinical effort using single cases highlighted individual differences regarding the mechanism of presented problems.

In more detail, clinical–experimental analyses of seemingly similar complaints revealed significant differences in structure, predisposing factors and learning histories. For example, one can detect complex interactions between presenting complaints and usually earlier learnt underlying maladaptive behaviours. Thus, as problem development in the biography of an individual can be highly ideographic it has been suggested that assessment strategies should go beyond analysis of the presenting complaint. In the light of these findings it was concluded that treatment strategies should be designed accordingly. Such thinking was hardly fashionable in the early days of behaviour therapy, when the research effort was directed at "symptoms" which required standardised techniques.

THE INITIAL INTERVIEW

The main purpose of the interview process is to collect *relevant* data, integrate these into a meaningful description and eventually formulate a model for explanation and prediction covering all presented problems. Wolpe & Turkat (1985) have listed the critical questions to be answered as follows:

- What are the problems this patient is experiencing?
- Which of any of these are behavioural problems (i.e. are any physiologically based)?
- If psychologically based, what are the functional relations between environment and behaviour?
- Why have these developed and persisted?
- What factors can produce change?

The style of interviewing is empathetic but can also be directive. The latter is usually rejected by dynamic or humanistic psychotherapists as "unethical manipulation". The issue is treated as a taboo and a scientific discussion of this "golden rule" is not encouraged. Turkat (1986), on the other hand, has argued that, if logic prevails, the whole therapeutic procedure should follow directive principles: after all it is the client who is looking for direction in order to cope better with his life problems. He further advances his case as follows:

> The directive style of interviewing as advocated here has often been the target of criticism. Such objections stem from theoretical notions which

seem to have little scientific basis. For example, the author has seen many beginning therapists berated by their supervisors for being "too directive". Often, they are accused of being non-emphatic and "threatening the fragility" of the patient. These assertions deserve some comment. First, one cannot be emphatic if one does not understand the specifics of a problem. It would seem that the most efficient way to understand is to ask direct questions. Second, the notion of a patient to be "too fragile" to handle direct inquiry has little scientific support. Descriptively speaking, the patient encounters daily the problems he or she is purported to be "too fragile" to discuss. The author finds that directness and openness seem highly valued by most patients. (p.127)

We prefer to teach initial interviewing in small group sessions with the patient and trainee therapist present. A great amount of time is spent in explaining the rationale and purpose of the interview to the patient. This involves clarification of his understanding and expectations of therapy, the procedure of the collaborative team approach, and his participation in an "active therapy". Unlike in classical psychiatric demonstrations, the patient becomes very much an active member of this group who may also ask questions or request further clarification. A blackboard is used to record all relevant information for reference of all participants.

DEVELOPING HYPOTHESES

To facilitate and direct case formulation, it is paramount to generate hypotheses of cause and maintenance of the problem behaviour under investigation. The role of hypothesis generation in the interview is twofold: (1) any information starting with the first contact should be utilised to develop hypotheses which (2) in turn form the basis for further questions designed to verify or reject adopted hypotheses. However, in a clinical context, experimental rigour, as was originally proposed by Shapiro (see Chapter 1) is normally not possible nor desirable. Thus, Turkat (1985) suggested, as a compromise, to confirm or eliminate untenable hypotheses by means of systematic questioning. In fact, even before, a similar strategy had already been practised and taught by Victor Meyer since the early 1960s.

As such a strategy can be highly subjective, that is, based on personal (life) experience as well as expert knowledge of cognitive–behavioural principles, it is important for the clinician continuously to review the process of hypothesis generation. For further evaluation, it seems appropriate to communicate this information with colleagues, trainees and patients in order to confirm the logical basis and achieve professional consensus. Obviously, this procedure must be described as "pseudo-experimental" as it involves interview logic instead of controlled experiments.

In consideration of complexity of life-styles and the idiosyncratic nature of problems, high standards of clinical skills, (life) experience and therapist ingenuity are called for. In most cases the clinician will have to perform a triple role: Develop sensible hypotheses on the information provided, define suitable questions and evaluate the outcome of this process all at the same time.

It is important that all information provided by the patient is accounted for. Discrepancies and contradictions need resolving, even if this means discarding otherwise suitable hypotheses and restarting the process.

Generating hypotheses begins at the very first contact with the client, i.e., the clinician may even use the initial impression to develop hypotheses as to what the problem may be. Turkat (1986) gives an appropriate illustration:

> The clinician scrutinises the manner in which the patient speaks, such as tone, pitch, style, choice of words and phrases, intensity, latencies between words, sentences, questions, and replies, searching for a clue. The clinician . . . also scrutinises the patient's physical presentation such as hairstyle, clothing, posture, motor activity, and so forth.
>
> . . . An example will help to illustrate this point. If [there is] a young man in the clinic lobby whose physical presentation includes poorly matched, ill-fitting clothes, unstyled hair, thick-rimmed eyeglasses, and uneasy movements and facial expressions when introduced to the therapist, then a preliminary general hypothesis of a social skills deficit is suggested. Depending on subsequent inquiry, one might hypothesise further certain consequences of this social skills deficit such as loneliness, depression, and so forth. (p.121)

Any bit of information provided by the client is treated in this way which provides guidance throughout the interview. As we progress towards the problem formulation (detailed below) we collect information in a systematic and logical manner. Therapists are encouraged to base questions on reasoned hypotheses and reject questions that do not fit these criteria. We typically find that inexperienced therapists often continue to interview over many sessions. Usually numerous topics are covered and eventually they find it difficult to make sense of the accumulated amount of information (Typical question to the supervisor: "what shall I do next?"). Also, it is not recommended to jump from topic to topic in a random fashion as this tends to lead to disorientation or even confusion, especially with trainees. Such interviewing styles are usually associated with inexperience, uncertainty, and lack of knowledge which recommends close guidance and supervision.

Thus, it is useful to conduct teaching sessions to demonstrate interviewing in a transparent manner with both trainee therapist and patient present. Hypotheses put forward are commented upon and discussed until consensus can be achieved. It seems particularly important to encourage trainees to formulate hypotheses which can be supported by the CBT framework.

Further, hypotheses may also be derived from sources other than information provided by the patient. All aspects of the immediate environment may be relevant, including key relations of the patient.

Finally, it is important to recognise that hypotheses at all stages of the interview may be wrong, and should always be supported by suitable data. On the other hand, open mindedness and flexibility are called for. For example, especially experienced therapists tend to develop biases based on preferred models of explanation leading to matching hypotheses. This fixation may subsequently lead to selective perception and direction in the interview, and may even include shaping of the patient's verbal behaviour.

Clinical illustrations for hypothesis generation and testing can be found in Turkat (1985, 1987).

PRACTICAL STEPS

To enhance practicality and operationalisation of the model, Lane (1990) proposed five basic phases for the assessment and treatment of children and adolescents, which allows for correcting feedback and continuous verification of the process by means of hypothesis generation and testing. An adapted version of this stepwise procedure can be found in Figure 2.1. The first three phases are conducted during the initial interview.

These steps shall be outlined in the following sections.

Defining Problems (Phase 1)

Also labelled as *descriptive analysis*, this phase is focused on the subjective statement of the patient. The main purpose is to understand what the client is considering as the main problem(s), why he is seeking help at this point in time, and what changes he may envisage. Apart from ethical considerations, in order to formulate valid hypotheses a detailed and personally meaningful description of present difficulties is sought. At UCL, we actively encourage clients to use their own "language" and

---

Phase One: Definition of Problems

1   Obtain statement of the problem from those involved

2   Clarify initial objectives of those involved

3   On the basis of initial information received, specify problems

Theme: A process of growing awareness aimed at a therapeutic consensus

Phase Two: Exploration

4   Hypotheses of cause and maintenance are generated

5   Multilevel cognitive–behavioural assessment is conducted

6   Data are collected to test hypotheses

Theme: The process is one of increasingly refined observations

Phase Three: Formulation

7   A formulation and intervention hypotheses are established

8   Discussion with participants and redefinition of objectives takes place

9   The adequacy of the hypotheses are checked and verified

Theme: The process is one of testing the hypotheses until an adequate explanation is available

Phase Four: Intervention

10   The procedures to be used are specified

11   An intervention contract is established

12   The agreed programme is enacted and monitored

Theme: The process is one of structured practice

Phase Five: Evaluation

13   Accomplished outcomes are evaluated

14   Any gains made are supported and enhanced, the programme is optimised and further objectives, if suggested, are persued

15   Continuing evaluation and review. Generation of further ideas to consolidate progress

Theme: The process is one of monitored achievement and support

---

Figure 2.1   Phases in the case formulation process

refrain from acquired jargon or interpretations of other professionals during the course of previous assessments or treatments. Already at this stage the patient is encouraged to express views and expectations regarding therapeutic change and outcome (to be reviewed after presentation of problem formulation). In cases which involve relationship problems (e.g. marital or family issues) it may be appropriate to obtain statements and opinions of other individuals involved. Discrepancies and conflicting information might have important implications both regarding motivation and outcome of therapy.

Consider the case of an obsessive–compulsive husband who disrupts marital life through intensive checking and cleaning rituals. As the situation becomes unbearable his wife might threaten divorce if he refuses to be treated for his problems. In cases like this a consensus about treatment goals has to be found before a modification programme can be envisaged. In other words we support a process of increasing awareness to achieve a consensus of all individuals which may get involved in the therapeutic process.

How do we get started in the initial interview? Routinely, we begin by explaining to the client the purpose of the interview and may discuss briefly various options of approaching behavioural problems (e.g. emphasising a psychological versus psychiatric approach). Depending on previous knowledge, we may also explain the nature of applied CBT: Stressing active participation of the patient, sharing the learning based rationale, pointing out responsibilities, contracts etc.

In case this is a teaching session involving trainee therapists one introduces each individual and facilitates adaptation to the situation. The patient is reminded that he is a volunteer and may only provide information he feels comfortable with. Finally, the patient is actively encouraged to participate in the interview by asking questions or making suggestions etc. Next, we may take some biographical details, e.g., age, sex, marital status, profession.

An adequate account of the way we start focusing on the presenting problem has been provided by Meyer & Turkat (1979):

> We begin typically by generating a list of all the behavioural difficulties the client is currently experiencing. Each problem is listed in general terms with the aim of generating an exhaustive list. The list of behavioural difficulties serves a variety of purposes such as structuring the clinical interview, specifying the range of problems the individual is experiencing, and, most importantly, providing the therapist with information for generating hypotheses. Preferably, the list of problems and subsequent information is recorded on a blackboard or some other medium which the client and

> therapist can visually refer to (as the wealth of information to be elicited is usually beyond memory capabilities). Visual inspection of the behaviour problem list often provides clues as to how the presenting complaints may be related and account for one another. If such relationships are discovered, then clinical efficiency is facilitated. For example, with a particular client it may be hypothesised that this person is depressed because he is sexually impotent. Consequently, for clinical expediency, sexual impotence will be examined first. In certain cases, the list of behaviour problems does not facilitate the formulation of such an hypothesis. Therefore, the most incapacitating behaviour difficulty is examined first. In either case, the next step in conducting the initial interview involves a developmental behaviour analysis of each individual problem the client is experiencing. (p.262)

In cases where it seems impossible to elicit a clear description of the main presenting complaint it can be appropriate to ask the client to list all problems in the session or as a homework task. Such compilation will facilitate hypotheses regarding relationships between simple complaints and might thus be helpful in detecting the underlying problem mechanism. Turkat (1986) provides an example for this: . . . assume the following list of problems is generated: (1) depression, (2) lack of friends, (3) excessive hand washing, (4) inability to leave the house, (5) difficulty sleeping, (6) excessive cleaning. The therapist attempts to find an explanatory hypothesis for all of these complaints. A striking hypothesis from the problems listed in this case is a *fear of contamination*.

Such a hypothesis is derived from the following type of thinking: The patient probably *washes her hands* and *cleans her house* excessively to prevent possible contamination by dirt, germs, and so forth. Further, she *avoids leaving her home* in order to prevent exposure to more contaminating stimuli. This results in *social isolation*, rumination about her predicament at night (which produces sleep onset *insomnia*) and thus, *depression*. Other problems predicted from the general mechanism of "fear of contamination" might include: avoidance of touching others, sexual problems, hosing down or vacuuming others when they enter her house (this is not as uncommon as it might sound), preventing others from entering her house, and so forth (p.123).

Functional Analysis (Phase 2)

The patient's statement of the previous phase normally inspires a host of hypotheses which can be investigated further. We shall now be able to outline the main problem(s) which should be subjected to extensive *functional analysis* in the first instance. The basic design of this analysis hardly requires further elaboration for the present context as it has been the major component of behavioural analysis since early formulations (learn-ing equation model; e.g. Kanfer and Phillips, 1970). However, more re-cently, tripartite response system analysis has been incorporated into this design to allow study of individual response modalities in a systematic manner. This seems appropriate as response systems have been shown to be highly interactive (e.g. Lang, 1979; Turkat, 1979). A graphic outline of the complete model is provided in Figure 2.2.

The clinician scrutinises each presenting complaint according these crite-ria. One attempts to identify relevant triggers regarding high (S+) and low (S–) probabilty. It is also important to determine whether the be-haviour is triggered by a *single stimulus* or has generalised to *cluster of related stimuli* which may be hierarchically organised.

Regarding the organism variable, it is useful to explore whether biolog-ical factors are involved with the reaction. For example, level of habitual arousal has been shown to be of predictive value for anxiety patterns following stress (Lader & Wing, 1966).

Most salient in the functional analysis is the examination of response sys-tems as illustrated above. This follows Lang's (1971) influential model which has proposed three related behavioural components: *verbal–cognitive, autonomic–physiological, and behavioural–motoric.* This concep-tualisation allows us to study contents as well as the interactive nature of these responses. For example, it is useful to identify the dominant response mode which may have causal impact on other systems. Such sequences may provide clues for design of subsequent treatment method. Or, as in the case of anticipatory anxiety, we may detect an enhancing interaction be-tween cognitive and autonomic variables (Meyer & Reich, 1978).

Further, it is of interest to know whether response systems are in a state of synchrony (high correlation) or desynchrony (low correlation) (Rachman & Hodgson, 1974). Such patterns can be highly ideographic, suggesting different treatment options. Decoupling synchronous systems can be a successful strategy to reduce anxiety, for example, by (cognitive) relabell-ing of autonomic cues. Also, systems should be assessed for

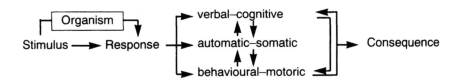

Figure 2.2   Functional analysis

(predisposed) dominant responses in individuals as one can often detect primary "cognitive" or "autonomic" responders (e.g. Bandura, 1977; Bruch, 1988). Part of this investigation should focus on the sequence of events, i.e. the way in which response systems influence each other.

The mode of assessment for response systems requires further consideration. We have found that self-report may yield different results as compared to direct measures. For example, we have detected significant discrepancies in the case of autonomic responses. To complicate things further, individuals tend to respond to stress in different modalities, i.e. some may show increase in "heart rate" whereas others respond with changes in "skin conductance". Modalities may not correlate and can vary independently (Bruch, 1988). To conclude, an analysis investigating response primary and sequences should provide important clues for the understanding of the problem mechanism. For example, an anxiety response which is initiated and dominated by the verbal–cognitive system may require different therapeutic focus (e.g. cognitive restructuring) as compared to a strong autonomic reaction (e.g. biofeedback). The arrows in Figure 2.2 indicate possible interactions.

Additional relevant parameters of each response system such as intensity, frequency and duration may also be studied to gain deeper understanding of the presenting complaint. This process is assisted by the *behaviour analysis matrix* (Table 2.1), which recommends additional assessment of cognitive, autonomic, and motoric components under antecedent and consequent conditions. These can be either behaviours or environmental events. A fuller discussion can be found in Turkat (1979).

The assessment of consequences is designed to clarify the operant-maintaining factors of the problem behaviour under investigation. It is important to identify whether there are conflicting short-term vs long-term consequences. For example, a social phobic might be able to reduce social anxiety by means of withdrawal and avoidance, which in the long run may to lead to complete isolation and subsequent depression. The balance between short-term and long-term consequences can also shed light on the level of self-control. Maladaptive self-regulation is operating

Table 2.1   The behaviour analysis matrix

	Antecedent	Behaviour	Consequence
Cognitive	X	X	X
Autonomic	X	X	X
Motoric	X	X	X
Environmental	X		X

when immediate reinforcement is preferred to long-term gratification, i.e. reduction of anxiety by means of substance abuse.

Lane (1990) has suggested a variety of additional strategies which can be employed in the exploration phase to enhance behavioural analysis further if suggested by appropriate hypotheses and if functional analysis appears inadequate. Although case formulation recommends adherence to the experimental approach, limitation to "traditional" behavioural methods of analysis is not necessary as long as complementary methods can be meaningfully employed within the model. For example, it may be appropriate to activate a deeply seated and avoided schema by means of emotive technique.

It is also important to observe that targets of analysis are not treated as isolated segments. Behaviour is continuous, i.e. a functional analysis should be conceptualised as part of a wider loop: consequences may become stimuli and so on.

As discussed already in the previous chapter, we do not recommend some of the very detailed and systematic, seemingly over-inclusive, analysis schemes (e.g. Kanfer & Phillips, 1970). Consistent with the the case formulation model, selection and focus on problem areas should be determined by hypotheses, as the potential number of investigations can be limitless. Apart from being time consuming, this may create an unmanageable and sometimes confusing array of data which may prove distractive when attempting a problem formulation. In the worst case scenario the purposeful, dynamic flow of the interview may get substituted by medical model style "pigeonholing". It has proved to be more useful to collect additional data at a later stage during treatment should information gaps become apparant.

DEVELOPMENTAL ANALYSIS (PHASE 2)

Next, a detailed history for each identified problem behaviour is taken. The usefulness of such etiologic assessment has been the subject of controversy amongst behaviour therapists and was treated with suspicion by early learning theorists (preferring the "here" and "now" focus), (e.g. Stuart, 1970) who sensed backsliding towards psychodynamic positions. Turkat (1986) has summarised the main arguments for the usefulness of the etiologic analysis:

> First, there is sufficient scientific and clinical evidence that one of the best overall predictors of future behaviour is previous behaviour. Second, in order to change a behaviour in a meaningful way, one must know the

potential causal and maintaining variables. Finally, one cannot prevent future behavioural problems unless one knows what the etiologic determinants are. In the initial interview, etiologic enquiry usually serves to either identify antecedents and consequences of relevance or to validate predictions from the hypothesised mechanism of disorder. In the former case, etiologic enquiry is used to *develop* an hypothesis about the mechanism of disorder. In the latter case, the clinician *predicts* what the history of the presenting problems are. In either case, every behavioural problem is examined from its very first occurrence through all changes in its development to the present. (p.124)

This analysis pertains to the onset circumstances, environmental influences, and also predisposing factors which may have contributed to vulnerability for specific complaints. Furthermore, all changes in manifestation of identified problems including antecedent and consequent conditions are monitored and interactions between different problem areas (if possible) carefully investigated. We have frequently observed that onset and current maintenance of disordered behaviours may be dependent on different stimulus and/or operant conditions.

Aetiologic information is usually also the main source for generating hypotheses about predisposing factors like biological vulnerabilities, earlier learned, deeply seated behaviours etc. Turkat (1985) illustrates this for the case of a "socially inept individual . . . he is likely to have had parental models for such behaviour (i.e. vicarious conditioning), promoting a lack of opportunity to acquire appropriate skills (operant conditioning) and, perhaps, traumatic consequences such as social rejection resulting in the present social anxiety (classical conditioning) problem" (p.30).

Particularly when working with complex cases we have often found evidence for early established maladaptive schemata which are likely to promote behavioural disorders. We have conceptualised this mechanism as deficient self-regulation (Bruch, 1988). Hypotheses arising from such observations have inspired an optional *schema analysis* which will be addressed in the next section.

SCHEMA ANALYSIS (PHASE 2)

Clinical observations and research evidence suggests that negative self-schemata are strongly related to maladaptive cognitive processing styles and interpersonal behaviours. In more detail, we have found excessive negative and pessimistic thinking, distorted attribution, low self-efficacy, social isolation and depression. This scenario of deficient self-regulation becomes self-perpetuating, a vicious cycle which can seriously undermine all therapeutic efforts and achievements; the main underlying mechanisms are faulty cognitive styles which prevent adaptive processing and appraisal of therapeutic progress and outcomes. As a consequence, the building of positive self-schemata is disabled.

Most of these features are typical for DSM IV, Axis II personality disorders which have received growing attention in recent years.

In clinical practice, such complications are not always obvious and sometimes difficult to explore, as self-schemata may operate in a *non-conscious* mode: Although self-schemata may promote inappropriate cognitive biases and behavioural complaints, clients are usually unaware of their automatic and continuous nature. In the long term, negative schemata may lead to maladaptive "personal theories" which are often responsible for maintenance of problems and resistance to treatment (Bruch, 1988; Young, 1990).

According to the self-schema model (Bruch, 1988) we have proposed that the pervasive maladaptive cognitive and behavioural patterns underlying presenting complaints should receive more attention. Obviously, this is subject to suitable hypotheses arising from the initial interview. For example, in analysing a client's early history in detail, hypotheses regarding basic anxieties and conflicts can be generated. Common basic anxieties include those associated with having to achieve good results in response to high standards or those associated with becoming independent from overprotective parents etc. In terms of conflicts, it may be hypothesised that the client is in an *approach-avoidance* conflict as basic anxieties associated with taking responsibility contrast with the consequences of avoiding responsibility (e.g. parental, social, or self-disapproval). A life-style often develops in response to such basic anxieties and conflicts. Such understanding usually aids the explanation of the onset and development of symptoms. This is especially true for complex cases, where the lack of traumatic conditioning events render explanations based on one principle of conditioning inadequate. Furthermore, a conceptualisation of problem behaviours which involves self-schemata and life-style can have predictive value with regards to "high risk" situations where exacerbation of symptoms or relapse might occur.

ADDITIONAL ISSUES (PHASE 2)

Finally, we are keen on establishing knowledge about the assets and potentials of patients. This prevents us from gaining a one-dimensional understanding of problems and may also provide important clues for involvement of the patient in treatment. For this purpose we assess areas of positive adjustment with particular emphasis on self-control skills. It may also of interest to find out whether clients can cope with their problems under certain circumstances or have done so previously and for what reasons.

This enumeration of analysis procedures for the initial interview cannot be complete. There are no limits for inventiveness as long as the general experimental strategy is followed. In principle, we try to keep assessment routines to a minimum and adopt a flexible, hypothesis-led approach. Although the client is regarded as the principal source of information, we might also consider it appropriate to use other sources, like direct observation in the natural environment or interviewing of partners, friends, or family members. Information which is inconsistent with prevailing hypotheses during interviewing must always be accounted for. This may be due to a wrong hypothesis, insufficient interview technique, or even manipulative behaviour of the client. It is recommended not to cling to hypotheses which cannot be supported. Also, it is not acceptable to employ selective interviewing to confirm favoured hypotheses. Should there be justifiable doubts about the honesty of a client, one might consider interviewing other individuals involved.

THE PROBLEM FORMULATION (PHASE 3)

The problem formulation assumes a central role as locus of data integration from which all further therapeutic steps should logically evolve. Meyer & Turkat (1979) have defined the problem formulation as a clinical theory which . . .

(1) relates all the client's complaints to one another, (2) explains why the individual developed these difficulties, and (3) provides predictions concerning the client's behaviour given any stimulus conditions. (p.261)

Meyer has argued against reductionism in behaviour therapy (Meyer & Liddell, 1977) and has stated that functional analysis cannot be regarded as sufficient for full understanding of behavioural problems—instead a conceptual system is preferred which approaches the whole person in cognitive–behavioural terms. Ideally, the ultimate question in behavioural analysis to be answered is: *Why has this individual at a particular point of time acquired this specific presenting complaint? how did the problem develop? which (underlying) conditions (if any) were instrumental? and what is the functional value of the problem for his life in general?* Such an analysis should also clarify any predisposing factors which may explain why a patients tends to behave in a particular way in a given situation or why a specific situation is more influential than another one.

By integrating data as gathered in the initial interview we hope to arrive at a comprehensive formulation to explain aetiology and maintenance of problem behaviours which should enable us to make predictions for specified situations. Subsequently, it is important to present and discuss the formulation with the client. In so doing one seeks approval, however, rejection is also considered as useful information as this may point to inconsistencies which require clarification. Turkat (1986) has recommended a checklist for this procedure: . . .

(1) Informing the patient that the clinician's formulation of the problem will be presented and that he or she should comment on its accuracy
(2) Stating what the presenting problems are
(3) [Stating] what the general mechanism of disorder is
(4) Illustrating how this mechanism is causing all the presenting problems
(5) Explaining why these problems developed, using examples provided by the patient
(6) Emphasising how these are (potentially) learned responses
(7) Outlining the range of treatment options
(8) Discussing all positive and negative consequences expected from each treatment option
(9) Predicting obstacles to successful intervention
(10) Stating whether or not the therapist can treat the patient, and if not, why not
(11) Asking the patient to comment on all that has been said
(12) Asking the patient what he or she believes would be the best option to follow
(13) Encouraging the patient to spend a week or so contemplating the formulation, its indications, and treatment options
(14) Answering any questions the patient asks. (p.125)

The other main purpose of a formulation is to provide guidance for all further therapeutic steps, that is to enable the therapist to decide on appropriate treatment strategies, determine priorities and sequencing, develop or select suitable techniques. For example, this would allow clarification whether the main complaint is isolated or supported by underlying problem behaviours acting as independent variables. We should also be able to explain why some individuals are vulnerable to stressful conditions which may lead to a variety symptoms whereas other appear immune.

In other words, clinicians using behavioural formulations based on a multilevel analysis do not have to rely on diagnostic decision trees or lists of developmental stressors. To conclude, factors that contribute to a valid problem formulation include (1) recognition of individual specificity, (2) multilevel analysis guided by cognitive–behavioural principles, and (3) the relation of symptoms to underlying schematas. The experimental method applied throughout this analysis serves as a guiding and integrating factor. In rare cases where a formulation cannot be achieved (when information is insufficient or unobtainable) one adopts a more pragmatic approach. Obviously, this can be expected to reduce therapeutic effectiveness greatly, especially when symptoms are treated in an isolated fashion.

CLINICAL EXPERIMENTATION (PHASE 3)

To verify the problem formulation, research-oriented methods should be employed, not least because of the proposed central importance for the ongoing therapeutic process. Obviously, clinical experimentation is not required as a routine measure, especially in simple cases where problems are formulated unambiguously and are generally agreed. Otherwise precise hypotheses should be delineated to be tested with *in vivo* experiments set under relevant stimulus conditions. The selection of procedures will depend on client variables, nature of hypotheses as suggested by the formulation, and inventiveness of the clinician.

In practical terms, the clinician should provide stimulation across all behavioural modalities and take appropriate measures covering all response systems. As outlined earlier, this can be useful for investigating response patterns, e.g. to determine discrepancies between verbal reports and motoric behaviours or to determine the dominant response mode.

This is important as response system interactions are responsible for misrepresentations of behavioural difficulties or competencies. Typical is faulty labelling of internal cues, for example, sexual arousal might be perceived as anxiety or emotional arousal as physical illness. At other times physiological cues may get exaggerated which is likely to promote the vicious cycle of *anticipatory anxiety* (operationalised as enhancing interaction of cognitive and autonomic variables).

Some other relevant measures might also be appropriate. These could pertain to information provided by other individuals involved, *in vivo* observations, self-monitoring data or "objective" questionnaire measures which should be carefully selected and must be relevant to the hypothesised problem. Naturally, converging evidence of multiple measures covering several dimensions will provide strong support for the problem formulation.

As this process is conceptualised to be continuous, the clinician can develop and test out further hypotheses if new information arises. In some cases discrepancies might arise and hypotheses cannot be verified. This can be caused by several factors including faulty information, a "weak" formulation, inappropriate hypotheses or unsuitable measures. In some circumstances reformulation of problem behaviours becomes necessary and clinical experimentation has to be repeated. If this does not solve the problem, additional information sources may be consulted or otherwise a pragmatic approach to treatment is adopted.

Finally, we like to emphasise that this experimental and hypothesis-guided procedure should not be confused with standardised psychodiagnostic test batteries, which we consider as inappropriate for a psychotherapeutic context where focus is on change processes. There should always be a sound reason why a particular measure is being employd. Typical examples for clinical experimentation have been provided by Turkat & Carlson (1984) and Turkat & Maisto (1985). A more detailed discussion of the method can be found in Carey and *et al.* (1984).

BASELINES AND MEASURES OF CHANGE (PHASE 3/4)

In addition to clinical experiments, validation of the problem formulation can be further enhanced by suitable quantitative measures which at the same time may serve as baselines for outcome evaluation. Such measures may range from questionnaire to rating scale type assessments. Once a set of measures has been selected, they may be used for repeated application at discharge and follow up.

For adequate evaluation, we recommend embracing the following dimensions: *client/expert; global/specific; short-term/long-term*. In more detail, outcomes ought to be evaluated *independently* both by patients and therapists; measurements should be directed both to specific *complaints* as well as *overall life adjustment* and, finally, *short-term treatments effects* should be balanced against *long-term changes*.

As cognitive–behavioural psychotherapists, we reject standardised psychometric test approaches based on trait personality conceptualisation as inappropriate as clinicians should be predominantly concerned about evaluating the therapeutic change process. Further, it is desirable to attempt long-term follow up for estimation of genuine independent functioning. Obviously, multidimensional assessments may yield discrepant results which need to be addressed in the overall clinical evaluation. For example, our own data show strong pre-treatment agreement, whereas discrepancies tend to be more typical for the follow-up stages. These issues ought to be discussed fully and disagreements need to be reconciled. Lane (1990) has provided some examples for suitable measurement techniques.

THE THERAPEUTIC RELATIONSHIP

Especially with complicated cases interviewing has to go beyond mere collection of data for assessment and formulation as motivation and compliance may be affected. For these reasons the establishment and enhancement of the therapeutic relationship should be given special attention. This issue has long been neglected in behavioural psychotherapy and it was only in recent times that more interest emerged. As the virtues of a positive therapeutic relationship hardly need further recommendations, we would like to emphasise a few points that appear particularly important in the context of *case formulation*.

In principal, we conceptualise the therapeutic relationship as an integral part of the whole treatment process and we recommend that this aspect should not be treated in an isolated manner. Thus, emphasis and direction of such relationships should be guided by the individual problem formulation and subsequent treatment requirements. Turkat and co-workers (e.g. Turkat & Brantley, 1981; Turkat and Meyer, 1982) have argued against standard enhancement techniques according to Rogerian principles (indicate *understanding* and demonstrate *empathy*), which appear to be endorsed by most clinicians (e.g. Goldfried, 1982), as being incompatible with individual problem formulations. Wolpe & Turkat (1985) provide a suitable illustration in support of their point:

> Unquestionably, one must be able to empathise with the patient if one is to be able to formulate the case. However, the question as to what demonstrable empathy is remains the basis of difference. We would argue that *accurate empathy is demonstrated when the therapist can accurately predict the patient's behaviour*. This difference in demonstrating empathy can be seen in the following example:
>
> PATIENT: I get very nervous when I leave the house by myself, I just feel as if I were going to pass out.
> ROGERIAN BEHAVIOURAL INTERVIEWER: It must be upsetting when this happens.
> PATIENT: Oh yes, I just want to run away.
>
> Here, the clinician has "demonstrated empathy" by providing a summary statement of how the patient must have felt during this situation. This can be compared with the response of the skilled behaviour analytic interviewer.
>
> PATIENT: I get very nervous when I leave the house by myself, I just feel as if I were going to pass out.

CASE FORMULATION INTERVIEWER: Do you also get this feeling of passing out in aeroplanes? (patient nods), trains? (patient nods), elevators? (patient nods), crowds? (patient nods), and if you can make it to a movie, you sit in the last row, the seat closest to the exit?
PATIENT: That's me, all right.

Here, the interviewer is testing hypotheses the validity of which demonstrates more accurate empathy than a simple pseudo-expression of understanding as advocated by Rogerian approaches. In this regard, for the case formulation clinician, the relationship to the patient is a means to an end; a good relationship exists if the clinician has created an environment for the patient which enables him to get the information he needs to make accurate predictions. (p.10)

The general conduct of our interview is open and natural. We try to avoid professional jargon which often makes clients feel uncomfortable. Clients are encouraged to intervene and ask questions if proceedings become unclear or confusing or if they feel misunderstood. The atmosphere is kept generally relaxed and there is also room for jokes which can have pleasant, counterconditioning effects on apprehension or even tension of clients. Perhaps more than other therapeutic schools we prefer an active and motivated client who is treated as a partner in achieving the behavioural analysis, problem formulation, and treatment programme. This entails that each significant step is discussed with the client and that one only proceeds if full agreement has been reached. Also, we consider it important to take the patient's point of view into account. Foremost, this includes discussion of formulation which has to be presented to the client in an understandable manner. Subsequently, before treatment commences, clients are explained the rationale of their programme and, at an intermediate stage, they are usually encouraged or even challenged to design and carry out their own treatments.

In other words, the therapeutic relationship is conceptualised to enable such active involvement. It seems crucial that the patient feels fully understood and supported with his problems. The way we can motivate and involve the patient will depend on his needs and competence, that is we may at times attempt a complementary relationship (e.g. acting as a primary reinforcer with a socially withdrawn and depressed patient) to achieve the desired behaviour. In case formulation this type of understanding and involvement seems more adaptive than non-specific Rogerian type of acceptance.

For these reasons, the initial interview must be regarded as a cornerstone for the development of appropriate relationships which predominantly seeks to involve and motivate the client. It is obvious that the therapist's style will be the main facilitator for this. In view of individual differences, standard enhancement methods are therefore never recommended. The role of the therapist is best guided by the problem formulation when deciding whether a non-directive or directive style should be adopted, even if this does not sound "politically correct" on the surface.

SUMMARY

To conclude, the *case formulation approach* is a dynamic, innovative, and goal-oriented process. It involves continuous collection of information and hypothesis testing and is guided at all times by principles of experimental psychology in general and cognitive–behavioural principles in particular.

The intent of this chapter was to give a brief introduction to this procedure. In all, we are aware that human behaviour is incredibly complex and that any psychological model will have severe limitations in explaining and predicting specific behaviours, such as clinical problems. Nevertheless we claim that this approach has been established as a useful clinical method with heuristic value.

More detailed clinical transcripts of the initial interview can be found elsewhere (e.g. Turkat, 1986; Meyer & Liddell, 1977). Frank Bond and David Lane have contributed clinical case demonstrations for this text which are related to the UCL case formulation model based on their personal styles. For good measure and balance we considered it desirable to invite some other distinguished clinicians, Windy Dryden, Gerald Davison and Michael Gann as well as Hans Reinecker to provide illustrations of their particular models of formulating and treating individual problems.

REFERENCES

Bandura, A. (1977) Self-efficacy: Toward a unifying theory of behavioural change. *Psychological Review*, **84**(2), 191–215.

Bruch, M.H. (1988) *The Self-Schema Model of Complex Disorders*. Regensburg: S Roederer.

Carey, M.P., Flasher, L.V., Maisto, S.A. & Turkat, I.D. (1984) The *a priori* Approach to psychological Assessment. *Professional Psychology*, **15**, 519–527.

Goldfried, M. (1982) Resistance and Clinical Behavior Therapy. In P.L. Wachtel (ed.) *Resistance: Psychodynamic and Behavioural Approaches*. New York: Plenum.

Kanfer, F.H. & Phillips, J.S. (1970) *Learning Foundations of Behaviour Therapy*. New York: Wiley.

Lader, M.H. & Wing, L. (1966) *Physiological Measures, sedative drugs and morbid anxiety*. London: Oxford University Press.

Lane, D. (1990) *The Impossible Child*. Stoke on Trent: Trentham.

Lang, P.J. (1971) The application of psychophysiological methods to the study of psychotherapy and behaviour modification. In A. Bergin & S. Garfield (eds) *Handbook of Psychotherapy and Behaviour Change*. New York: Wiley.

Lang, P.J. (1979) A bio-informational theory of emotional imagery. *Psychophysiology*, **16**, 495–512.

Meyer, V. (1957) The treatment of two phobic patients on the basis of learning principles. *Journal of Abnormal Psychology*, **55**, 261.

Meyer, V. (1970) Comments on Yates: Misconceptions about behaviour therapy: A point of view. *Behaviour Therapy*, **1**, 108–12.

Meyer, V. (1975) The impact of research on the clinical application of behaviour therapy. In R.I. Thompson and W.S. Dockens (eds) *Applications of Behaviour Modification*. New York: Academic Press.

Meyer, V. & Liddell, A. (1977) Behavioural interviews. In A.R. Ciminero, K.S. Calhoun and H.E. Adams (eds) *Handbook of Behavioural Assessment*. New York: Wiley.

Meyer, V. & Reich, B. (1978) Anxiety management—The marriage of physiological and cognitive variables. *Behaviour, Research and Therapy*, **16**, 177–182.

Meyer, V. & Turkat, I.D. (1979) Behavioural analysis of clinical cases. *Journal of Behavioural Assessment*, **1**, 259–69.

Rachman, S. & Hodgson, R. (1974) I. Synchrony and Desynchrony in Fear and Avoidance. *Behaviour Research and Therapy*, **12**, 311–318.

Stuart, R.B. (1970) *Trick or Treatment: How or when Psychotherapy fails*. Champaign, ILL: Research.

Turkat, I.D. (1979) The behaviour analysis matrix. *Scandinavian Journal of Behaviour Therapy*, **8**, 187–189.

Turkat, I.D. (1985) *Behavioural Case Formulation*. New York: Plenum.

Turkat, I.D. (1986) The behavioural Interview. In A.R. Ciminero, K.S. Calhoun and H.E. Adams (eds) *Handbook of Behavioural Assessment* (2nd edn), New York: Wiley-Interscience.

Turkat, I.D. (1987) Invited case transcript: the initial clinical hypothesis. *Journal of Behaviour Therapy and Experimental Psychiatry*, **18**(4), 349–356.

Turkat, I.D. & Brantley, P.J. (1981) On the therapeutic relationship in behaviour therapy. *The Behaviour Therapist*, **4**(3), 16–17.

Turkat, I.D. & Carlson, C.R. (1984) Symptomatic versus data based formulation of treatment: The case of a dependent personality. *Journal of Behaviour Therapy and Experimental Psychiatry*, **15**, 153–160.

Turkat, I.D. & Maisto, S.A. (1985) Application of the experimental method to the formulation and modification of personality disorders. In D.H. Barlow (ed.) *Clinical Handbook of Psychological Disorders*. New York: Guilford.

Turkat, I.D. & Meyer, V. (1982) The behaviour–analytic approach. In P. Wachtel (ed.) *Resistance: Psychodynamic and Behavioural Approaches*. New York: Plenum.

Wolpe, J. & Turkat, I.D. (1985) Behavioural formulation of clinical cases. In I.D. Turkat (ed.) *Behavioural Case Formulation*. New York: Plenum.

Young, J.E. (1990) *Cognitive Therapy for Personality Disorders: A Schema-focussed Approach*. Sarasota, Florida: Professional Resource Exchange.

CHAPTER 3

Understanding persons in the context of their problems: a rational emotive behaviour therapy perspective

Windy Dryden

I have grave reservations about the terms "case formulation" and "case conceptualisation" that are currently in vogue in cognitive–behavioural psychotherapy, and will explain why presently. Why then have I agreed to contribute to this book? For two reasons. First, because I think that coming to an overall understanding of a client in the context of his or her problems can enhance the effectiveness of therapy and second, because having an REBT-oriented contribution to this book will help redress the continuing marginalisation of REBT in the cognitive–behavioural literature.

My fundamental objection to the terms "case formulation" and "case conceptualisation" is that the use of these terms perpetuates the objectification of clients. In short, a complex, unique person is objectified as "a case" and I strongly object to this practice. For this reason, in this chapter, I will speak of understanding the person in the context of his/her problems (UPCP) instead of using the phrase "making a case formulation". I do not know (or indeed care) whether or not other REBT therapists share my reservation about the terms "case formulation" and "case conceptualisation". If this book is about nothing else it is about respecting the individuality of persons and as a person who is also an REBT therapist, I claim the same respect for myself. What I bring to this chapter, then, is an idiosyncratic approach to understanding persons (who happen to be clients) in the context of their problems based on REBT principles (Walker, 1997). I will

Beyond Diagnosis: Case Formulation Approaches in CBT.
Edited by Michael Bruch and Frank W. Bond.
© 1998 John Wiley & Sons Ltd.

approach this task as follows. First, I will present and discuss the framework that I use for UPCP. Second, I will apply this framework to highlight the work that I did with a particular client that is particularly relevant to the focus of this book. And finally, I will show how my UPCP guided my clinical thinking in treatment planning with a selected client. Let me stress at the outset that I have sought and received the permission of my client to do this as long as salient features of her situation are disguised. I have shown her the first draft of this chapter and she is satisfied with the modifications that I have made to protect her confidentiality.

This is not the place for me to discuss REBT theory in depth (see Dryden, 1994a; Ellis, 1994 for such a discussion). However, in order to understand what follows you will need to understand REBT's ABC assessment framework. Here is a thumbnail sketch of this framework.

"A" refers to the activating events that a person focuses on. These can be (i) actual or inferred; (ii) past, present or future or (iii) external or internal. "B" refers to the beliefs that the person holds about these events. As we will presently see, these beliefs may be irrational/unhealthy or rational/healthy. Finally, "C" refers to the consequences of holding these beliefs. These consequences may be emotional, behavioural and/or cognitive.

Before I consider the factors that need to be considered in developing a UPCP, I want to make the following point about its sequential place in the practice of REBT. Some approaches to cognitive–behaviour therapy consider that it is important to "formulate a case" before making therapeutic interventions. REBT does not advocate this position. Rather, it holds that it is equally possible and sometimes desirable to construct a UPCP after one has taught the client the ABC model of REBT and used this model to help the client with some specific problems. Indeed, I often find that teaching clients the ABC framework helps them to guide my UPCP since they are thus oriented to look for information that I need to formulate such understanding. However, other clients will respond more readily to REBT interventions once they have an overall understanding of themselves in the context of their problems. Thus, REBT adopts a flexible approach to developing a UPCP with respect to when this is done with different clients.

THE FACTORS THAT NEED TO BE CONSIDERED IN DEVELOPING A UPCP

In this section, I will outline and discuss the factors that need to be considered when understanding a person in the context of his or her problems. While these factors are heavily influenced by REBT theory, I do draw upon other cognitive–behavioural concepts. In the section, I will demonstrate how I developed a UPCP with a client using the factors which I will now discuss in general terms.

Basic Information and Initial Impressions

If you receive referrals from GPs and psychiatrists, you will often receive basic information about clients before meeting them. While this information is second hand, it is important to consider because it will often contain relevant demographic information, family history and a developmental account of the client's past and present problems. If your clients are largely self-referred you will need to gather this information yourself. This information is important to consider in developing a UPCP since it places your client in a wider context.

You will also develop initial impressions when you meet your client and even when you speak on the phone to make an appointment. While you should regard such initial impressions tentatively, they can be useful in helping you to confirm or reject your beginning attempts to formulate a UPCP.

The Importance of Developing a Problem List

I agree with Persons (1989) in her book on "case formulation" in cognitive therapy that it is important to develop a list of the client's problems when one is working to develop a UPCP. This is not an accepted practice in REBT, but I find it to be one of the ways that Beck's cognitive therapy has enhanced my practice as an REBT therapist. I also agree with Persons (1993) that it is useful to have these problems expressed in the client's own words whenever possible unless their words lack the necessary specificity for a working problem list. In this case, the therapist needs to paraphrase these problems in a way that more clearly elucidates them.

Having a clear idea of the range of problems the client wants to work on in therapy at an early stage, rather than working on a problem as soon as the client identifies one (an unfortunate practice, but a common one amongst novice REBT therapists) gives therapy a sensible direction based on an emerging UPCP.

Identifying Goals for Therapy

I have been very much influenced by Bordin's (1979) tripartite view of the working alliance in my practice of REBT. Bordin argues that one of the hallmarks of effective therapy is that the client and therapist have shared ideas about the goals of therapy. However, there is another reason why asking for the client's goals is useful early in therapy. Doing so often reveals quite a lot about the client's problems, unhealthy beliefs and possible obstacles to therapy. Thus, if a client says that one of her therapeutic goals is never to be anxious again, this may reveal something important about her problem, her attitude to being in control (for example) and the likelihood of her becoming disillusioned with therapy (which in this case is very high).

Developing a List of Problem Emotions (or Cs)

The client's problem list may or may not contain specific information about which problematic emotions the client experiences. If this information is not provided in the problem list, then I find it useful to discover what these problematic emotions are at a fairly early stage of therapy since such a list will provide important clues about other aspects of the client's cognitive–affective–behavioural dynamics.

REBT theory clearly discriminates between healthy negative emotions (HNEs)—such as concern, sadness, healthy anger, remorse, disappointment, sorrow, healthy envy and healthy jealousy—and their unhealthy counterparts. These unhealthy negative emotions (UNEs) are anxiety, depression, unhealthy anger, guilt, shame, hurt, unhealthy envy and unhealthy jealousy.

At an early stage of therapy I like to know which of these UNEs are involved in my client's problems. I refer to these as the client's problem emotions. These occur at "C" in the ABC framework.

Developing a List of Problematic Critical As

As I mentioned earlier, As represent activating events in the ABC framework. In particular, REBT therapists are keen to identify those As about which clients disturb themselves. These are known as critical As (Dryden, 1995). These are best identified when the client's unhealthy negative emotions are known. There are twelve major ways of identifying critical As (see Dryden, 1995, for a discussion of these methods). In striving to develop an accurate UPCP, it is important to identify broad categories of critical As. Examples of these general categories are: disapproval, injustice, failure and uncertainty.

REBT therapists generally begin therapy by working on specific examples of client problems. However, in developing an accurate UPCP, I tend to ask a client who has identified a specific example of disapproval, for example, to what extent he experiences difficulties in dealing with disapproval in other areas of his life. For the purposes of developing a UPCP, I work from the specific to the general on each specific problem the client identifies.

Identifying Core Irrational/Unhealthy Beliefs

According to REBT theory, four irrational or unhealthy beliefs lie at the centre of psychological problems. These four beliefs are known as demandingness, awfulising, low frustration tolerance and depreciation of self, others and life conditions. In REBT practice, with its early focus on specific client problems, the therapist tends to identify specific irrational beliefs. However, as I have already mentioned, in working to develop an accurate UPCP, I tend to move quickly from the specific to the general in an attempt to gain an overall understanding of the range of my client's problems. Thus, I endeavour to discover which of the client's specific irrational beliefs are representative of more general core irrational beliefs. Identifying core irrational beliefs (which are unhealthy beliefs that the client holds in a variety of situations) tends to accompany attempts to identify general problem emotional Cs and general categories of problem–critical As.

In identifying core irrational/unhealthy beliefs, I strive to understand whether these beliefs reflect ego disturbance or non-ego disturbance. Basically, self-depreciation beliefs are a distinguishing feature of ego-disturbance and LFT and awfulising beliefs are distinguishing features of non-ego disturbance where self-depreciation beliefs are either absent or peripheral. As I have discussed elsewhere identifying demands on their own do not help the REBT therapist to judge whether the client's problem is an example of ego disturbance or non-ego disturbance (Dryden, 1996a).

Identifying Dysfunctional Behavioural Cs

Dysfunctional behavioural Cs are either actions or tendencies to act which accompany unhealthy negative emotions. As I have shown elsewhere (Dryden, 1995), certain classes of actions and action tendencies (defined as tendencies to act which may or may not be transformed into overt actions) accompany specific unhealthy negative emotions. While there are recurring actions and action tendencies which accompany specific UNEs, in developing a UPCP I am keen to identify the client's idiosyncratic dysfunctional behavioural Cs. These responses tend to be consistent with the UNEs and the unhealthy, irrational beliefs that underpin them.

Identifying the Purposive Nature of Dysfunctional Behaviour

REBT theory owes a debt to the work of Alfred Adler and the latter day Adlerians in that it recognises that behaviour can be purposive. My own work in developing a UPCP leads me to ask the person whether his or her dysfunctional behaviour helps:

(1) to initiate an emotional state;
(2) to stop an emotional state;
(3) to avoid an emotional state;
(4) to reduce the intensity of an emotional state;
(5) to intensify an emotional state;
(6) to maintain emotional state;
(7) to elicit a response from the physical environment;
(8) to elicit a response from the interpersonal environment or;
(9) to act in a way that is consistent with personal values, standards and goals.

Identifying Ways in which the Person Prevents or Cuts Short the Experience of Problems

It is a feature of human beings that because we find our problems painful, we are strongly motivated to prevent ourselves from experiencing them. We are also similarly motivated to cut short our problems once we have begun to experience them. In developing a UPCP, I actively probe clients to discover their idiosyncratic ways of preventing the onset of problems or cutting them short once they have begun to be experienced.

Without an understanding of these two categories of client functioning, I am disadvantaged in my planning of REBT treatment strategies.

Identifying Ways in which the Person Compensates for Problems

It also happens that clients may function in ways that help them to compensate for having their problems. A common example of such compensatory behaviour was identified by Adler (1927) who showed that striving for superiority can often be a compensation for feelings of inferiority. This mechanism and the two described above represents the client's "protective shell" which serves to protect the client from the unhealthy psychological pain that he would feel if he experienced the full impact of his problems.

Identifying Meta-emotional Problems

REBT theory has for many years held that people frequently experience meta-emotional problems, i.e. they experience emotional problems about their emotional problems. Thus, I want to find out how clients feel about each of their problem emotions. As I have discussed elsewhere (Dryden, 1990a), the presence of meta-emotional problems complicates the work that my client and I will do on their original problems. Identifying meta-emotional problems helps me to understand the type of obstacles I may experience in my work with the client's original problems. Such understanding helps me to plan to circumvent these obstacles.

Identifying the Cognitive Consequences of Core Irrational/ Unhealthy Beliefs

In the ABC framework, "C" not only stands for the emotional and behavioural consequences of holding beliefs at B, it also stands for the cognitive consequences of these beliefs. When a person holds unhealthy, irrational beliefs then she tends to think in ways that are overly negative and distorted (Bond & Dryden, 1996). These cognitive consequences are generally inferential in nature and often serve as new "As" in subsequent ABC episodes. Furthermore, REBT theory holds that people implicitly bring their irrational or unhealthy beliefs to events at "A" with the result that these beliefs influence the inferences that are made at "A". Thus, a person who believes that he must succeed perfectly at important tasks brings this belief to performance-based situations, and may conclude that he has failed when objectively he can be said to have performed well, but not perfectly well, at the task in question.

In developing a UPCP, I look carefully at the cognitive consequences of irrational or unhealthy beliefs and see how they relate to inferences that the person makes in problem situations.

Identifying the Manner of Problem Expression and the Interpersonal Responses to these Expressions

It is a truism to say that people are social beings, but this can often be forgotten when one focuses on cognitive phenomena and, to a lesser extent, behavioural phenomena. When a client experiences a problem, I want to know how she expresses this when in the presence of others. Does she ask others for reassurance when she is anxious or does she put on a "brave face", for example?

Once I have discovered the client's routine ways of expressing her problems to others, I endeavour to identify how these others respond to these problem expressions. Do they, for example, offer reassurance when the client asks for it? And if the client puts on a "brave face", do others notice this and if so, how do they respond? REBT is an interpersonal-oriented therapy, but this feature has not received as much attention in the REBT literature as it warrants. An understanding of the client's interpersonal world, as it is relevant to her problems, is important in two ways. First, this knowledge helps me to decide how much attention I need to place on helping the client to communicate her problems more functionally and second, it alerts me to the possible inclusion of one or more of the client's significant others in therapy.

Identifying the Client's Health and Medication Status

Clients are not only psychological beings, they are also biological beings and as part of developing a UPCP, it is important to understand their health and medical status. Thus, I want to know what their general health is like and whether or not they have any illnesses that may impact on their psychological problems.

I want to know whether or not they are currently taking medication, the daily dose of any such medication and their attitude towards taking these drugs. In addition, I determine whether or not their psychological symptoms warrant further psychiatric or physical investigations. Thus, some clients show biological signs of severe depression and are not currently on psychotropic medication. In these cases I refer the clients for a psychiatric evaluation.

Developing an Understanding of Relevant Predisposing Factors

As I have mentioned elsewhere (Dryden, 1996b), REBT does not have an elaborate theory of the acquisition of psychological disturbance. It argues that people are not disturbed by events, but bring their tendencies to disturb themselves to events. This being said, it is useful in developing one's UPCP to identify the predisposing factors that may have contributed to the origin of the client's problems.

The difference between contributory events (or what I call critical As) and predisposing factors is as follows. Contributory events are current events which trigger the client's unhealthy, irrational beliefs that underpin current problems, whereas predisposing events are usually past events which influenced (but did not cause) the development of his irrational beliefs. Predisposing factors are usually similar in theme to critical As.

Predicting the Person's Likely Responses to Therapy

I agree with Persons (1993) who argues that an important feature of her case formulation approach to cognitive therapy is to use this formulation to help her predict the client's likely response to therapy. I attempt to do this as well by drawing upon (i) the UPCP; (ii) the person's previous attempts to solve problems, including her utilisation of previous therapy and (iii) the person's interpersonal and learning styles as these are relevant to the therapy situation.

Negotiating a Narrative Account of the UPCP for Consideration with the Client

I also agree with Persons (1993) that it can be helpful to put one's UPCP in narrative form to the client for consideration, feedback and refinement. Sometimes I do this in writing, particularly when the UPCP is complex, but more often I do this verbally. Like Persons, I see the UPCP as fluid and open to refinement at any point in therapy. A rigid adherence to one's UPCP is not only bad therapy, it is also against the flexible nature of REBT.

Let me now show how I developed a UPCP with a particular client.

UPCP IN ACTION

Basic Information and Initial Impression

Jane Smith was at the time I saw her a 36 year old single woman who was referred to me after a brief hospitalisation for anxiety and depression. The referral letter from her psychiatrist mentioned that she worked as a nursing sister in a rehabilitation unit and that she was regarded as a model practitioner and administrator. Jane had two younger brothers and her parents were still alive and constantly looked to her for emotional support. She was generally regarded as the strong person in the family and her two younger brothers often used her as a counsellor when life became too stressful for them. This was her first hospitalisation and she had no previous recorded history of psychological problems. She smoked thirty cigarettes a day, drank three units of alcohol a week and had no experience of taking mood-altering drugs.

When she called me to make an appointment she was very keen to know how long therapy would last. While this is a reasonable request for a client to make of a therapist (Dryden & Feltham, 1995), I was struck by the insistence with which Jane made her enquiries. I very much agree with Persons (1993) that all client communications are grist for the UPCP mill and while REBT and CBT therapists do not analyse their clients' every utterance for deeper meaning, as may be true of some of our more enthusiastic psychoanalytic colleagues, we certainly have our eyes and ears open for information which may help us to deepen our UPCP. Rather than develop a specific, albeit tenuous hypothesis about what Jane's insistence might mean, I noted the experience as potentially valuable for my UPCP.

Jane's Problem List

I helped Jane to develop the following list of problems that she wanted to address in therapy. I should make clear that most of these items were developed in the first two sessions, but others were added as therapy proceeded.

(1) unable to control my feelings;
(2) overwhelmed with the demands of my job;
(3) unable to say no to people in my work and in my personal life;
(4) having to put on a brave face with people;
(5) unable to commit myself to men;
(6) afraid of falling in love;
(7) unable to show weakness;
(8) afraid of feeling anxious and depressed;
(9) scared of falling apart;
(10) expecting those I am close to to know how I feel without my having to tell them;
(11) expecting others to know that I am stretched and not add to my burden.

Jane's Goals for Therapy

Jane's goals for therapy were as follows:

  (1) to be able control my feelings;
  (2) to develop healthy boundaries at work and in my personal life;
  (3) to be able to say no to people in my work and in my personal life;
  (4) to be honest about my feelings with people;
  (5) to be able to commit myself to men;
  (6) to allow myself to fall in love;
  (7) to be able to show weakness;
  (8) to deal constructively with feeling anxious and depressed;
  (9) to allow myself to feel out of control without being so scared of it;
(10) not to expect those close to me to know how I feel if I don't tell them;
(11) not to expect others to know when I am stretched if I don't tell them.

Jane's List of Problem Emotions (or Cs)

Jane identified the following emotions as being problematic for her:

(1) anxiety;
(2) depression;
(3) shame;
(4) guilt;
(5) hurt;
(6) unhealthy anger.

Jane's Problematic Critical As

Jane identified the following critical As as being problematic for her:

(1) when I am not in control of my feelings;
(2) when I am asked to take on more responsibility at work when I am stretched;
(3) letting people down at work and in my personal life;
(4) when I am asked if I feel all right when I am under stress;
(5) if a man who I like asks me out;
(6) thinking about being in a love relationship;
(7) when I do not feel strong emotionally;
(8) when I watch TV programmes when people have emotional problems;
(9) when those close to me do not understand how I feel without my having to tell them.

Jane's Core Irrational/Unhealthy Beliefs

I helped Jane to identify her core irrational beliefs, by first helping her to analyse a number of specific ABCs and detecting a number of her specific irrational beliefs. I then took these specific irrational beliefs and asked Jane to consider to what extent she held these beliefs in other relevant situations. In particular, I asked her to use the items on her list of problematic critical As as a guide. In this way Jane and I developed the following list of her core irrational or unhealthy beliefs. In presenting these beliefs I have indicated which is an example of ego disturbance and which of non-ego disturbance.

(1) I must be able to cope with anything that life throws at me and if I do not, I am a weak, defective person (ego disturbance belief).
(2) I must feel in control and it is terrible if I don't have this feeling (non-ego disturbance belief).
(3) I must not appear to be weak to others and if I do, I am a weak defective person (ego disturbance belief).
(4) I must have the approval of others and if I do not this means that I am inadequate (ego disturbance belief).
(5) I must not be badly treated by others and if I am I can't bear it (non-ego disturbance belief).

Jane's Dysfunctional Behavioural Cs

The following is a list of Jane's dysfunctional behavioural Cs grouped by her problem emotions:

(1) When Jane feels anxious, she tends to:
  (a) smoke;
  (b) praise people who she thinks may disapprove of her;
  (c) hold on to things to steady herself;
  (d) distract herself with work-related activity.
(2) When Jane feels depressed, she tends to:
  (a) smoke;
  (b) withdraw from others;
  (c) eat junk food.
(3) When Jane feels ashamed, she tends to:
  (a) smoke;
  (b) withdraw from others.
(4) When Jane feels guilty, she tends to:
  (a) smoke;
  (b) withdraw from others;
  (c) blame herself in the presence of others.

(5) When Jane feels hurt, she tends to:
  (a) smoke;
  (b) sulk.
(6) When Jane feels unhealthily angry, she tends to:
  (a) smoke;
  (b) bang doors.

The Purposive Nature of Jane's Dysfunctional Behaviour

Jane's dysfunctional behavioural Cs served three major purposes:

(1) To gain a sense of control
  (a) smoking;
  (b) holding on to things to steady herself;
  (c) withdrawing from others;
  (d) distracting herself with work-related activity;
  (e) sulking.
(2) To get rid of disturbing feelings
  (a) smoking;
  (b) withdrawing from others;
  (c) distracting herself with work-related activity;
  (d) eating junk food
  (e) banging doors.
(3) To ward off or neutralise interpersonal threat
  (a) praising people who she thinks may disapprove of her;
  (b) withdrawing from others;
  (c) blaming herself in the presence of others.

How Jane Prevents or Cuts Short the Experience of her Problems

In my work with Jane, I identified a number of ways in which she prevented or cut short the experience of her problems. While some of these methods are the same as those employed by Jane in the sections on irrational/unhealthy beliefs and dysfunctional behavioural Cs, the difference is that in those sections all the methods were behavioural in nature and were brought into play when Jane experienced the full force of her problems and associated feelings, while in this section the methods employed by Jane were a mixture of cognitive and behavioural and they were brought into play either to prevent the onset of her problems or to cut them short as soon as they had begun to be experienced.

Here are the methods that Jane employed to prevent or cut short the experience of her problems and associated feelings:

(1) Behavioural
    (a) smoking;
    (b) withdrawing;
    (c) immersing herself in work-related activities;
    (d) volunteering for activities;
    (e) agreeing to do whatever is asked of her at work;
    (f) contacting others who have problems and helping them with these problems;
    (g) going to the gym to work out;
    (h) telling others who show concern for her that she is fine;
    (i) turning down the offer of dates from men whom she finds attractive.
(2) Cognitive
    (a) imagining times when she felt strong and in control;
    (b) thinking that she is tired or physically ill rather than emotionally disturbed;
    (c) planning reorganisations at work;

How Jane Compensates for her Problems

The following are ways that Jane compensates for her problems:

(1) taking on more work
(2) being strong for others
(3) teaching stress management classes at work
(4) applying to join the Samaritans

Jane's Meta-emotional Problems

As discussed above, meta-emotional problems are emotional problems that the person has about her original problems. Here is a list of Jane's meta-emotional problems:

(1) shame about not coping and feeling depressed;
(2) anxiety about feeling anxious and not "feeling in control";
(3) anger at herself for needing the approval of others.

The Cognitive Consequences of Jane's Core Irrational/ Unhealthy Beliefs

The following are the cognitive consequences of Jane's core irrational/ unhealthy beliefs. I have listed these under each core irrational belief.

(1) I must be able to cope with anything that life throws at me and if I do not, I am a weak, defective person (ego disturbance belief)
  (a) thinking that others will disapprove of me if I let them know that I am not coping;
  (b) thinking of my emotional problems as weaknesses;
  (c) when I am feeling out of control, seeing others as strong and myself as weak.

(2) I must feel in control and it is terrible if I don't have this feeling (non-ego disturbance belief)
  (a) failing to acknowledge that I am under stress;
  (b) when I do acknowledge that I am under stress, overestimating the chances that I will lose control and the degree of loss of control that I will experience;
  (c) thinking that there are only two positions: being in full control or being out of control;
  (d) underestimating my ability to cope with slight or moderate loss of control.

(3) I must not appear to be weak to others and if I do, I am a weak defective person (ego disturbance belief)
  (a) overestimating the negative consequences of "appearing weak" to others (e.g. being reprimanded at work or losing my job);
  (b) overestimating the degree to which others view one negatively.

(4) I must have the approval of others and if I do not this means that I am inadequate (ego disturbance belief)
  (a) overestimating the amount of disapproval that I will experience from others;
  (b) viewing objectively neutral responses from others as signs of disapproval;
  (c) thinking that when others give me a positive response it is not honestly meant and that they have an ulterior motive. This is particularly the case when I do not think that I deserve the positive response;
  (d) thinking that when I show a "weakness" in public everyone will notice and look down on me.

(5) I must not be badly treated by others and if I am I can't bear it (non-ego disturbance belief)
  (a) thinking that if others treat me badly then I must have done something really bad to warrant it and will get into serious trouble as a result;
  (b) thinking that if others profess to care about me, then they will be able to tell when I am under stress and treat me appropriately.

Jane's Manner of Problem Expression and the Interpersonal Responses to These Expressions

Jane's way of dealing with her problems was basically to internalise them. Since she was very adept at hiding her feelings and erecting a facade of being strong and coping, others did not realise that she was experiencing problems. Since she cultivated and successfully communicated an "I am strong" persona, people at work continually came to her with their problems and asked her to take on difficult problems because they were sure that she would be able to cope.

In her personal life it was a similar story. Jane was known in her family and among her friends as a "veritable rock" who could take everything that life could throw at her "and then some" as one of her friends put it. She was also known to be a good listener and to offer sound advice if needed. Consequently, her family and friends would seek her out if they had problems which was quite often. Since they saw her as a "veritable rock" it rarely occurred to any of her family or friends to enquire about her well-being other than a cursory "how are you?" Even when she was under extreme stress she used to answer such queries with an automatic "I'm fine". Later in therapy Jane and I humorously referred to this as meaning, "I'm Fragile, Insecure, Nervous and Edgy!"

Establishing Jane's Health and Medication Status

Jane's health was generally good apart from periodic bouts of bronchitis exacerbated by smoking. The referring psychiatrist had not prescribed any medication for Jane's anxiety and depression partly because he did not think that her symptoms were severe enough after her discharge from hospital and partly because Jane was not keen to take drugs. This was not surprising given her core irrational belief that she had to be in control.

Jane's Relevant Predisposing Factors

As I mentioned earlier, predisposing factors are of importance in my UPCP in helping to explain the past context for the development of the client's unhealthy irrational beliefs. They differ from contributory events in that the latter are present events which trigger her presently held irrational beliefs that underpin her current problems. I call these contributory events, critical As. Critical As (or contributory events) are usually similar in theme to predisposing factors.

Jane's predisposing factors were as follows.

(1) From quite a young age, Jane's parents looked to her for her emotional support. This intensified as her two younger brothers grew up and began misbehaving both within the family and outside. In addition, Jane's brothers always looked up to her and frequently sought guidance from her. These predisposing factors were influential in leading Jane to see herself as the strong one in the family and the others as needing support. Early in therapy, Jane remarked that she developed the idea fairly early on that she had to be strong or the family would fall apart. REBT theory argues that these predisposing factors explain why Jane developed a keen desire to be strong, but we also have to take into account Jane's understandable human tendency to transform this strong desire into a devout demand.

(2) From Jane's account it seems as if her parents compensated for their own problems and vulnerabilities by deriding others outside the family for being weak. Jane reported that for as long as she can remember, she had two beliefs about emotional vulnerability. First, it was to be despised as it proved that the person was weak, spineless and defective. This was the attitude that Jane developed towards herself and, to a lesser extent, to people that she didn't know. Second, when people in her family and those whom she knew showed that they were struggling to cope, they were to be understood and helped. This view contributed to Jane's compensatory strategy of proving to herself that she was strong by helping others who were not. She would not have helped them if she had despised them.

REBT theory argues that Jane introjected (i.e. believed without question) her parents' views about weakness and about some of those who display it and actively carried these ideas into her adult life.

It may be that Jane was temperamentally suited to be active and helpful to others, a factor which also has to taken into account when developing a UPCP. REBT theory has a bio-social view of the development and maintenance of psychological problems and does not only look for environmental predisposing factors but also for biologically based ones.

Predicting Jane's Likely Response to Therapy

Given what I knew about Jane, I predicted that she would respond to therapy as follows:

(1) Since one of Jane's core problems concerned "feeling" out of control and her need to be in charge, I predicted that she would be attracted

to REBT because of its emphasis on self-help and its preference for forming egalitarian, adult–adult therapeutic relationships between client and therapist. Furthermore, investigations of her learning style indicated a good fit between her orientation towards independent learning and REBT.

(2) However, since she abhorred the idea of not being in emotional control, being in therapy could be a constant reminder of her defectiveness about being weak. If this shame-based belief became strongly activated, then Jane might be tempted to terminate therapy prematurely. In any event, her cognitive dynamics would suggest that she would want a brief therapeutic contract. Corroborating evidence for this came from Jane's initial contact with me by telephone. If you recall, I was struck by her insistence to know how long therapy would last before we had even met.

Negotiating a Narrative Account of the UPCP with Jane

The following is a narrative account of my understanding of Jane in the context of her problems. The account is one that has been refined by the client and appears in the first person at the request of the client herself.

My main problem is that I have a rigid attitude about being strong. This attitude leads me to be scared of losing control emotionally and to feel ashamed if I can't cope. I also need others to approve of me and think that they will not do so if I show that I can't cope and if they were to learn that I have emotional problems. In particular, this has meant that I have shied away from committing myself to men I like because I fear that they will reject me if they see the real me.

The roots of these problems go back to the role that I took on in my family. I was seen as, and took on the role of, the strong one in the family and concluded that I had to be strong to keep the family from disintegrating. I need to rethink this role if I am to look after myself.

I have developed a number of strategies to prevent myself from confronting what I see as my weak side. First, I take on too much work. This has the effect of leading me to feel overly stressed, but I do it to prove to myself and others that I can cope. Second, I feel strong when others turn to me for help even though it adds to my burden and creates more problems than it solves. Third, I have developed a number of ways to gain a sense of control and get rid of disturbed feelings. I recognise that these strategies don't work for me in the long term. Fourth, I have developed a number of ways of getting approval, but again these ways don't work for me in the long term.

I recognise that I need to accept myself as a person who has strengths and weaknesses, and to tolerate feeling stressed long enough to deal with these feelings in more productive ways than I have managed at present. In particular, I need to develop healthy boundaries at work and in my personal life and to honestly admit to myself and others that I can't be strong all the time. I also need to take risks with people and particularly with men and to get over my fear of being rejected by them.

While I want to help myself as quickly as possible, I recognise that therapy will take longer than this and I need to guard against bringing my "need to be strong" patterns to therapy.

You will note that while this narrative summary is fairly complete, it does not contain all the above elements of the UPCP. The purpose of the narrative summary is to paint a picture of the client's main problems and relevant associated factors rather than to include everything.

Before I discuss using the UPCP as a guide to therapy with Jane, let me say a few words about the relationship between the UPCP and psychiatric diagnosis. Basically, my view is the same as Persons' (1993) who has said that a psychiatric diagnosis may be useful for communicating with other clinicians, but it is insufficient for detailed treatment planning because it fails to describe the person's mechanisms underlying his or her problems in sufficient depth. It also fails to include the breadth of a person's problems. I also think that a psychiatric diagnosis unwittingly increases the risk that the client will become objectified and become equated with his diagnosis. In this vein, I frequently hear people described as "borderlines", for example. As I mentioned at the beginning of this chapter, I am passionately against anything that objectifies persons who seek therapeutic help and thus, I do not employ psychiatric classification systems such as the DSM-IV in thinking about my clients and as an aid to treatment planning and therapeutic intervention. It is for these reasons that I choose not to speculate about Jane's psychiatric diagnosis.

USING UPCP AS A GUIDE TO THERAPEUTIC INTERVENTION WITH JANE

In this concluding section, I will show how I used the UPCP to guide my thinking about selecting therapeutic strategies and techniques with Jane. I will not discuss what I actually did with Jane in therapy since this falls outside the scope of this chapter; rather, I will outline briefly my therapeutic intentions and clinical thinking.

I believe that it is important to be explicit with clients about my clinical thinking so that I can involve them fully in therapy. I thus view therapy as a partnership between myself as therapist and my client. This view is particularly important in the work that I plan to do with Jane because my UPCP led me to conclude that she is likely to terminate therapy prematurely in that being in therapy is likely to be interpreted by her as evidence that she cannot cope and this will trigger her core irrational belief that she must be able to cope and if she doesn't, she is defective. As I noted above, one of Jane's characteristic ways of cutting short the experience of shame that accompanies the activation of this core irrational belief was withdrawal from other people, expressed here by terminating therapy prematurely. I plan to raise this issue with Jane early on in therapy and to check with her if she had such thoughts about cancelling sessions, for example.

As I have just expressed, it is my practice to involve clients in treatment planning. This does not preclude me from offering them my views about how we might best proceed. In this way, I strive to develop and maintain an effective working alliance between my clients and myself (Bordin, 1979). I thus plan to raise with Jane the possibility of working initially on her meta-emotional problems so that she can begin to accept herself as a fallible human being who has strengths and weaknesses and so that she can begin to tolerate more effectively the experience of being out of control without being overwhelmed by such experiences.

Early on in therapy, I plan to use bibliotherapy and I will suggest that Jane read one or two of the self-help books that I have written based on REBT principles. For example, I will probably recommend that she should read my book entitled *Ten Steps to Positive Living* (Dryden, 1994b) which is a step-by step guide to basic REBT principles. Later, I may suggest that she reads *Overcoming Shame* (Dryden, 1997) and certain key chapters from *Beating the Comfort Trap* (Dryden & Gordon, 1993) which focuses on non-ego disturbance problems.

This reading and the cognitive work that I imagine we will do in early sessions will underpin the behavioural changes that I will encourage Jane to make. For example, I plan to help Jane to begin to say no to unreasonable requests to take on extra workload and to withdraw from the role of being counsellor to her family members. This behavioural work will also be preceded by my helping her to challenge her core irrational belief about being approved.

In disputing her core irrational beliefs I plan to make liberal use of therapist self-disclosure. Thus, I plan to share instances of how I struggled with similar core irrational beliefs to Jane's, how I challenged these beliefs and the difference that changing these beliefs made to my own life. The reason why I think such self-disclosure may be particularly potent with Jane is that it will serve to equalise the relationship between us and ensure that her shame-based beliefs about being weak for having problems do not interfere with therapy. In using therapist self-disclosure it is very important to monitor the impact that these disclosures have on the client. If it transpires that Jane reacts negatively to the first instance of such disclosure then I would not persist with this type of intervention (Dryden, 1990b).

As Jane makes progress in tolerating her feelings of not coping, I plan to encourage her to desist from using the strategies she employs to prevent, cut short and get rid of feelings of being out of control. In doing so, she will be able to use cognitive disputing of core irrational beliefs that I will have taught her before encouraging her to let go of these counterproductive strategies.

Then, I plan to teach her the effects that her core irrational beliefs have on her subsequent thinking and show her how she thereby creates many of her critical As. Once she has accepted and understood this point, I plan to encourage her to share with others when she is feeling vulnerable and to take risks in her relationships with attractive men. In addition, I plan to help her to challenge any negatively distorted inferences that remain. This last point is in keeping with REBT theory which states that it is important to challenge and change irrational beliefs at B before challenging and changing inferences at A. However, this sequence is not a rigid one and if it needs to be reversed in Jane's case, I will not hesitate to help her to correct some of her distorted inferences before working with her to replace her irrational beliefs with rational ones.

CONCLUSION

REBT therapists have written extensively on general strategies and techniques that can be used with a broad range of clients (Grieger & Boyd, 1980; Wessler & Wessler, 1980) and have been very explicit about how to work with clients on specific problems (Dryden, 1990a). However, there is a dearth of material in the REBT literature on how to understand clients in the context of their problems and how this understanding may inform the development of individualised treatment plans. It is my hope that this chapter will encourage other REBT therapists to take this important clinical topic further.

REFERENCES

Adler, A. (1927) *The Practice and Theory of Individual Psychology.* New York: Harcourt, Brace.
Bond, F.W., & Dryden, W. (1996) Modifying irrational control and certainty beliefs: Clinical recommendations based upon research. In W. Dryden (ed.), *Research in Counselling and Psychotherapy: Practical Applications.* London: Sage.

Bordin, E.S. (1979) The generalizability of the psychoanalytic concept of the working alliance. *Psychotherapy: Theory, Research and Practice*, **16**(3), 252–260.

Dryden, W. (1990a) *Rational–Emotive Counselling in Action*. London: Sage.

Dryden, W. (1990b) Self-disclosure in rational-emotive therapy. In G. Stricker and M. Fisher (eds), *Self-disclosure in the Therapeutic Relationship*. New York: Plenum.

Dryden, W. (1994a) *Invitation to Rational–Emotive Psychology*. London: Whurr.

Dryden, W. (1994b) *Ten Steps to Positive Living*. London: Sheldon.

Dryden, W. (1995) *Preparing for Client Change*. London: Whurr.

Dryden, W. (1996a) *Inquiries in Rational Emotive Behaviour Therapy*. London: Sage.

Dryden, W. (1996b) Rational emotive behaviour therapy. In W. Dryden (ed.), *Handbook of Individual Therapy*. London: Sage.

Dryden, W. (1997). *Overcoming Shame*. London: Sheldon.

Dryden, W. & Feltham, C. (1995). *Counselling and Psychotherapy: A Consumer's Guide*. London: Sheldon.

Dryden, W. & Gordon, J. (1993) *Beating the Comfort Trap*. London: Sheldon.

Ellis, I. (1994) *Reason and Emotion in Psychotherapy. Revised and Updated*. New York: Birch Lane Press.

Grieger, R. & Boyd, J. (1980) *Rational–Emotive Therapy: A Skills-based Approach*. New York: Van Nostrand Reinhold.

Persons, J. (1989). *Cognitive Therapy in Practice: A Case Formulation Approach*. New York: Norton.

Persons, J. (1993). Case conceptualization in cognitive-behavior therapy. In K.T. Kuehlwein and H. Rosen (eds), *Cognitive Therapies in Action: Evolving Innovative Practice*. San Francisco: Jossey-Bass.

Walker, A.P. (1997) Managing counter-transference and achieving appropriate self-disclosure: A new model from REBT. Workshop held as the annual UKCP conference (July).

Wessler, R.A. & Wessler, R.L. *The Principles and Practice of Rational–Emotive Therapy*. San Francisco: Jossey-Bass.

CHAPTER 4

The reformulation of panic attacks and a successful cognitive–behavioral treatment of social evaluative anxiety

Gerald C. Davison and
Michael K. Gann

In recent years there has been increasing interest among psychologists and other social scientists in social constructionism, an epistemological approach that emphasizes the observer's/scientist's active role in defining reality. Consistent with a lively interest in cognitive science, the core constructionist assumption finds its roots in the observations of ancient philosophers as well as in the writings of poets and playwrights. Shakespeare put the idea this way: "There is nothing either good or bad, but thinking makes it so" (*Hamlet*, Act 2). And constructionism has been explicated of course by many current social philosophers (e.g. Gergen, 1994). While the extreme position can lead to an undesirable solipsism—there is no external reality worth worrying about—the message seems to us relevant and important for clinical psychologists. We have put the issue as follows in a discussion of constructive assessment in therapy with homosexuals:

> . . . clients seldom come to mental health professionals with problems as clearly delineated and independently verifiable as what a patient brings to a physician . . . a client usually goes to a psychologist or psychiatrist in the way described by Halleck (1971). That is, the client is unhappy; his life is going badly; nothing seems to be meaningful; she's depressed more than her life circumstances would seem to warrant; his mind wanders when he

Beyond Diagnosis: Case Formulation Approaches in CBT.
Edited by Michael Bruch and Frank W. Bond.
© 1998 John Wiley & Sons Ltd.

tries to concentrate; unwanted images intrude on her consciousness or in her dreams. The clinician *transforms* these often vague and complex complaints into a diagnosis or assessment, a set of ideas about what is wrong and, usually, what might be done to alleviate what is wrong. I would argue, then, that psychological problems are for the most part *constructions* of the clinician: our clients come to us in pain, and they leave with more clearly defined problems that we assign to them (Davison, 1991, pp.142–143).

A constructionist approach was taken in the case described in the present chapter. As will be shown, the nature of the referral was transformed very early in the therapy. A treatment program was then devised that was consistent with the reformulated clinical problem. The orderly and favorable course of therapy is consistent with the proposition that the reformulation of the patient's problem was useful. It is of course impossible to prove that the kind of positive outcome reported here would not have arisen with other assessment and therapeutic strategies, but the following case report is, we believe, of heuristic and demonstrational value.

NATURE OF THE REFERRAL

The first author was teaching a graduate clinical course in psychological intervention several years ago and had decided to have as the practicum component of an otherwise theory- and research-based seminar his treatment of an ongoing patient in the program's teaching clinic. The clinic director arranged for the therapist to see a female patient whose problem was described by a social worker she had been seeing as panic attacks. This therapist believed her patient would profit from a behaviorally oriented treatment, possibly systematic desensitization. The social worker described her approach as psychodynamic and family systems-oriented, so she did not feel qualified to embark upon the kind of behavioral treatment that she considered appropriate for her patient. (It is worth noting that the referring therapist's view of desensitization as the best intervention for panic attacks was not consistent with the research literature, which supports a treatment aimed at exposure to interoceptive stimuli like accelerated heart rate intentionally created by the patient in session and then reduced by various coping techniques such as relaxation, e.g. Barlow, 1988.)

The patient, whom we shall call Marie, agreed in writing to have all sessions with GCD videotaped and made available for use in professional training contexts. This she did because she hoped that this complete archiving of her treatment might help in educating future clinicians and thereby assisting other patients.

ASSESSMENT AND REFORMULATION

The first session of this therapy was perhaps the most critical. The referring clinician and the patient came together to our training clinic for the initial consultation, and with the patient's permission, there was a brief preliminary session with the social worker alone so that she might provide some context for the referral.

The social worker had been seeing the patient for ten months and described her as a 39-year old thrice-married full-time high school drama instructor and part-time actress who, as a recovering alcoholic, had been abstinent for 18 months. She had been complaining of what both the social worker and the patient referred to as "panic attacks," and these were marked by elevated heart rate, perspiration, and what the patient called "mind-fucking" cognitions. The social worker described the patient also as suffering from low self-esteem and a high need for approval.

A question in the therapist's mind before even seeing the patient was whether these "panic attacks" were uncued. Before the initial consultation, the therapist was prepared to embark on a therapy program drawn from the work of Barlow and his associates on panic disorder (Barlow, 1988), but consistent with his behaviorist assumption that unrealistic anxiety is usually triggered by identifiable environmental antecedents, he embarked in the preliminary interview with the social worker on a line of questioning that, he believed, might lead to a reformulation of the problem.

We learned from the referring therapist that Marie had a long history of sensitivity to criticism, dating back to childhood experiences with a "hypercritical" mother. This prompted GCD to ask whether criticism could be an important cue for Marie's "panic attacks": "Does she react with this extreme anxiety when she perceives she might not do well? Are there other situations in which she experiences the anxiety?" Answers by the social worker and, later in the session, by the patient herself, yielded support for our evolving hypothesis that criticism, or social evaluation, might be a powerful cue for sometimes extreme bouts of anxiety which the patient and the social worker were labeling panic attacks.

After speaking with the referring therapist for about half an hour, GCD spoke with Marie without her therapist present. Marie readily engaged the therapeutic situation with energy and intelligence. She presented as an attractive, intelligent, articulate person who was strongly motivated to make maximum use of the weekly sessions that GCD was able to offer her during the coming semester as part of his graduate course. She showed considerable emotional lability in this session, tearful one moment, reflective and composed the next. Despite the inevitable intrusiveness of the session being videotaped, including the presence of a third person in the room to monitor the videotaping, Marie and the therapist managed readily to concentrate on the therapy process itself.

As a follow-up on the briefing with Marie's clinician, our first line of questioning with the patient focused on determining if specific situations could be linked to her feelings of intense anxiety. Some excerpts will illustrate:

> THERAPIST: Are there things that trigger greater or lesser degrees of anxiety? For instance, I understand that you feel anxious during auditions.
> PATIENT: Auditions or any other kind of situation when people might criticize me.
> T: Would you describe yourself as sensitive to criticism? Can a negative remark stay with you for hours, even a day or two?
> P: Definitely. I have always been that way since I was a child. My mother was very critical. . . . I can hear her nagging. . . .
> T: Can you recall a recent situation that was very troubling? One in which you were very anxious about criticism?
> P: Yeah, a few months ago I auditioned for an industrial shoot. When I got there I heard that everything had gone wrong that day. There were technical problems and [problems also with] the house they chose for the location. I got very anxious and worried about doing a good job so everyone would feel better. I could feel my heart pounding and my hands were sweating.

From this exchange, GCD began to construct a theme of extreme interpersonal performance anxiety/sensitivity to criticism. "Panic attacks", especially in the sense of uncued bouts of extremely high anxiety, did not seem as useful a way to construe the patient's predicament as anxiety reactions to a range of specific and specifiable situations. The patient found the therapist's use of the descriptor "thin-skinned" very apt to refer to her sensitivity to criticism. Marie reported a long learning history dating back to her childhood experiences with a nagging mother. She also tended to blame herself for anything around her going awry. For example, if technicians at a shoot were unhappy, she would see it as her fault and her responsibility to make things right. Critical—but also neutral—reactions from people to her presence or to her actions were perceived as signs of danger.

In response to direct questions, Marie also expressed certainty that the "panics" she experienced never occurred out of the blue. And as the first session continued, she began referring to them as anxiety feelings rather than an panicky feelings. Furthermore, as she began to see some orderly relationships between her anxieties and specifiable events in her environment, she derived reassurance that she was not, as she had been fearing, losing her mind (a not infrequent associated symptom of panic disorder). The lack of evidence for panic disorder marked by recurrent uncued panic attacks, coupled with an emerging picture of a woman who had for years been extremely concerned about pleasing others and very fearful of being criticized by them, gave further support to the reformulation of the patient's difficulties as centering around high levels of social evaluative anxiety.

The therapist observed to the patient that high levels of nervous tension punctuated by extreme anxiety ("panic attacks") in response to social evaluation were understandable, given that she was an actress often going to auditions. As the therapist learned in succeeding sessions, auditions and acting in general provide a very thin schedule of positive reinforcement and a very concentrated schedule of punishment. At the same time, he agreed with her judgment that her anxiety reactions were much greater than the situations warranted and that they were probably interfering with her ability to perform as well as she was capable of.

DESIGNING AN INTERVENTION BASED ON THE REFORMULATION

Because the therapist considered systematic desensitization as a strong possibility for treatment, he inquired into past experiences that the patient might have had with relaxation training. She reported that she had done Hatha Yoga and considered herself fairly proficient at achieving a state of relaxation when she put her mind to it in a controlled environment. This boded well for her learning progressive relaxation that would be applied in desensitization. Her background as an actor suggested to the therapist that she would have no trouble in the imaginal role-playing that is intrinsic to desensitization (whereby an imagined event has to be the functional equivalent of an actual one).

During the second session, additional questioning provided further evidence in support of that hypothesis, pursuing an allusion by the patient about the fear of the unknown:

> T: Does the fear of the unknown have anything to do with not knowing what to do, a fear of harm that might befall you?
> P: I'm aware of something physiologically that happens to me, the excessive sweating, the adrenaline flowing, and I don't know why that happens. I think it comes down to "they won't like who or what I am. . . . I don't know what any other actors' insides are like but I can't imagine spending the rest of my life feeling what I have over the past year. I always compare myself

to other people. I look around and see that they all seem fine and I'm about to pass out. I am dying inside from the anticipation. One way I judge the appropriateness of how I feel is to see how others are feeling.

"People-pleasing" and sensitivity to criticism go hand in hand with assertiveness problems, and Marie was no exception. She readily agreed that she had great difficulty expressing her needs and disagreeing with others. Whether time would permit a focused approach to nonassertiveness was doubtful, but the therapist harbored the belief that reducing her concern about the opinions of others would likely have a beneficial effect on her nonassertiveness.[1]

At the end of the second session, the therapist asked Marie to gather data for their collaborative project as an important first step in efforts to reduce her interpersonal anxiety. She was asked to write down situations or events where she found herself getting more anxious "than you believe the event warrants". Feelings of anxiety, therefore, were construed for her as useful tools for treatment, cues that would help in the formulation of a therapy that would target her excessive anxiety in reaction to a range of specific and specifiable situations.

By this point the therapist was considering a cognitive intervention based on Ellis (1962, 1993). Because rational–emotive behavior therapy focuses on internal monologues and (sometimes unverbalized) assumptions that reflect an overly demanding, perfectionistic attitude towards the self and/or the environment, the therapist began to ask the patient to consider what goes through her mind when she becomes anxious. Therefore, in addition to the self-monitoring of external events that seemed to trigger unwarranted anxiety, Marie was asked to try to take notice of what she was thinking about while she was feeling inappropriate anxiety. The therapist was thus laying the groundwork also for a cognitive therapeutic approach to complement desensitization. The following exchange illustrates how this self-monitoring assessment was presented to the patient:

> T: What someone says or does is the external situation so write that down [in the coming week as soon as possible after it happens]. But an important part is also what *you* bring to the situation. It's very important and useful to know what the thoughts are when you feel anxious. Start from your feelings as a signal to gather data. Include your "self-statements" or things you say to yourself.
> C: Subtext. In acting we call it subtext.[2]

GCD emphasized the distinction between useful and maladaptive anxiety so that Marie would not be concerned that she would "lose her edge" in behaving under the pressure of acting auditions. In other words, the goal of the therapy would not be to render her unconcerned about the quality of her performance, unable to "get up for" an acting challenge, rather it would be to teach her ways to avoid the debilitatingly high degrees of anxiety that had been preventing her from performing at her best and that had been making her role as an aspiring actress little better than a living Hell. This theme was discussed again towards the end of treatment, when Marie was beginning to feel a good deal less anxious generally and in social evaluative situations in particular. To drive the point home, the therapist described the inverted-U function in experimental psychology, whereby optimal performance is at a point of moderate arousal; too little arousal can contribute to a lackadaisical performance while too much can interfere with the expression of talents and skills that the person possesses. This metaphor seemed to make a great deal of sense to Marie and helped her adopt not only a realistic view of therapy but an adaptive one as well.

In collaboration with the patient, the therapist generated the hypothesis that a reduction in sometimes high levels of performance anxiety and sensitivity to criticism would be of material benefit. In the interests of making maximum use of the limited time available, the therapist presented to the patient a two-pronged approach: systematic rational restructuring, an imagery-based strategy for implementing Ellis's rational–emotive behavior therapy (see Goldfried & Davison, 1976, 1994, chapter 8); and taped systematic desensitization, Wolpe's imagery-based method for reducing anxiety (Wolpe, 1958) and adapted for audiotaped presentation (Goldfried & Davison, 1976, 1994, chapter 6). They would be combined on audiotape in order to accommodate the time restriction (an academic semester). The cognitive component would be directed at altering cognitions in a manner that would lessen the patient's catastrophizing and absolutist attitudes towards acting and other situations in which she could be unfavorably evaluated/criticized. The desensitization component would aim to break the links between specifiable anxiety-provoking situations and what might be non-cognitive mediated autonomic reactions that had been classically conditioned to inherently innocuous situations or situations of less than monumental import. While there are empirical data attesting to the efficacy as well as clinical effectiveness of both strategies, the *combination* of the cognitive and desensitization components was new in the therapist's practice and, to his knowledge, not previously (or since) reported on.[3]

Using the information gathered between sessions by the patient, the therapist worked with her over several sessions to create a 19-item anxiety hierarchy that represented her anxiety disorder (in DSM-IV terms, she would probably have been given a diagnosis of social phobia). A sampling of these items will illustrate this central aspect of the therapy. The numbers in parentheses represent the patient's rating of the aversiveness of the item on a 100 point subjective rating scale, where a rating of "1" indicates that the situation would evoke or has evoked no anxiety at all in real life, and "100" indicates that the situation is or would be as anxiety-provoking as she could imagine anything being. The fact that some of the ratings appear very precise (e.g. 59 instead of 60) is a result of items sometimes clustering within a general range and of the need to rank-order them. Note: while the construction of an anxiety hierarchy is usually seen as an aspect of treatment, it is in fact as much a part of the clinical assessment for it involves the fine-grain specification of the patient's anxiety-related clinical problems.

> At school, you are having a production meeting for the musical. You've done your work, and other people are reporting being on schedule, too. (15, easiest item)
>
> After a Twelve-Step meeting, you're inviting Mary and Ingrid to have lunch at your house. (25)
>
> Arriving for the shooting of the industrial [a training film], you are parking your car on the street near the house where the shoot is going to be. (30)
>
> As you enter the house for the shooting of the industrial, the casting director asks you who you are. You tell her who you are. (40)
>
> At home, you are putting on your make-up as you get ready to leave for the production company audition. (48)
>
> You've just arrived at the production company audition and you're scoping out the competition. (59)
>
> You're walking down a long hall in heels on your way to the production company audition room. (62)
>
> At the reading for the play, you're a few beats late with your first entrance. (65)
>
> At the industrial shoot, the director is yelling at you to get together with the continuity director and clean up the dialogue. (68)
>
> You're sitting around your dining room table with Kathy, Marion, and your daughter. You, Marion, and your daughter are smoking. Your husband comes in then quickly turns on his heel, goes into the kitchen, and bangs around some to show his displeasure. (80)
>
> At the reading for the play, you're making an entrance and realize that you didn't turn the page and you now have to find your place in the script. (92)
>
> At the industrial shoot, you're working with the continuity director to clean up the dialogue, and she is having you repeat each sentence often until you get it correct. (95, most difficult item)

It should be noted that the nature of the hierarchy itself is constructive in nature. That is, we have never viewed a specific anxiety hierarchy as the only or best one for a given patient at a given time. Knowing that a person is, as here, exceedingly sensitive to criticism does not in itself dictate those situations to which she will be desensitized or otherwise taught to cope with. An anxiety hierarchy or any other group of situations in a patient's life are, in our view, best seen as a sampling from an infinite number of situations that could be represented. We put the matter thusly many years ago in a discussion of desensitization:

> [We view themes pursued in therapy] as a *conceptualization* of the therapist. We have long ago stopped asking ourselves whether we have "truly" isolated a basic anxiety dimension of our clients. Rather, we ask ourselves how best to construe a person's difficulty so as to maximize his gains. In other words, rather than looking for the "real hierarchy," we look for the *most useful* hierarchy. This has important implications, not the least of which is the freedom to attempt to reconceptualize various client problems in terms amenable to desensitization. . . . The clinician must ask himself what the implications are likely to be should a particular desensitization actually succeed. For instance, will a person depressed about her lack of meaningful social contacts be happier if her inhibitions about talking to people are reduced by desensitization [in contrast to suggesting she find different people to associate with, for example; and/or trying to change her relationship with her husband, etc.]? Looked at in this way, the clinician would seem to have both greater freedom and greater challenge in isolating anxiety dimensions. (Goldfried & Davison, 1976, 1994, p.115)

Recall that the therapist was planning also a cognitive intervention based on Ellis. As noted earlier rational–emotive behavior therapy deals with internal monologues and assumptions that reflect an overly demanding, perfectionistic perspective on life. The therapist therefore began to ask the patient to consider what goes through her mind when she becomes anxious. This kind of discussion took place at various times during the first few sessions.

The anxiety hierarchy constructed with Marie was used in an imagery-based procedure that combined systematic desensitization and the cognitive approach of Albert Ellis. The desensitization component entailed instructing the patient to relax away even the slightest degree of tension elicited by a given aversive image. Relaxation was thereby seen as a coping response to anxiety per the self-control desensitization strategy originally proposed by Goldfried (1971).[4] The cognitive component involved first providing the patient with and then later encouraging her to develop on her own self-statements that reflected a less demanding, less absolutistic view of her interactions with others. For example, to deal with the item, "You're phoning your friend Jane to borrow an outfit for the production company audition," the therapist asked her to cope with the tension by saying silently to herself, "While it would be nice for the outfit to be great and for the audition to go well, it's not a catastrophe if things don't go perfectly." The patient imagined each item twice, the first time using relaxation to lessen her anxiety, the second time using a coping self-statement to control her tensions.

An aspect worth noting is the degree of *choice* that we indicated this combined treatment was designed to give her. That is, we proposed to her that one of the most frightening and daunting consequences of being exquisitely sensitive to negative evaluation—especially when one's life is full of such challenges, as hers was because of her acting—was that one felt tugged and pulled and dominated by external events. Learning ways to cope with such anxiety should lessen the feeling that one is helpless. Also, inherent in cognitive therapy, as with humanistic and existential therapies, is the guiding and core assumption that people do not react so much to what the world serves up to them, rather they can learn to choose to *construe* the world in a particular way (within practical and sensible limits, of course). The therapy, then, was aimed at increasing the range of choices she might have. Significantly, this discussion in the fourth session led to the patient crying, a reaction she said arose from feeling the relevance of the choice issue and allowing herself to have some hope that she could achieve more freedom in her emotional life than had been the case for many years.

The combined desensitization–REBT therapy in imagination was carried out across five sessions, with the therapist presenting items serially to the patient in groups of between two and four in session and making a tape of these presentations. This exercise occupied no more than half of a given session, with the patient instructed to practice with the tape between sessions. There was always discussion of the patient's experiences with each tape at the beginning of the following session, and then time was available to talk about related issues.

THE PROGRESS OF THERAPY

A number of events took place during the therapy that indicated that our particular construction of the patient's problems and the intervention based on it was proving useful. The importance of attending to the patient's self-talk was underscored in the fourth session, when she came in with a report of an audition that week having gone well because she had tried not to "beat up on myself" as she usually did when things were not going as well as they "should." She found herself realizing that she would be unlikely to get the part because she looked too young for it. With this pressure removed, she was able to relax and ended up auditioning very well. This experience, unplanned by the therapist, gave her insight into the role of self-talk and of not taking a "musturbatory" attitude towards a challenge and confirmed the therapist's developing belief that a cognitive approach would be useful as part of the therapeutic intervention.

Practicing relaxation with audiotapes was also facilitated by the patient's developing ability to refrain from demanding perfection of herself. She reported in the seventh session that she was able not to worry about how well she was doing with the practice and as a consequence was able to see it as less of a challenge to be perfect and more as something to enjoy, focusing on the process and not the desired outcome.[5]

In the ninth session she reported a good audition and attributed it to two factors: she knew beforehand that she had the part, and she saw that it was someone else's role that was to be decided on during the audition, not hers.[6]

During the thirteenth session, she recounted being able to deal with some stressors in a less agitated way than usual and made the following comment:

> The good side of all this [dealing with stressful situations] is that I feel so good about situations that come up that before would have made me very nervous and very anxious that haven't. I've had very quick clarity on the ability to put it into perspective and judge what my role is . . . I'm not getting emotional and I know I couldn't have done that last year . . . I was at a party where everyone was singing. One of the songs was an audition song of mine and everyone stopped singing because I was singing so well. When they stopped, I could feel my anxiety just go right up but I was able to continue singing and bring it down again.

In the fifteenth session, Marie commented that the hierarchy items she had worked with the preceding week seemed "silly" to get upset by. These were items that she had ranked as moderately anxiety-provoking.

In the second-last session, Marie said she was on her way to an audition and was, to her pleasure, looking forward to it as an occasion to apply her newly learned relaxation and cognitive restructuring skills.

While the therapeutic contract called for a time-limited therapy aimed directly at her "panic attacks," other themes were developed and discussed to some degree during the 17 sessions of treatment. Each of these themes could well have occupied our time, and each of them could have been construed as relevant to the "panic attacks". One such theme was problems the patient and her husband were having with one of the patient's daughters, a 17-year old suffering from an eating disorder. This naturally added to the stress that the patient had sought help for. Also a source of concern were conflicts with her husband, which seemed to be centered around his overbearing attitudes towards family finances. Coupled with this was a lack of assertiveness in the patient, something she herself traced to her traditional southern upbringing, constraints and limitations that she chafed under as a co-equal breadwinner in the marriage. And finally there was the continuing battle against a drinking problem that both she and her husband had been waging with help from AA. When she entered therapy with us, she had been abstinent for a year and a half.

These are issues which, as noted, were the subjects of discussion from time to time and would, under ordinary circumstances, have demanded greater attention in our therapy. The unease that the therapist experienced in paying little concentrated attention to these problems was alleviated by the knowledge that the patient was maintaining therapeutic contact with the referring social worker, who, it should be mentioned, watched the videotapes of the treatment and conferred periodically with us.

The last session, the seventeenth, took place five months after the initial consultation and included the referring therapist in a review of the course of the treatment. The social worker, who had seen Marie several times during the course of our therapy with her, confirmed our positive judgment of her general anxiety level and her ability to deal with stressful situations without the panic that had been the basis of the original referral to GCD. The audition that Marie had gone to immediately following the preceding session, along with a second one that week, had both gone very well. As she put it: "I just nailed both those auditions. I feel the anxiety creeping up and I use it for the auditions. It's just not unmanageable . . ."

At this wrap-up, the therapist encouraged Marie to practice with the relaxation tapes about once a week and also with the last couple of desensitization–REBT tapes (which dealt with the most difficult hierarchy items) in order to keep these newly acquired cognitive skills fresh and available to apply to the stressors in any person's life. "It's like staying in good physical condition. . . . It takes repetition and drill," GCD observed. Marie would begin seeing her social worker therapist once again to work in particular on her marital stress, and the plan was for her to phone GCD for a two-month follow-up session.

This session in fact took place. Marie was continuing to have good auditions and was even getting some paid acting jobs. She commented jokingly that on one voice-over she was doing, she was feeling so relaxed that the director told her to "put more of an edge on it." She had no trouble doing so. Her home situation continued to pose major challenges—her daughter's bulimia and ongoing conflicts with her husband—but she expressed confidence that, with the continuing help of her social worker therapist, she would be able to cope adequately. In general, she saw herself as less of a pawn and more of an assertive person with legitimate rights and the means to achieve them.

A second follow-up session five months later was planned and took place, constituting a seven-month follow-up. At this meeting the gains already noted seemed to be holding. She was continuing to audition and to get jobs, and was planning to leave her teaching job in order to focus more on her acting career. She described her marriage in very positive terms and was having less frequent sessions with the social worker. She and her husband were continuing to attend AA meetings regularly. At the end of the session, GCD reminded her that slip-ups were inevitable and that she would be well advised to see them as temporary and a part of normal daily life.

A letter 18 months later and a phone call two years after that, or about three years after termination, confirmed that things continued to be going well. She had taken a management position at a large upscale department store in Los Angeles and asserted that her social evaluative anxiety was gone. This had given her, she said, a sense of self-empowerment that was having generalized positive effects in her life.

SUMMARY

This case study illustrates the manner in which a presenting complaint of panic attacks was reformulated into a theme of social evaluative anxiety. This construction of the patient's problem led to a two-pronged approach: systematic desensitization and rational–emotive behavior therapy, combined in a novel imaginal therapeutic procedure that was conducted largely via audiotapes made over several consulting sessions and used in daily at-home practice by the patient. In this procedure, relaxation and positive self-statements were applied by the patient as self-control ways to ease tension in a range of social evaluative situations, most especially auditions for this part-time actress. As with most people who commit to psychotherapy, this patient had other problems as well, among them a continuing battle against problem-drinking, a bulimic daughter, problems of nonassertiveness, and a marriage that showed some signs of strain. The time-limited nature of the therapy reported here precluded dealing with these issues, but the stress occasioned by them seemed to benefit from the anxiety-reduction procedure as did much as the interpersonal performance anxiety that was the target for intervention. A follow-up of almost three years suggested that the treatment gains were being maintained and that the patient was succeeding in coping well with life's inevitable stressors.

NOTES

1. Nonassertive patients always pose a process problem for the therapist, namely, a concern that the patient will agree with interpretations and other statements of the therapist when, in fact, she doesn't. It is always good practice to make an extra effort with such patients by pointing out the importance of their expressing their needs and disagreements openly in session. This not only facilitates the treatment but also provides an opportunity for the patient to experiment with being more assertive. In this therapy we watched for opportunities for the patient to disagree with us and were gratified to find some. For example, during the relaxation training, Marie brought up problems she was occasionally having and reported at-home practice sessions that did not result in her feeling more relaxed after listening to a tape than she was beforehand. Also, there were many occasions when she expressed a difference of opinion about the therapist's interpretation of an event. Another sign that the patient was prepared to tell the therapist things she believed he would rather not hear was a comment in the twelfth session when she reported that listening to the desensitization-REBT tape the previous week had been "boring" and that she had experienced resistance within herself about working with the tape on a daily basis, as had been prescribed. (The therapist construed her boredom as a positive sign, to wit, that the hierarchy items were becoming easier for her to cope with.)
2. Notice how the patient immediately grasped the importance of a person's ongoing dialogue with herself. The therapist made clear on this and other occasions the connections and similarities between what was going on in their therapy together and what an actor is familiar with and uses to enhance her work.
3. The nature and role of clinical innovation have been reviewed previously by us (Davison & Lazarus, 1994, 1995; Lazarus & Davison, 1971).
4. There are many ways to conceptualize the mechanisms underlying the effectiveness of systematic desensitization. If the effects derive from counterconditioning (cf. Davison, 1968; Wolpe, 1958), then relaxation is viewed as a response that is substituted for anxiety. As implemented here, we focused on the coping aspects of relaxation as suggested by Goldfried (1971), but the strategy we followed would also satisfy the procedural requirements of counterconditioning.
5. Not always considered when teaching patients relaxation is the attitude that is best suited for acquiring this skill, and we believe that reports of "relaxation-induced anxiety" (Heide & Borkovec, 1984) may arise from overlooking this variable. We have made it a practice to spend time before a first induction explaining the mind-set that is helpful in deriving benefit from this training. Discussion centers around such themes as viewing relaxation as a skill that requires patience and practice, understanding new sensations like tingling in the fingers as good signs rather than something to be alarmed about, and emphasizing that the patient retains ultimate control over what is happening.

Most relevant to Marie were two "rules": adopting the set of "going with" the process rather than focusing on the outcome, and not seeing the training as an achievement situation, viz., "Especially with clients who are concerned about how they are doing, it is important to point out that this is not a testing situation and not something that they have to work at in a dogged, grim fashion" (Goldfried & Davison, 1976, 1994, p. 84). Indeed, as with trying to "achieve an orgasm", to pursue relaxation with steadfast resolution seems to interfere with the goal.

6. It is interesting that positive outcomes were being reported *before* intentional work on the anxiety hierarchy had been undertaken. While one never knows how to explain changes in a single case study, we attribute these glimmerings of improvement to several possible factors: (1) the ubiquitous placebo effect, considering especially the big build-up that the referring therapist had given the patient prior even to coming to our training clinic for the first session; (2) reassurance that her "panic attacks" were not just coming out of the blue, that they were ultimately controllable, and that they did not signify that she was losing her mind; (3) and the discussions that had begun in the second or third sessions about the philosophy of rational–emotive behavior therapy, in particular the desirability of making fewer absolutistic demands on oneself and one's environment. With respect to the last point, it sometimes occurred to us that we were not so much telling Marie anything new as we were endorsing a way of approaching challenges that she already understood but had been reluctant to adopt.

REFERENCES

Barlow, D.H. (1988) *Anxiety and its Disorders: The Nature and Treatment of Anxiety and Panic*. New York: Guilford.

Davison, G.C. (1968) Systematic desensitization as a counterconditioning process. *Journal of Abnormal Psychology*, 73, 91–99.

Davison, G.C. (1991) Constructionism and therapy for homosexuality. In J. Gonsiorek and J. Weinrich (eds), *Homosexuality: Research Findings for Public Policy*. Newbury Park, CA: Sage.

Davison, G.C., & Lazarus, A. A. (1994) Clinical innovation and evaluation: Integrating science and practice. *Clinical Psychology: Science and Practice*, 1, 157–168.

Davison, G.C. & Lazarus, A.A. (1995) The dialectics of science and practice. In S.C. Hayes, V.M. Follette, T. Risley, R.D. Dawes and K. Grady (eds), *Scientific Standards of Psychological Practice: Issues and Recommendations* (pp.95–120). Reno, NV: Context Press.

Ellis, A. (1962) *Reason and Emotion in Psychotherapy*. New York: Lyle Stuart.

Ellis, A. (1993) Fundamentals of rational–emotive therapy for the 1990s. In W. Dryden and L. Hill (eds), *Innovations in Rational-Emotive Therapy*. Newbury Park, CA: Sage.

Gergen, K. (1994) *Toward Transformation in Social Knowledge* (2nd edn). Newbury Park, CA: Sage.

Goldfried, M.R. (1971) Systematic desensitization as training in self-control. *Journal of Consulting and Clinical Psychology*, 37, 228–234.

Goldfried, M.R. & Davison, G.C. (1976) *Clinical Behavior Therapy*. New York: Holt, Rinehart & Winston.

Goldfried, M.R. & Davison, G.C. (1994) *Clinical Behavior Therapy*. Expanded edition. New York: Wiley.

Halleck, S.L. (1971) *The Politics of Therapy*. New York: Science House.

Heide, F.J. & Borkovec, T.D. (1984) Relaxation-induced anxiety: Mechanisms and theoretical implications. *Behaviour Research and Therapy*, **22**, 1–12.

Lazarus, A.A. & Davison, G.C. (1971) Clinical innovation in research and practice. In A.E. Bergin and S.L. Garfield (eds), *Handbook of Psychotherapy and Behavior Change* (pp.196–213). New York: Wiley.

Wolpe, J. (1958) *Psychotherapy by Reciprocal Inhibition*. Stanford: Stanford University Press.

CHAPTER 5

Using a case formulation to understand and treat a person with generalised anxiety disorder

Frank W. Bond

In this chapter, I first discuss, briefly, the case formulation approach that we employ at University College London (UCL). I then describe how I used this approach to understand and treat a person's psychological problem. This case example will hopefully demonstrate how the UCL case formulation (CF) analyses a person's problem(s), and how this conceptualisation guides the client's treatment. (Unless otherwise indicated, the term "case formulation" or "CF" refers to the specific approach that is employed at UCL.)

The CF is based upon Meyer's (e.g. 1957) idiographic analyses of people who had multiple problems, including what the *Diagnostic and Statistical Manual for Mental Disorders*, Fourth Edition (DSM-IV, 1994) would label as Axis II or personality disorders. Bruch (Chapter 2, in this volume), Bruch & Meyer (1993), and Meyer & Turkat (1979) describe the CF thoroughly. I present only a summary of it here, but the case example, discussed below, shows, in detail, how the CF is actually used to understand and treat clients' problems.

THE CASE FORMULATION APPROACH

Assessment of Biographical Details

Not surprisingly, perhaps, the CF first asks for information concerning the age, marital or partner status, and profession of the clients. The clinician

Beyond Diagnosis: Case Formulation Approaches in CBT.
Edited by Michael Bruch and Frank W. Bond.
© 1998 John Wiley & Sons Ltd.

can obtain other, relevant biographical details, when enquiring about the historical development of people's presenting problem(s) (see below).

Client's Statement of His or Her Current Difficulties and Treatment Goals

In this part of the CF, the clinician asks clients to summarise, in their own words, the difficulties that they are currently experiencing. The clients are strongly encouraged to describe how *they* see their problems, not how others (e.g. family, friends, and professionals) perceive them.

In order to treat their problems effectively, the clinician attempts to have clients specify their difficulties in concrete terms. For example, if a client says that his problem is, "my life has no meaning", the clinician can help him to clarify this statement by asking questions such as, "What does that mean to you?", "Can you give me an example of how your life has no meaning?", and "How does a lack of meaning in your life affect the hopes and goals that you have?". With these and/or other relevant questions, the client and clinician may be able to describe his "lack of meaning", in the following problem statements: The client: (1) hates his job, but does not think he can get another one, (2) is lonely, and (3) feels pressure from his friends and family to accomplish certain goals (e.g. be happy, get a partner, and be sociable). With these problem statements, which constitute the target problems, it is possible to know, in fairly concrete terms, what this client means when he says that his life has no meaning.

Specific problem statements are sought in this CF, because they form the basis upon which the client's goals of treatment are detailed. With concrete statements, it is easier to produce specific goals, and the more specific the goal, the greater the probability is that the client can achieve it. For example, if the above client states that he wants to find "meaning" in his life, he and his clinician may have difficulty designing interventions to help him to achieve this goal. If, however, the client consults his explicit problem statements, he might be able clearly to specify his goals. For instance, the above client may determine that he wishes to (1) get another job, (2) find more friends, perhaps even a partner, and (3) be able to assert himself in front of his family and friends. As can be seen, these goals are clear enough so that interventions can be developed that can help a client realise these objectives.

Functional Analysis of Each Target Problem

A functional, or causal, analysis attempts to identify the variables that cause psychological problems (Cone, 1997; Skinner, 1953). To conduct this analysis, clinicians detect (1) the stimuli that occasion (2) the client's responses, or dysfunctional behaviours. Lastly, they identify (3) the consequences that result from the responses. Turkat (1979) suggests that clinicians should detect stimuli and consequences on the cognitive, physiological, motor, and environmental levels; and, they should assess responses on the cognitive, physiological, and motor levels. Radical behaviourists insist that dysfunctional behaviours (i.e. responses) cannot be divorced from the stimuli that trigger them and the consequences that follow from them (Skinner, 1974). Thus, the complete stimuli–responses–consequences (S–R–C) event, or contingency, constitutes a problem behaviour, not just the dysfunctional responses. A separate functional analysis should be established for each target problem.

In detailed interviews, clients can often provide the information necessary to construct a functional analysis. At times, however, clinicians may wish to observe the client amongst the actual stimuli that may occasion his or her target problems. For, in this context, clinicians can obtain a very detailed view of the stimuli, responses, and consequences that constitute the client's problems. Obtaining information from an *in vivo* examination may be particularly helpful, when the client is unclear about elements that comprise the S–R–C, or when the S–R–C components are complex (e.g., in an obsessive–compulsive problem). The case example, presented later, details a complete functional analysis.

Historical Development of Each Target Behaviour

After obtaining the necessary functional analyses, clinicians should acquire information as to how the client's target behaviours developed. This history should include details on if and how his or her problem was previously addressed by health care professionals. I should like to make clear that, in my view, understanding how a problem developed is different from knowing how a person acquired a problem. To elaborate, information about problem development is knowledge about how the client (and perhaps a partner or a family member) views the progress of his or her presenting difficulties (e.g. "It became worse when I lost my job"). In contrast, information about problem acquisition is knowledge about how a problem started in the first place (e.g. a biological vulnerability and an unpredictable early life). Of course, in obtaining a developmental history of a disorder, clients may offer opinions as to why a problem began. Their explanations, however, whilst needing to be noted and respected, may not necessarily be correct or complete. Likewise, it is probable that a clinician's hypotheses as to how a person acquired a problem are, if not inaccurate, then at least functionally false; that is, the hypotheses "are a very small part of the picture and they are based on a great deal of ignorance" (Hayes, 1995, p.62).

Hypotheses as to how people acquired problematic behaviours are also unhelpful, because they are unverifiable and, thus, unscientific. To illustrate, if a clinician thinks that parental modelling, for example, caused certain dysfunctional behaviours, it would be impossible to test this hypothesis. Furthermore, knowledge about problem acquisition is unlikely even to improve the treatment of a disorder (Poppen, 1989). For, unfortunately, variables that caused current, psychological problems cannot be changed, because they occurred in the unalterable past. (However, the present variables that maintain these problems can be modified, and this is, of course, the goal of psychotherapy.) It is thought that problem development, not problem acquisition, is the better focus for forays into a person's past; because, information on the former, unlike the latter, can be employed usefully to inform treatment (see Chapter 9 for a detailed example). As can be seen, unlike Meyer & Turkat (1979) and Bruch & Meyer (1993), who developed the current CF, I do not think that historical material can be usefully used to construct valid or even scientific hypotheses as to how a person acquired his or her problem.

Behavioural Formulation

In the CF, information from the functional analyses is summarised in what is called the "behavioural formulation" (Meyer & Turkat, 1979). Furthermore, in this formulation, a clinician should hypothesise as to how the responses in the contingencies are maintained. If, a rule, or a cognition, is thought to underpin people's dysfunctional responses, as many radical behavioural and cognitive behavioural therapists believe (e.g. Beck, 1976; Catania, Matthews & Shimoff, 1990), it is very important to hypothesise as to what maintains the unhelpful rule. For, in therapy, the clinician needs to select or devise interventions that can modify the variables that maintain this rule. (Cognitive–behavioural therapists who do not subscribe to radical behaviourism can, throughout this chapter, substitute the word "belief" for the word "rule"; because, for the purposes of this chapter, both terms are interchangeable.) As can be seen, the behavioural formulation is a crucial component of the CF, because it guides the selection and even development of therapeutic interventions. The case example, later, presents a behavioural formulation and shows how it directs the treatment process.

Clinical Experimentation

Since the behavioural formulation plays such an important role in the therapeutic process, clinicians need reasonably to ensure that the hypotheses that it specifies (i.e. the functional analyses and the rule) are tested and found to be valid. Furthermore, the clinician should be prepared to alter aspects of the functional analyses or rule, based upon the results of his or her experimentation.

There are, of course, many ways to test the behavioural formulation. For example, clients can, over a week, record the occurrence, frequency, triggers, and/or consequences of target responses, in order to test the functional analyses. In addition, over a week, clients can record the thoughts that they have in specific circumstances (e.g. Beck *et al.*, 1979), so that their hypothesised rules can be examined. At times, it may be necessary for the clinician or some other person (e.g. the client's partner) to monitor directly the clinical experimentation. For instance, such oversight may be helpful when a client has severe anxiety and is unable to record his or her responses and/or thoughts accurately. However, it is accomplished, clinical experimentation helps to ensure that the behavioural formulation is as correct as possible. When the clinician believes that it is, he or she can have confidence in using it as the primary guide for treatment planning and implementation.

Treatment Goals

In this section, the behavioural formulation is translated into the therapeutic goals. For example, if the formulation hypothesises that a rule maintains a person's unhelpful behaviours, a treatment goal should be proposed in this section. This goal might be: the client needs to develop a new rule. In this section, the clinician should also specify how the goal will be accomplished. For instance, a new rule can be developed by providing structured and repeated learning experiences. The treatment goal(s) should be able to achieve the client's goals that are stated in the section, "Client's statement of his or her own difficulties and goals".

When selecting therapeutic techniques, treatment goals can usefully form the basis upon which alternatives are selected. Specifically, any viable alternative should produce an affirmative response to the question, "Does this technique help to achieve any or all of the therapeutic goals that are detailed in this section?" If the answer to this question is "no", then the technique should not be employed. As can be seen, the behavioural formulation, translated into the treatment goals, forms useful selection criteria for therapeutic interventions.

Outline of the Treatment Programme

This section describes some of the actual therapeutic techniques that are employed. Depending upon the amount of detail required, the techniques, and how they are implemented, can be discussed in sub-sections.

Treatment Evaluation

Consistent with behavioural and cognitive behavioural psychotherapies, the CF emphasises that psychological treatments should be evaluated. Ideally, this evaluation takes the form of single-case experimental designs (Barlow and Hersen, 1984) that employ valid and reliable measures. Of course, such rigorous evaluations are not always possible or ethical. Nevertheless, clinicians would do well to employ some type of treatment evaluation strategy. For instance, it may be sufficient to document the frequency and duration of compulsive responses, when treating a person who suffers from obsessive compulsive problems. In addition, tracking Beck Depression Inventory (BDI; Beck et al., 1961) scores over time might prove helpful in assessing a client's depressive affect. For a client who is not a part of a research project, a clinician needs only to show that the person is getting better. Demonstrating that it is the therapy, itself, that is producing the change would be desirable, but it is certainly not necessary.

The measures that are employed to evaluate treatment effectiveness are documented in this section. It should also be noted here when and how often these measures are taken. If a clinician is employing a single case experimental design, he or she can describe it in this section.

The following case study is presented in the form of the CF approach that I just detailed. It should show how this approach helped to construct my understanding of this person's problem, and how I employed this conceptualisation to develop the treatment programme that is described below.

CASE STUDY

Assessment of Biographical Details

Juan (a pseudonym) was a 23 year-old, single, male from Spain who was assessed at University College London Medical School (UCL) on 20 March 1996 (which is really the incorrect year). At the time of the assessment, he was a final-year student at a London University. His general practitioner made the referral.

Juan's Statement of his Current Difficulties and Goals

Juan said that his main problem was that he felt overwhelmed by negative thoughts for much of the day, every day. He noted that once he encountered negative thoughts, it was very difficult to draw his attention away from them, to decrease their perceived importance, or to control them.

Juan also reported that he experienced another problem: he often coordinated when he ate breakfast and when he left his flat. Specifically, he often avoided leaving his flat until two hours after he had eaten breakfast. Juan stated that the reason for this avoidance was that he was afraid that he would vomit when he was amongst people.

Juan's goal was to decrease the "stranglehold" (his own term) that his negative thoughts had on him. When asked to elaborate on this statement, Juan noted that he believed that he could not get rid of his negative thoughts, entirely; however, he did want to become less upset by them and feel less helpless to do anything about them, when they occurred. Juan wanted to achieve this goal soon so that he could begin to concentrate effectively on revising for his final exams.

Regarding his fears about vomiting, Juan stated that he believed that if his overall negative thinking had less of a stranglehold on him, his concerns regarding vomiting would decrease. In addition, Juan maintained that he would be able to concentrate effectively on his revision, if he were not so bothered by all of his negative thoughts. Consistent with his thinking, we agreed that work on negative thoughts regarding vomiting and revising would be subsumed under the goal of becoming less upset about negative thoughts, in general.

Functional Analysis of Juan's Negative Thoughts

From interviewing Juan, it appeared that the following rule (or verbal stimulus that specifies a contingency) occasioned the responses that constituted his primary problem. This rule was: when I think that I may fail in my professional or social life, I must establish complete control over my emotions, thoughts, and behaviour. If I cannot, then I will be a failure, and if anyone is around me, they will see what a failure I am. Juan's problem with distressing, negative thoughts is now described in a functional analysis.

Stimuli

The stimuli that set the occasion for Juan's unhelpful responses (described below) were: negative thoughts regarding potential failure in his professional or social life. These "failure" thoughts typically centred around the prospect of: (1) doing poorly on his exams or in his later professional career, (2) never having a girlfriend because he worked too hard, and (3) being perceived as unsuccessful. These negative failure thoughts typically occurred in the morning (during breakfast), at night when he was revising, and during the weekend when he was revising but really wanted to be with his friends. Juan's negative thoughts about failure were not typically present when he was interacting socially.

In accordance with contemporary, radical behavioural accounts of rule-governed (or cognitively controlled) behaviour (e.g. Catania, Matthews & Shimoff, 1990; Catania, Shimoff & Matthews, 1989; Hayes and Hayes, 1989), it was hypothesised that exposure to negative thoughts regarding potential failure elicited Juan's rule: when I think that I may fail in my professional or social life, I must establish complete control over my emotions, thoughts, and behaviour. If I cannot, then I will be a failure, and if anyone is around me, they will see what a failure I am. Upon contact with his rule and negative thoughts regarding potential failure, Juan then followed his rule (i.e. he engaged in what is termed "rule-governed behaviour") by attempting to control his emotions, thoughts, and behaviour.

Responses

Juan's responses were divided into three categories: cognitive, autonomic, and motor:

(1) *Cognitive responses.* Juan reported that he began to have incessant and uncontrollable thoughts about failing in his professional and/or social life. If Juan had just eaten, and he had to go out of his flat, he thought that he would vomit. If he was with other people, he was afraid that they would perceive him as a failure. If he blushed in front of others, he believed that they would think that he was lying about something and then think that he was a failure. When these thoughts occurred, Juan tried to challenge the validity of them, and "think them through" (a control strategy).

(2) *Autonomic responses.* Juan stated that he felt his heart beating fast, and his palms sweating. Very occasionally, he reported that he became nauseous.

(3) *Motor responses.* Juan maintained that, if he was in the presence of other people, he would leave the situation as fast as possible. If he could not escape it, then he would try to divert attention away from himself so that he did not feel like the centre of people's attention. He noted that his strategies for doing this varied, depending upon the context. If Juan had just eaten, he would often avoid leaving his flat

until he relaxed and felt certain that he would not vomit. (Establishing this certainty typically took about two hours.)

Consequences

Juan reported that his responses did not often "make him feel better". In fact, he stated that he typically felt even more out of control and distressed after trying to get rid of his negative thoughts. In addition, he maintained that his negative thoughts and his autonomic responses did not often cease upon responding in the above ways. Juan noted that a long-term consequence of his responses was that he did not socialise as much as he used to and was, therefore, feeling isolated and alone.

Developmental History of Juan's Problem with Negative Thoughts

Before June 1995, Juan stated that he had been a very social and "pretty relaxed" person. He said that, whilst he always wanted to excel, he rarely felt anxious about failing, because he always "put in the necessary time". Juan reported that he first started to feel anxious about his negative thoughts regarding potential failure around June 1995. He stated that his worries centred around failing to maintain the high grade levels that he had achieved during his first two years at university. He noted that it was important for him to continue to do very well at university, if he was to be accepted on a postgraduate course in the United States. Whilst his negative thoughts and anxiety occurred sporadically in June, Juan recalled that they became more frequent as the summer progressed. By the end of summer, he reported that he found himself "constantly" having negative thoughts and anxiety about potential, academic failure.

During the autumn of 1995, Juan stated that his negative thoughts and anxiety were "always there". In addition, Juan noted that, on 22 November 1995, he vomited after eating breakfast. He reported that he did not know why this happened, and, after that episode, he stated that he was very concerned that he would vomit one day when he was amongst other people. In fact, Juan became so concerned about this that, by December 1995, he said that he found himself skipping meals (by 20 March 1996, he stated that he had lost 10 kg). By the end of 1995, Juan maintained that he hardly ever ate outside of his flat, and, having eaten, he would remain in his flat for at least two hours.

Juan stated that this avoidance behaviour, regarding eating and leaving his flat, occurred only when he had negative thoughts regarding potential failure. Since, however, he had these negative thoughts more increasingly, he found himself in this avoidance pattern most of the time. Juan maintained that this pattern made it very difficult for him to live "normally". Furthermore, it made him feel "out of control", which, he noted, increased his negative thinking about potential failure.

Juan stated that he had had a medical examination in July 1995, and it revealed that he was physically healthy. In fact, he reported that he had always been physically healthy and was rarely ill with flu or colds. Juan reported that his parents were both physically and psychologically healthy. Regarding his professional and social life, Juan stated that he expected more from himself than his parents expected from him.

Behavioural Formulation

Juan's primary problem was that he was feeling overwhelmed by negative thoughts regarding professional failure for much of the day, almost every day. He stated that once he experienced negative thoughts, he found it very difficult to draw his attention away from them, decrease their perceived importance, or control them. When Juan did feel overwhelmed by his negative thoughts, he coordinated when he ate and when he left his flat, because he was afraid that he would vomit when he was amongst people. It appeared that Juan's "eating problem" was contingent upon the presence of negative thoughts, regarding potential failure (i.e. the primary problem). He and I conceptualised, therefore, that his eating problem was a manifestation of the primary problem.

I hypothesised that when Juan experienced negative thoughts regarding potential failure, a rule was elicited that specified how he should respond to these negative thoughts. Juan's rule that occasioned his responses was: when I think that I may fail in my professional or social life, I must establish complete control over my emotions, thoughts, and behaviour. If I cannot, then I will be a failure, and if anyone is around me, they will see what a failure I am. I posited that this rule maintained Juan's unhelpful responses, which were outlined in the above, functional analysis.

I hypothesised that Juan's rule was maintained in the following way. Specifically, Juan stated that his responses did not often provide relief from his negative thoughts and emotions. It is likely, however, that his rule-governed responses made him feel better often enough to negatively reinforce his rule. This negative reinforcement,[1] therefore, maintained his rule (and the probability that he would follow it).

Clinical Experimentation

Juan thought that the behavioural formulation reflected his problem accurately. Although his endorsement was important, it was, of course, necessary to examine further the validity of his functional analysis and rule. To this end, for one week, I asked Juan to complete a chart, whenever he experienced his primary problem. On this chart, he was asked to record the situation in which he found himself, when he encountered his primary problem. Specifically, he was asked to note down his thoughts, feelings and actions at the onset of the problem. He was next requested to identify his responses to the primary problem (i.e., his thoughts, actions, and physical sensations). Lastly, he was asked to identify the immediate and longer-term consequences of his responses. Results from this one-week examination were consistent with his functional analysis and rule. I thought it acceptable, therefore, to base his treatment programme, described below, upon his behavioural formulation.

Throughout the course of therapy, I wished to monitor carefully Juan's primary problem, in order to ensure that it was improving. To this end, I employed two measures. Firstly, since the aim of therapy was to decrease the stranglehold that Juan's negative thoughts had on him, I developed a one-item measure to assess the strength of this stranglehold. This item read, "To what extent did your negative thoughts have a stranglehold on you this past week?". This item was attached to a nine-point Likert-type scale, with one indicating "to no extent", and nine denoting, "to a great extent".

The second measure that I employed to monitor Juan's primary problem was the State-Trait Anxiety Inventory (STAI; Spielberger, 1983). This measure assesses "the subjective, consciously perceived feelings of tension and apprehension, and heightened autonomic nervous system activity" (Spielberger, 1983, p.3). Research (e.g. Eysenck, 1992; Wells and Matthews, 1994) has shown that the STAI is a good predictor of generalised anxiety disorder (GAD), as defined by DSM-III-R. Since Juan fulfilled the DSM-III-R and DSM-IV criteria for GAD, I considered the STAI to be an appropriate measure of change for his primary problem. Juan's scores on the "stranglehold" measure and the STAI are discussed below. Finally, I should note that these two measures were administered at each therapy session.

Treatment Goals

The first goal of treatment was to prevent Juan from performing behaviour that was governed by his "failure" rule. (Recall that this behaviour involved controlling his thoughts and emotions). By not performing his rule-governed behaviour, he would no longer receive the negative reinforcement that maintained his unhelpful rule. This lack of reinforcement would eventually decrease the control that the unhelpful rule had over his behaviour. The second treatment goal was to have Juan contact contingencies of positive reinforcement.[2] Regarding the first goal, I thought that I could stop Juan from following his "failure" rule by showing him that: (1) by following it he was (negatively) reinforcing it (as just described); and, (2) he was unable to do what it specified. That is, he could not establish complete control over his emotions and thoughts. Since he could not do this, and he was reinforcing his failure rule by trying to do so, it was best for him to stop trying to exert this control.

To accomplish the second goal, I needed to show Juan that, although he could not control his thoughts and feelings effectively, he could control other behaviours (e.g. whether or not he contacted his friends). Furthermore, some of these controllable behaviours had consequences that could provide him with a sense of well-being. To put it another way, the two treatment goals entailed encouraging Juan to exercise conscious and purposeful control in areas where it was effective and life-enhancing (e.g. revising for exams or visiting friends); and, to exercise acceptance and toleration in areas where conscious and purposeful control was ineffectual or even harmful (e.g. in preventing or stopping thoughts and emotions) (Hayes, 1995).

Outline of Treatment Programme

Consistent with the behavioural formulation and the treatment goals, the following treatment programme was developed for and administered to Juan. This programme is outlined now, and important aspects of it are detailed in the following section.

In session, Juan was asked first to reflect on the fact that controlling his thoughts about potential failure had not been helpful in attenuating his incessant fears. He then spent one week recording the strategies that he employed to control his thoughts and emotions that centred around potential failure. He also noted how effective these control strategies were in helping him to feel better. Through this exercise, Juan was able to see that attempting to control (i.e. avoid, or stop) his negative thoughts and feelings surrounding failure was not helpful to him. He was then taught an alternative strategy to help him cope with his negative thoughts and emotions. It was used to achieve the first treatment goal that was discussed in the previous section.

This new strategy has been called, variously, comprehensive distancing (Hayes, 1989), acceptance (Hayes, 1994), disconnected mindfulness (Wells & Matthews, 1994), and passively letting go (Bond and Dryden, 1996). In applying this strategy, I first taught Juan how to be mindful of (or to watch, or accept) his thoughts and feelings that surrounded potential failure. Through practice, he saw that he could accept these unpleasant thoughts and feelings without having to change, avoid, like them, or otherwise act on them.

To achieve the second treatment goal, discussed above, Juan and I considered the following. Specifically, could he achieve his current, daily goals (e.g. revising for exams and visiting with friends), even though he still had thoughts and feelings about potential failure? By testing out this question, he soon saw that he did not have to control his thoughts, in order to achieve his goals. By accomplishing his goals, Juan made contact with contingencies of positive reinforcement; and, it appears that this contact made Juan happier, less anxious, and less bothered by his thoughts and feelings regarding failure.

Details of the Treatment Programme

I now describe Juan's first two sessions in some detail, because it was during these that the core element of the treatment programme was described and enacted. Following this fairly detailed presentation, I provide a summary of his last four sessions. Juan's six treatment sessions extended over a two-month period from 25 March to 21 May 1996.

The Assessment Session

At the assessment session on 19 March, Juan stated that he was unable to revise for his exams, which were in May. He said that his negative thoughts regarding failure prevented him from studying effectively, and he was scared that he was going to fail his exams. Juan reported that this fear of failure prompted him to seek therapy when he did. For the following session, which was to be the first treatment session, I asked Juan to notice the strategies that he employed to cope with his negative thoughts. In addition, I gave him the assessment chart, described above, so that I could test the hypothesised functional analysis and rule.

Session on 25 March

At the first treatment session, Juan reported that he had done his homework. He said that when he tried to control his thoughts by avoiding them or distracting himself from them, they became worse. Reasons for this pattern were discussed, and they centred around the formulation that was presented above. These reasons were discussed at length, and in a way that he could understand.

When Juan clearly recognised that trying to control his negative thoughts made him feel more out of control and anxious, I presented the acceptance strategy to him. One way that I did this was through a metaphor, which I took from Hayes (1995). It is called the Willingness Scale Metaphor.

> Imagine there are two scales, like the volume and balance knobs on a stereo. One is called "negative thoughts and emotional disturbance". It can go from 0 to 10. The other is called "willingness", and it can also go from 0 to 10. Check and see if it isn't the case that the posture you're in now, what brought you in here, was this: "This negative thoughts and emotional disturbance scale is too high. It's way up here and I want it down here and I want you (the therapist) to help me to lower it, please." Now, there's also this other scale; it's been hidden in the past, but we're going to look at it now. This other scale, the willingness scale, is really the more important of the two, because this is the one that makes the difference. When discomfort is up here at 10, and the willingness scale is down at 0, then this means that you're trying hard to control your thoughts (and negative emotions), to make them go down, and you're unwilling to experience these negative thoughts and emotions; and, when you are unwilling to experience these thoughts and emotions, then by definition, this means that your negative thoughts and feelings are something to be uncomfortable about. So, what we need to do in this therapy is shift our focus from the negative thoughts and emotional disturbance knob to the willingness knob. You've been trying to control your negative thoughts (and negative emotions) for a long time, and it just hasn't worked. It's not that you weren't clever enough; it simply does not work, for anybody. Instead of trying to do something that just cannot work, why don't we turn our focus to the willingness scale, and let it go up, and stop trying to control the negative thoughts scale (Hayes, 1995, p.43) . . ., which you have seen is not controllable. You may see that, once you stop trying to control something that you cannot control, then you will be in a better position to focus your attention on controlling those things that you can control, like studying for your exams.

When I presented the acceptance strategy to Juan, I showed him that it is necessary to control and eliminate negative thoughts and emotions only if they impede the realisation of one's goals. If they do not impede such goal attainment, then they need not be controlled and eliminated before one's goals can be achieved. To relate this concept to Juan's life, I stressed to him, in many different ways, that he could attempt to revise for his exams, even though he was experiencing negative thoughts and emotions. That is, he did not have to get rid of his thoughts and feelings that centred around potential failure, before he could begin achieving his goals.

Juan appeared to grasp the whole acceptance concept very well. In fact, he stated that he had tried to control and eliminate his negative thinking for so long, using so many techniques that he had read about, that he was not hopeful that he could do it. Thus, when I said to him that it was not necessary to eliminate his negative thoughts before he could get on with his life, he appeared much more hopeful.

I explained to Juan that his thoughts and emotions are records of his life experiences: ones that he cannot change, but that he can add to. I told Juan that if he accomplished his short-term goals, then these successful experiences would affect his records (i.e. his thoughts and emotions). These experiences would not eliminate his previous records, which he needed to accept, but they would be pleasant additions that could affect his well-being (Hayes, 1995).

In order to practise the acceptance strategy, I asked Juan if he was willing to do a homework assignment, during the following week. Specifically, I asked him if he would eat breakfast, and then, within ten minutes of finishing, leave his flat and go to the library. I recommended that, when his negative thoughts came, he should check his emotional willingness scale and employ other acceptance techniques that we discussed in the first treatment session. In doing this assignment, daily, I asked Juan to see what happened when he accepted his negative thoughts and feelings, whilst going to the library and revising.

I should note that, in each session, I made several attempts to ensure that Juan understood fully what we were discussing. For example, when conveying concepts such as the one's mentioned above, I employed, primarily, socratic questioning (e.g. Beck and Emery, 1985). In this case study, the heavily socratic nature of our therapeutic interaction is not conveyed, due to space considerations. To ensure further that Juan understood the concepts that we were discussing, I asked him the following question, at least two times per session. One of these times was always at the end of the session. The question was: "I know that we have just discussed a lot of concepts, and I want to ensure that I have explained them well to you. So, would you mind summarising for me the important points of our discussion?" Juan consistently showed that he understood the main points of our discussion; and, when he did not, this question helped to identify those points that were opaque to him.

Session on 2 April

During the week following his first treatment session, Juan reported that he was able to leave his flat and go to the library, within a half-hour of having eaten. Juan maintained that he was able to leave his flat "so quickly", because he employed the acceptance strategies that we discussed during the first treatment session. Through socratic questioning, I placed great emphasis on how he was able to achieve his goal of going to the library to revise, even though he had negative thoughts whilst he was walking to the library. Juan stated that, soon after beginning to study at the library, his negative thinking, to his surprise, stopped, and he was able to concentrate on his revision.

After discussing the homework assignment, Juan stated that he was better able to handle his negative thoughts about failing his exams. He noted, however, that he could not apply the acceptance strategy to his thoughts about failing in his career. Through socratic questioning, I showed Juan how he could do this, using the acceptance techniques that he already knew. In addition, I also taught him another one, which employed imagery. Called "At the cinema", this acceptance technique required Juan to watch his negative thoughts, as if they were on a cinema screen, and he were sitting in the audience. As an audience member, he was to let the film (i.e., his negative thoughts) roll. He was not to stop the film. for he was not the projectionist. He was not to edit the film, for he was not the editor. Nor was he to re-shoot the film, for he was not the director or the head of the studio. He was only an audience member, and therefore he was only to watch the film unfold.

Juan practised this imagery exercise in session and stated that he thought that it would be very helpful to him. (Consistent with this statement, he later said that it was the most helpful *technique* that he had learnt in therapy.) Towards the end of the session, I showed Juan how he could use the "at the cinema" technique in conjunction with the others that we had discussed at the previous session.

I encouraged Juan to use "at the cinema" when he had any negative thoughts about failure. In addition, I recommended that he spend ten minutes a day looking at these thoughts, using this technique. Thus, he was to let his negative failure thoughts role, without trying to control them in any way; that is, without trying to "edit" them, "re-direct them" or "stop" them. I also asked Juan to carry out the same assignment that he had done the previous week.

Sessions on 30 April, 7 May, 14 May, and 21 May

Due to Juan's Easter holiday, which he spent at his home in Spain, we did not meet for four weeks. At the first session after this holiday (i.e. 30 April), Juan reported that he had worked diligently on the homework assignments, and he was able to revise successfully for his exams. During the four last sessions, we discussed, at great length, how he could apply the acceptance strategy to different areas of his life. Indeed, the overarching goal of these last sessions was to show Juan how he could handle his negative thoughts and feelings, in every situation, by employing the acceptance strategy. Furthermore, in accordance with the treatment goals, I wanted to ensure that he realised when control was useful and when it was not. Specifically, I stressed that acceptance worked well when control was not possible (e.g. with his internal events). In contrast, however, I emphasised that control was the better option, when it had the potential to be enacted effectively (e.g. when revising for an exam, or accomplishing a task).

During these last four sessions, Juan's feelings of anxiety received greater and more direct, therapeutic attention. Although his anxious feelings had attenuated significantly by this time, they were still present and unpleasant. I taught him, therefore, how he could apply the acceptance strategy and techniques to his anxious feelings. By this stage of therapy, Juan appeared to understand the acceptance strategy very well, and he was able to apply it effectively to his feelings of anxiety.

A few days before his exams, Juan reported that, at times, he began to experience very negative thoughts about failure. He noted, however, that he was able successfully to employ the acceptance strategy when these thoughts came. I told Juan that it was normal to experience negative thoughts and feelings during such naturally stressful times as final exams. Moreover, I emphasised that it appeared that he was able to cope effectively with his negative thoughts, even during such a stressful time. In particular, through socratic questioning, Juan realised that, despite his momentary periods of high negative arousal, he continued to revise for his exams. Upon reflection, Juan stated that he had improved significantly, and he was able to provide, without prompting, many examples of how he had applied the acceptance strategy successfully.

Juan reported that he was able to cope well with his negative thoughts during the ten days that he sat his exams. His last two therapy sessions occurred just after he sat an exam, and, on both occasions, Juan said that he was happy that he had taken his exams and handled his thoughts and emotions so well. In addition, he believed that he had performed acceptably on his exams, and he said that he was proud of his performance.

Throughout the six therapeutic sessions, we spent a great deal of time discussing how Juan could apply the acceptance strategy to all of his negative, internal events. At the last session, however, we elaborated upon this concept in great detail. Juan was very keen to know how he could maintain and further the gains that he had made during his two months in therapy. To this end, I used socratic questioning to show him that he could use various acceptance techniques, including "at the cinema", daily. As indicated above, Juan had found this technique to be very helpful to him, and therefore I encouraged him to use it every day for at least five minutes. The rationale for this suggestion was that this exercise would serve as a reminder to Juan that he should employ the acceptance strategy during his daily life.

During the last session, I asked Juan to summarise the main elements of the acceptance strategy and to discuss how he could apply them to other problems. Juan was able to do this very well, and he noted that he wanted to use this strategy in his social life. He stated that his social life had been satisfying before he became distressed about his thoughts of professional failure. He said that when this occurred, he soon became concerned about failing in his social life. Juan maintained, however, that this worry was not nearly as disturbing as his fear had been about failing professionally. The session ended with Juan outlining a plan as to how he could apply the acceptance strategy to his negative thoughts about failing socially.

Therapy ended when it did, because Juan finished university and moved home to Spain. He spent the summer there, before going to the United States to take up a place on a postgraduate course.

Treatment Evaluation

The measures of change that I employed in Juan's treatment indicated that his target complaints improved during the course of therapy. As noted above, these self-report questionnaires were the "stranglehold" question, and the STAI. As will be recalled, the "stranglehold" question is a one-item measure that I developed in order to assess the degree to which negative thoughts interfered with Juan's life during the previous week. Such assessment was seen as critical, because the goal of therapy was to decrease the "stranglehold" that Juan's negative thoughts had on him. The one item on the questionnaire read, "To what extent did your negative thoughts have a stranglehold on you this past week?" This item was on a nine-point Likert-type scale, with one indicating "to no extent", and nine suggesting "to a great extent". As can be seen in Figure 5.1, Juan's scores on this measure dropped from a 9, at the first treatment session, to a 3, at the last treatment session. This very positive, two-thirds drop in the degree to which negative thoughts interfered with Juan's life was reflected in his own comments about his improvement.

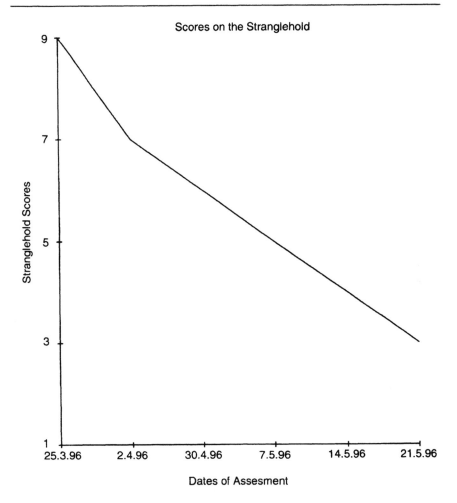

Figure 5.1   Encores on the stranglehold question

The second measure of change that I employed in Juan's treatment was the STAI. I chose to use this, because, as noted above, it has been shown to be a very good predictor of GAD (Eysenck, 1992; Wells and Matthews, 1994). Since Juan fulfilled DSM-III-R and DSM-IV's criteria for GAD, I saw the STAI as an appropriate measure of change for his primary problem. Regarding this measure, and as can be seen in Figure 2, Juan's STAI-S score dropped from 71 at the assessment to 46 at the last session. (The increase between 30 April and 21 May is non-significant (Spielberger, 1983).) In addition, his STAI-T score dropped from 57 at the assessment to 36 at the last session, which can also be seen in Figure 5.2. According to

Spielberger (1983), these drops in STAI scores indicate very significant decreases in both state and trait anxiety. These indicators reflected Juan's self-reports of becoming less disturbed by his negative thoughts and feelings, as the treatment sessions progressed.

Each measure of change employed in Juan's treatment indicated that his target problems improved considerably over the course of therapy. At our last session, I asked Juan whether or not this conclusion (derived from these measures) was consistent with his perception concerning the degree to which his target problems had improved during the course of

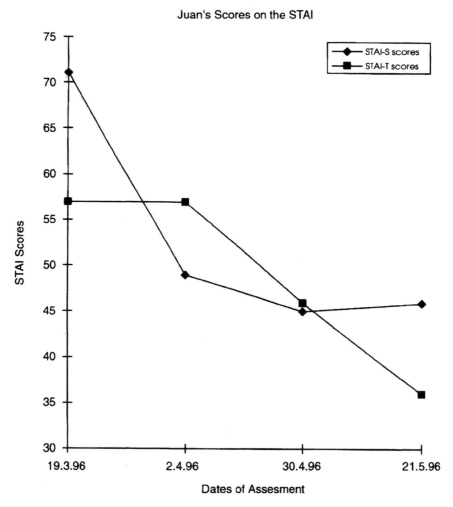

Figure 5.2 Juan's scores on the STAI

therapy. Juan said that it was. In addition, this conclusion was also consistent with my perception regarding the degree to which Juan's target problems had improved.

SUMMARY

Hopefully, this chapter showed how the case formulation approach, employed at UCL, constructs people's problems. Moreover, I hope that the case study demonstrated how a client's treatment programme should stem directly from information that is detailed in the CF. Proponents of CFs believe that, by basing a client's treatment on an idiographic conceptualisation of his or her problems, clinicians can provide the most effective interventions for a particular person's problems. Confirmation of this hypothesis, however, awaits empirical inquiry.

NOTES

1. As may be recalled, "negative reinforcement" describes the *removal* of stimuli (e.g. social derision or pain), if a particular response occurs in a given type of situation. These stimuli also must be responsible for *increasing* the probability of the particular response (Skinner, 1953).
2. As a reminder, "contingencies of positive reinforcement" describe an event in which stimuli are *presented* (e.g. social interaction or praise), if a particular response occurs in a given type of situation. These stimuli also must be responsible for *increasing* the probability of the particular response (Skinner, 1953).

REFERENCES

American Psychiatric Association. (1994). *Diagnostic and Statistical Manual of Mental Disorders* (4th ed.). Washington, DC: Author.

Barlow, D.H. & Hersen, M. (1984). *Single Case Experimental Designs: Strategies for Studying Behavior Change* (2nd edn). New York: Pergamon.

Beck, A.T. (1976). *Cognitive Therapy and the Emotional Disorders.* New York: Meridian.

Beck, A.T. & Emery, G. (1985). *Anxiety Disorders and Phobias: A Cognitive Perspective.* New York: Basic Books.

Beck, A.T., Ward, C.H., Mendelson, M., Mock, J.E. & Erbaugh, J.K. (1961). An inventory for measuring depression. *Archives of General Psychiatry*, **4**, 561–571.

Beck, A.T., Rush, J., Shaw, B. & Emery, G. (1979). *Cognitive Therapy of Depression.* New York: Guilford Press.

Bond, F.W. & Dryden, W. (1996). The effect of control and certainty beliefs on inference formation: Clinical implications from research. In W. Dryden (ed.), *Research in Counselling and Psychotherapy: Practical Applications.* London: Sage Publications.

Bruch, M.H. & Meyer, V. (1993). The behavioural interview. *Psychopathologia*, **11**(3), 167–186.

Catania, A.C., Matthews, B.A. & Shimoff, E. (1990). Properties of rule-governed behavior and their implications. In D.E. Blackman and H. Lejeune (eds), *Behaviour Analysis in Theory and Practice: Contributions and Controversies*. Hove, UK: Lawrence Erlbaum Associates.

Catania, A.C., Shimoff, E. & Matthews, B.A. (1989). An experimental analysis of rule-governed behavior. In S. C. Hayes (Ed.), *Rule-Governed Behavior*. Nevada: Context Press.

Cone, J.D. (1997). Issues in functional analysis in behavioral assessment. *Behaviour Research and Therapy*, 35(3), 259–275.

Eysenck, M.W. (1992). *Anxiety: The Cognitive Perspective*. Hove, England: Lawrence Erlbaum.

Hayes, S.C. (1989). *Rule-Governed Behavior*. Nevada: Context Press.

Hayes, S.C. (1994). Content, context, and the types of psychological acceptance. In S.C. Hayes, N.S. Jacobson, V.M. Follette, & M.J. Dougher (eds.), *Acceptance and change*. Reno, NV: Context Press.

Hayes, S.C. (1995). *Acceptance and Commitment Therapy: A Working Manual*. Unpublished manual.

Hayes, S.C. & Hayes, L.J. (1989). The verbal action of the listener as the basis for rule-governance. In S.C. Hayes (ed.), *Rule-Governed Behavior*. Nevada: Context Press.

Meyer, V. (1957). The treatment of two phobic patients on the basis of learning principles. *Journal of Abnormal Psychology*, 55, 261.

Meyer, V. & Turkat, I.D. (1979). Behavioural analysis of clinical cases. *Journal of Behavioural Assessment*, 1, 259–269.

Poppen, R.L. (1989). Some clinical implications for rule-governed behavior. In S.C. Hayes (ed.), *Rule-governed Behavior*. Nevada: Context Press.

Skinner, B.F. (1953). *Science and Human Behavior*. New York: The Free Press.

Skinner, B.F. (1974). *About Behaviorism* London: Penguin Books.

Spielberger, C.D. (1983). *State–Trait Anxiety Inventory*. Palo Alto, Ca: Mind Garden.

Turkat, I.D. (1979). The behaviour analysis matrix. *Scandinavian Journal of Behaviour Therapy*, 8, 187–189.

Wells, A. & Matthews, G. (1994). *Attention and Emotion: A Clinical Perspective*. Hove, England: Lawrence Erlbaum.

CHAPTER 6

Context focused analysis: an experimentally derived model for working with complex problems with children, adolescents and systems

David A. Lane

THE CHILD WHO WOULD NOT BE IGNORED

For thirty years I have been concerned with issues faced by children and adolescents within the school system and the community. This has included issues of drug misuse, delinquency, child abuse, learning difficulties, and emotional and behavioural problems.

One group of children has consistently occupied my thinking for much of that period. This consists of the children who, in spite of all the efforts of psychotherapy, psychology, education, social work or the law, fail to change in the ways expected of them. Attempting to understand them has shaped my approach to diagnosis and psychotherapy. It is, therefore, with them that this chapter must start. The first section of this chapter identifies the process by which I came to reject the use of diagnostic models such as DSM. The move from diagnosis to individual formulation was so critical to our success that it deserves some attention.

The 1970s saw an increasing concern with the problem of disruption in schools and rising levels of delinquency in our communities. Numerous schemes began to appear to work with disruptive children. Many of these

Beyond Diagnosis: Case Formulation Approaches in CBT.
Edited by Michael Bruch and Frank W. Bond.
© 1998 John Wiley & Sons Ltd.

had as their origin existing theoretical models that had influenced adult psychotherapy. Children and adolescents were identified, diagnosed (as maladjusted) and consigned to special schools, often many miles away from their homes. Pathology was seen as rooted in the child, their history, and in malfunctioning families. The notion that environments might be disabling, that behaviour might be a function of context or that professionals might be part of the problem rarely surfaced. This was in spite of the efforts of those sociologists and psychologists who identified the discriminatory role of education and psychology in system processes (Jackson, 1977; Jones, 1972; Herrick, 1971). They also ignored the debate on the ineffectiveness of psychotherapy for both adults and children. (Eysenck, 1952; Rogers, 1963; Colby, 1964; Carkhuff & Berenson, 1967; Goldstein, 1971; Rachman, 1971). The major form of provision for children, "the child guidance centre" was attacked as "expensive, ineffective and wrongly conceived" (Tizard, 1973), as was our approach to labelling children as "maladjusted" (Lawrence, 1973). Teachers complained about the role of psychology in assisting them in dealing with children beyond control. This created a crisis for psychological provision but also led to the emergence of new forms of intervention.

It was against this background of uncertainty that I found myself in the early 1970s seeking to find ways to work effectively with childhood behaviour problems. I experimented with the emerging behavioural methods and found a degree of success. As I became more successful I was confronted by teachers who presented examples of children with whom they said I would not be able to deal—the "impossible child"—for whom everything had been tried and failed. I found that I could not ignore such children if the credibility of my efforts were to remain intact. Consequently I embarked on a detailed study, of the factors giving rise to the predisposition, precipitation and maintenance of problems in such groups. The results led to the emergence of new forms of intervention (in the creation of "resource continuum" (Topping, 1983) and "behaviour support" (Gray et al., 1994) models at the Islington Educational Guidance Centre) and replication studies in a number of centres in the UK. One of the clear conclusions from the studies and long term follow up data collected over 15 years was that the label applied was predictive of long term outcome but that the diagnostic labels were inadequate for designing interventions. Within one diagnostic label a variety of contributing factors were present that impacted on therapeutic success. The application of the label also varied based on factors outside of the child, varying between practitioners. It was necessary, if the plea of our teachers and parents was to be answered, to develop a model of analysis capable of identifying key factors in each referral and then designing interventions to meet them.

That was more than twenty years ago, so does it matter any more? Within the UK, the last five years have seen a dramatic and unprecedented rise in the number of children suspended from schools for behaviour problems and much agitation amongst the major political parties and teaching unions. Two decades of research and official government reports point clearly to continuing failures but also to the features that mark out effective provision. Yet even the official reports seem to be ignored in the headlong rush for new answers. Disputes about the concept of what works, with difficult and delinquent children, remain.

This chapter will outline the diagnostic problems that confronted our original study; briefly review the analysis that emerged; and outline through a case study the model of psychotherapy that was developed to address the problems of the impossible child. In doing so I hope to demonstrate the usefulness of an individualised case formulation approach for developing ways to conceptualise problems and generate therapeutic interventions.

Who Defines Whom

An adult who self-refers to a therapist is in a different position from that of a child. A child is referred by a parent, teacher, or some other agent. The question of how the referral happens, the label used and the point at which this label is removed, is not a neutral issue. The issue of diagnostic labelling is critical for the child and will impact on their long term future. It is not enough to argue that the label might be a good fit or assist communication between professionals. It has very real consequences, and if it is to be used, any justification for its use must outweigh the harm that it can do.

A number of factors will influence the referral decision. These include resource differences between localities, attitudes of teachers and social workers and psychologists towards their role, and the attitudes of support services. The label applied carries with it the attitude of the referring agent. That attitude is absent from any system of classification of the child's behaviour, yet it will vitally affect referral decisions and the long term outcome. It is now apparent that we must consider the role of the school and professionals in generating and perpetuating the problems for which children are labelled and excluded. (Lane, 1978; Rutter et al., 1978; Galloway et al., 1982; Mortimore, 1988; Keise, et al., 1993) This means that five seemingly simple questions pose complex answers.

(1) Who is the client?
(2) How does the person become a client?

(3) What is the focus of the intervention?
(4) Where will the intervention take place?
(5) What models underpin the intervention?

The idea of experts intervening for another's good forms the cornerstone of much therapy. However, if we ask these questions there are alternative ways to view the relationship. Cunningham & Davis (1985) describe the expert model, in which the professionals view themselves as in control of the decision making process, a consumer model in which the professional assists the client to make their own decisions and a transplant model which lies somewhere in between. This raises a number of questions about the roles played by service providers. Callias *et al.* (1992) identifies a variety of ways in which children may come to be labelled. They may be placed (social control model) referred (expert gatekeeper model) or assessed (in a partnership model). The model of that analysis may be individual (focused on pathology within the child), systems based (focused on pathology within natural groupings), or ecological (based on analysis of all contributing factors in the environment). The issues raised by Callias and her colleagues are all the more important for the fact that ethnic minority children are found to be over represented in units operating placement models (Shearer, 1983; West *et al.*, 1986; Keise *et al.*, 1993). Diagnosis is not neutral.

For example, the Warnock Committee (1978) recommended early identification of children with problems so that help could be offered. Yet, as several writers have pointed out, there can be negative consequences in being picked and "red tagged" early in life (Scheff, 1966; Clarizio, 1968; Scheff & Sundstorm, 1970; Ullman & Krasner, 1975). Even without professional intervention most behavioural difficulties ameliorate, so why mark out the child?

Individuals can be led to view their behaviour in terms of a sick role, through a process which is supposedly for their own good, but which may operate as a social control mechanism (Ford, *et al.*, 1982; Adams, 1986; Lane & Miller, 1992; Keise *et al.*, 1993). The relationship between the actor, the behaviour and an observer who is in a position of power who can apply the label is crucial to this tagging process. If a consumer model (Miller and Lane, 1993) is seriously to be preferred, then the power relationships must be addressed and the process through which a definition emerges must be recognised as a negotiated social exchange, not one of supposed neutral expert labelling.

A number of issues were apparent in the way the process of defining problems emerged in my work for the Islington Educational Guidance Centre. The idea that a number of agents had the power to impact on the decision was recognised and taken into account. The child was seen as one of those agents and therefore their view had to be incorporated. A solution had to be found to resolve the power imbalances. We initially tried to do so by operating within the framework of "exchange theory", (a model that incorporated behavioural and sociological concepts, Coser & Rosenberg 1969) through "contract therapy" (Lane, 1972). Thus the process by which definitions emerged was one of negotiation between the parties involved. In order to deal with power inequalities, an "open file" system was instituted, borrowed from earlier work (1973) which two of the staff (David Lane and Fiona Green) had originated elsewhere (see Cohen, 1982; Lane & Green, 1990).

The Conflict Between Diagnosis and Negotiated Therapy

The process we used to negotiate areas of concern could conflict with the diagnostic labels applied by professional groups working with us. Specific issues arose for us in applying diagnostic labels. These will be illustrated by reference to DSM 11 (since that was the model current at the time we were developing our approach) although some of the same issues are apparent with DSM 1V. In our original work several alternative diagnostic models were evaluated for possible use and found to be wanting.

The children referred to us as "impossible" represented a small sample of approximately 10% of the total of around three thousand children seen over a ten year period. They were popularly referred to by teachers as the impossible 1% of pupils. This was a more or less accurate figure. Originally, we used an administrative basis for the definition. The pupils had to be presenting difficulties of conduct in school sufficient to require additional specialist help. These difficulties had to be of at least two years' standing. Specialist help having been provided (in practice our pupils averaged over four previous failed interventions before arriving with us), the behaviour had to be not sufficiently improved for the school to rate the behaviour as improved. (Those familiar with the literature on spontaneous remission will understand the need for the two year proviso (Eysenck, 1952; Rachman, 1971).

They fell predominantly within the ninth DSM category of "behaviour disorders of childhood and adolescence", and excluded children with transient disturbances (category eight) or specific single difficulties (category seven). However, a number of the pupils could also find themselves categorised under section ten as socially maladjusted, or dyssocial. The single most applicable label would be unsocialised aggressive reaction of childhood, but the majority would also be categorised within group delinquent reaction. Two diagnoses of themselves are not problematic with DSM. The matter is resolved by listing first the most urgent or the most serious. Unfortunately, that decision depends heavily on the context in which the assessment was being made. For example, if the psychologist had been retained by the courts for a forensic report following criminal activity, the delinquent aspects required the most urgent attention. At the same time the educational psychologist retained by the school would be far more concerned with covert and hostile disobedience, physical and verbal aggression, destructiveness and bullying, that is, unsocialised aggressive reaction. The immediate threat of school expulsion made this the most urgent matter. Given the number of different agencies and previous interventions to which our pupils had been subjected, such conflicts between the psychological reports were not uncommon.

We had committed ourselves to defining problems in a way that could be shared and agreed between all parties; exploring problems in a way that led directly to a formulation of the controlling factors; using that understanding to create a detailed intervention; and creating a framework to ensure effective evaluation. The diagnostic models seemed woefully lacking for our task in terms of reliability, validity and utility.

Processes in DSM and other diagnostic tools both were dominated in the 1970s, and are again dominated in the 1990s, by the professionals' need to communicate with each other rather than a genuine partnership with the child. Professionals talk of ascertaining the wishes and feelings of the child or assessment of risk within families by eliciting the child's and parent's view. The process used is, nevertheless, constrained by professional need and in extreme cases consists of lengthy lists of predetermined questions asked of the child and parent. There are gallant efforts by many practitioners to give due weight to the concept of partnership, but they frequently become bogged down in the bureaucracy. The weight of decision making lies with the professionals and parents and children are denied rights of access to information (Widlake, 1993; Scherer, 1993).

The reasons for this are clear. Diagnostic systems are concerned to apply a categorical label (clinical or risk related). That label enables the professional to act on the basis that the threshold criteria have been reached to authorise (state) intervention. Diagnostic labelling may be inappropriate to therapeutic work with children, adolescents and their carers.

To resolve this our assessment scheme had to be reconstructed within the exchange framework. This led on to the possibility of negotiating definitions of problems through the use of discrepancy between the views of the parties on questionnaire and observational data together with the individual's view of where he or she was and where they wanted to be.

Performance Discrepancy as a Definition

At best an individual or a social system comes to define a problem through an awareness that something is wrong. This may be through feedback from others or from themselves but the individual/system gains a sense of performance error. "This is not how it should be, feel, look, act", and something can only be defined as a problem when the performance error is recognised.

Three elements received particular attention in the performance discrepancy framework. One, the actual behaviour that constituted the error had to be defined and agreed. Two, the objective to be met, that is the new behaviour to be attempted, had to be agreed. Three, the role each of the involved parties was to play, had to be agreed.

Therapy became a process in which each party created definitions of the performance error, came to a shared understanding of their concerns and thereby recognised why they could no longer co-exist. If they agreed that change was necessary they generated new compatible behaviours that would restore their relationship (social exchange).

Exploring the Paradox

If our concern was to develop a partnership-based model why bother with a consideration of diagnosis at all? Our attempts through research to look at groups of children labelled as "impossible" rather than to concentrate solely on individualised assessment, represented what many saw as a distraction from the main vision of the Islington Educational Guidance Centre. Our vision was to create a school-focused model of analysis and intervention. (Kings Fund, 1975). However, teachers, social workers, psychologists, psychiatrists and the courts continued to present such children to us. They seemed to have features in common and some attempt to explore the nature of their impossibility became inevitable. We were originally looking at the definition from the referring professional's perspective but there was a contradiction between that and the negotiated practice of the Centre. This meant that we would also need to look at the pupils' definitions and also at the process by which a shared definition (that is, a shared concern) could emerge if change was going to be possible. Our long term attempts to unravel the features that determined impossibility led to the increasing use of experimentally derived models in shaping our practice. The long term data indicated that some categories of behaviour were predictive of long term outcome. Behaviour did predict behaviour. Outcome was in large measure a feature of the label rather than the therapy applied. This was a confusing paradox for us.

It took a long time for us to unravel how the various features of the behaviour exhibited, the life experience and personality of the child, the characteristics of the school, family and peers, the patterns of intervention, the labelling of the child, discourse about the child/problematic situation and the role of fortuitous events, all related to each other.

Finally the paradox was resolved, for while it was true that a diagnostic label predicated future outcomes, it was in part self-fulfilling. Once applied it had an effect independent of objective evidence for its occurrence. There remained considerable evidence for continuities in behaviour, but equally compelling evidence of discontinuities. Even impossible children were not "bad" in all situations at all times. Children could be grouped within diagnostic categories and this had a value in our research endeavours. To do so in individual cases added little to intervention planning, generated negative consequences, and any gains were outweighed by the disadvantages (Lane, 1990).

Our task was to generate models of analysis that were sensitive to the variety of factors that generated and maintained inappropriate behaviours, contextually relevant, addressed power inequalities, and fostered a partnership for change.

Diagnostic models such as DSM had no place in our therapeutic work.

Where Next?

This is what the process looks like from the perspective of a research model. How might it be put into practice? How will the process of analysis be carried out? What will the intervention process look like? Will it work in practice? What outcome can we expect, from undertaking what looks like a great deal of work? I will now attempt in this section of the chapter to answer these questions by reference to a case study.

A CASE STUDY IN CONTEXT FOCUSED ANALYSIS

Context Focused Analysis—a Framework for Intervention

Context focused analysis was derived from four sources of knowledge:

1. Detailed therapeutic work with several thousand children, their families and their schools, by myself and professional colleagues in Islington and elsewhere, has generated much information.

2. The experimental work carried out over fifteen years has evaluated factors that generated and maintained problematic behaviours and situations based on research studies of both referred and non-referred comparative samples of participants.
3. Theoretical models having some basis of support in the research literature have been carefully evaluated.
4. The networked meetings organised by ourselves and others enabling a lively exchange of ideas between practitioners, and joint training events between our students and other centres (notably Didsbury College Manchester, the Institute of Education, Middlesex Hospital and University College Medical School) have generated critical analysis of emerging ideas.

The framework presented here remains recognisable from Lane (1974) and EGC (1975) (although less so from the 1969 (Lane, 1969) model) but the complexity of tools that can be brought to bear on an analysis is now much greater. Originally the model was effective at individual analysis and understanding the impact of the environment (behavioural/ environmental models) but less effective when we were asked to work in the other direction analysing environments and their impact on people (social/radical analysis). The tools for undertaking both now exist. Thus we can tackle disabling environments and change them as well as assist individuals in a process of change.

The potential to work with both the environment and the individual is made possible by selecting the tools for the job rather than being constrained by one theoretical position or diagnostic system. The point at which the analysis starts depends upon the aim of the intervention and the tools used vary according to the context. But in each case the intervention is based around three simple principles.

1. The focus of the analysis is to seek to understand the context in which one rather than an alternative behaviour occurs (hence the name, "context focused analysis").
2. Each of the participants (child, parent and professionals) are joint partners in generating that understanding (co-researchers).
3. The focus for change is based on the agreed formulation (the contextual understanding of why the behaviour occurs) and might include any of the constituent parts of that understanding. (Thus the child's school is equally likely to be asked to change its practice, as is the child or parent likely to be asked to change their own.)

The process involves using a behavioural/cognitive analysis but within an ecological philosophy. It must be remembered that behavioural analysis has within its origins a strong emphasis on environmental management.

Background Information at Referral

John, aged 15 years, is the youngest of five children. His father was in regular work and provided for the family but had always been aggressive towards the children according to the mother's and child's accounts. She used to intervene to prevent the children being hit, but gave up after receiving beatings herself. She reported that the father had a poor relationship with all the children. Attempts over the years to involve the family in family therapy failed. The older brother had been suspended from school for bullying and was increasingly involved with the police. John spent several months in hospital in his early years, for a series of operations to correct birth defects. He remembered that period clearly, and his feelings of fear. Difficulties with language development added to his problems. Speech therapy over several years, two years in a specialist unit for language difficulties and, later, a period in a unit for the "emotionally disturbed", preceded his transfer to mainstream secondary education. At this time, he was still a non-reader and had poorly developed social skills, although his speech had improved. He developed a severe stutter at the age of 12. He had been seen by three different psychologists, and the family was previously referred to a Child Guidance Clinic for assessment and therapy. Social work reports were available.

He was, over a period of three years, becoming increasingly involved in violence and vandalism and, subsequently, football hooliganism. His school felt that they could no longer contain him, and he received a series of suspensions. Referral to a residential adolescent unit was proposed as a final step. There remained a reluctance by his mother to see her son sent away from home. Prior to taking that step, his social worker and school between them decided to refer to the Islington Education Guidance Centre for assessment and recommendations.

1. *How is the behaviour to be defined?* The definition phase establishes the shared concern.

It is clear that the behaviour of the child must be carefully defined in the context in which it occurs. That change in behaviour may not be recognised raises important questions about the objectives of those involved. A variety of people are making the decisions, including the child. Each person able to influence the outcome may have to be included in the definition of the problem. Discrepancies between their views may be the appropriate point to start a change process. A contract for change may be necessary to enhance that process. The role each party is to play in the change process may have to be defined as part of the contract.

A definition phase based on social exchange concepts would represent the obvious starting point for a change process. Participants take events they share and describe them. We seek descriptions of specific events seen as exemplars of the concern. The distinction between behaviour as observed (which can include self reports of thoughts and feelings as well as overt actions) and explanations for why the behaviour occurs is maintained. Participants describe events (in phase 1) and offer hypotheses on cause separately (in phase 2). The meaning they each attach to the events is important but it is critical that agreement on what took place precedes examination of its meaning.

Our analysis in the first phase tries to establish an understanding of three areas.

Step 1. We establish the views of the significant partners in the problematic situation on the behaviours that occur that give rise to the assumption that something needs to change.

The first difficulty is to identify the partners. For us it is all of those who have a stake in the outcome, the child, parent, teachers, other professionals and other children, in fact all who are victims or beneficiaries of the behaviour. It is important to recognise that behaviour might be overt, or covert, but if it is capable of measurement in some way it would be included. It is also the case that behaviour is both complex and dynamic. Participants will offer explanations that include their perspective on the behaviour, explanations of why it occurs, their frustrations about the difficulties caused, objectives for change and ideas on change, all mixed together. We are asking them to generate their stories about events, the way in which they see (construe) the world. These constructions are the starting point for the analysis to follow. As we believe that we are all partners in finding a solution it is important to initiate the participants into the role of co-researchers. We start by explaining to them that the research process requires separation of the problematic behaviours from explanatory theories. The stories are de-constructed, separated out into parts for analysis. We explain what behaviours look like and we agree ways in which we can each help to identify and record them.

Step 2. The views of the significant partners on their objectives for change are identified.

The concept of performance error assumes that the partners have some view of how they want things to be different. It may be partially formed, or not appear to be related to the behaviour in question. It may contain alternative agendas. We do, however, strive to assist them to gain some sense of what it is that they want to be different. We assist them to review the objectives in terms of feasibility, expectation, organisational/resource constraints, etc. We do so not to judge their views but to help them to look at and evaluate their own views. We found early in our work with children and families that they often preferred to focus on the objectives for change. They wanted to forget past difficulties and disputes with the school and agree solutions for the future. For such clients we started with the objectives for change, using analysis of problems only in so far as it assisted understanding of change. The focus was on what needed to be different and hypotheses for change.

Step 3. The views of the significant partners on the role they want to play in the process are explored.

We explore with each partner, what role they expect to play in the process, and the limits they place on their involvement. Once the information on these three areas has been gathered we convene a series of meetings to examine the data and try to identify areas of shared understandings. It is like creating a set of Venn diagrams. Sets are defined, the information is assigned to set membership, overlaps are recognised, and attempts are made to redefine the information to ensure that all parties have some sense of a shared concern. That concern is subsequently explored. We do not rush this stage. Taking time to define, re-define and negotiate, in itself often changes the perspective of those involved and enables them to see that change is not impossible. Individuals come to see that the other parties have views that just might have some validity. They are moving towards an agreed "story". At the very least we work to an agreement that the behaviours defined are worth exploration to seek an understanding of why they occur or what needs to change.

John—It must be remembered that for John this was the end of the road: unless change occurred he was to be permanently excluded from school. We started by identifying the key players and their views on the noteworthy behaviours. The deputy head of his school, the teacher with responsibility for him (year head), a sample of other teachers, his remedial teacher, his mother, social worker and psychologist and John were asked to identify their primary concerns. There was a mixture of explanatory theories contained within the statements, and to assist the teachers to concentrate on behaviours a standard questionnaire (BSAG, Stott, 1975) was also used by the teachers and John.

The teachers split into two groups. One group saw no redeeming qualities in John. They described him as:

A fearless violent boy who will attack any enemy. He has committed a number of acts of vandalism. Cannot cope with the general school situation. Aggressive and bullying. Attacks other children without cause. Fantasises about violence and talks about hurting people. Very disturbing. Called "mad John" by his peers, because he is fearless in gang fights. His animal cunning is increasing. On a power trip. On a high. Gets agitated and then violent. Has attacked teachers. Refuses to follow instructions from teachers, disobedient, rude, disrupts lessons, moody, sullen, provocative and aggressive. Dumb insolence. Has point blank refused to do as told by the deputy head. A violent bully. He should be caned, suspended, prosecuted or preferably "strung up".

The second group identified similar problematic behaviours but also described other behaviours:

Can be a friendly and likeable boy. Can get on well with his peers. Perfectly pleasant and co-operative in one to one situations with most teachers. Works well in class with some teachers. Works hard and tries to overcome his learning difficulties. Made good progress in his remedial class and as a result no longer needs to attend. (John had established a very good relationship with the special needs teacher in the school, who made a determined and successful attempt to teach him to read.) It must be noted that a number of other teachers felt there were positive aspects in his behaviour, although they neither accepted nor tolerated his bullying.

The teachers identified 21 behaviours of concern on the BSAG (which would have placed him in the "maladjusted" category) marked particularly by severe over-reactive behaviours. These included items such as "flies into a temper if provoked", "attacks other children viciously", "frequently absent", "Damage to public property" (although it was noted that he respects private property). They also identified three possible neurological indicators and mild indicators of depression.

The more positive teachers stated that they wanted him to stay in school and benefit from learning but only if there were no more incidents. They were prepared to co-operate in designing a programme and would be prepared to examine all aspects of the situation and take necessary action.

John also marked himself on the BSAG and identified 31 behaviours of concern (which would place him in the "severely maladjusted" category). This included most of those marked by teachers but also additional behaviours related to delinquency, peer group deviance, distractibility and hyperactivity, with the addition of strong indicators of depression (additional to those identified by the teachers). He also marked three indicators of possible neurological involvement.

His descriptions of his own behaviour were more specific than the teachers. He described beating up particular children who insulted him. He stated that this was not bullying as they deserved it. He described occasions when he had insulted and "pushed past" certain teachers who were winding him up. He described his main concern as not getting thrown out of school because it would upset his mum. He also described his sadness at not being in the remedial class any more and offered the reason as his bad behaviour. He said he was bored in lessons, and was picked on for his stutter in front of the class which made him mad. He said that when he left lessons feeling mad he smashed things up. He *identified a number of teachers he liked because they were fair, did not mimic his stutter, and helped him to learn. He said that he was extremely depressed about his situation and felt he should be put away somewhere that would control his behaviour.*

John was prepared to take whatever course of action that was suggested to him as long as someone took control of him.

His social worker described him thus:

He functions at an immature level, and has always fantasised about violence and now engages in violence. He is also likeable and friendly, but restless and unable to accept even the slightest reprimand. He seems to split good and bad feelings completely and cannot link the two in any adults, peers or himself. As a result he likes and co-operates with some and rejects others. He feels that he must be put away since if he was surrounded by adults who controlled him he could change.

His social worker was prepared to co-operate in a programme and felt that behavioural contracting would work as it introduced some level of control.

The psychologists' reports added little information to what was known in terms of behaviour but referred to him as a passive bewildered boy who had difficulty making sense of his environment. He needed a secure framework to help him to make sense of the world. Various placements were suggested, but the current psychologist saw himself as having no active role in the process.

His mother recognised the problems exhibited at school and expressed her desperation that someone help him as she feared for his future. She also identified that she babied him and prevented him from becoming independent although she knew that he needed to do so. She wanted him to learn to control his behaviour and saw her role as supporting the professionals to help him.

The mixture of information provided a starting point for discussion to try to identify actual behaviours of concern and to work towards achieving a shared concern. However, the descriptions were too generalised (apart from examples provided by John). The process of trying to see connections between the various descriptions began. Three situations of violence were identified for consideration since they represented potential areas of overlap (behaviours could potentially be grouped into three sets—"Venn diagrams"):

1. bullying other children—set 1;
2. attacks on certain teachers—set 2;
3. fights in other contexts—set 3.

Selecting these areas does not imply they are more serious or urgent, they simply represent possible overlaps (sets) about which shared concerns can be reached. It is usually more effective to start with agreed areas and then work towards areas of disagreement. His year head and John were asked to identify actual incidents that they both remembered, could recognise as the same occurrence and could describe in detail. Their respective stories were elicited and compared. In each case they were prompted to describe what happened, not offer explanations for what happened.

Three other patterns were identified as currently ill-defined but were potentially sets. These included:

4. *behaviours labelled as depression;*
5. *behaviours labelled as working co-operatively;*
6. *behaviours labelled as a need for control.*

Set 1—bullying

His teacher described a number of incidents, for example:
- *Another younger boy called him a scallywag and he kicked him in the kidneys and face.*
- *He hit a boy who disagreed with a friend of his.*

John described both incidents but offered more detail.

- *This kid was mouthing off and kept taking the Mickey out of me, micky taking my stutter and trying to act big. I hit him to shut him up and because if I let him get away with it he would do it again.*
- *The other boy was trying to act big and was putting my mate down, so I hit him.*

There was little disagreement about the various incidents but whereas John saw his reaction as appropriate to the situation, his teacher saw it as an excessive inappropriate response. For the teacher it was bullying because John used his strength to intimidate others, for John it was deserved punishment, not bullying. It matters little which account is "true", they represent differing incompatible ways of viewing the world leading to relationship breakdowns.

Set 2—Attacks on certain teachers

His teacher described him pushing a teacher to the ground and kicking him. He also recounted an incident in which John was shouting at a teacher and punched him. This arose from a situation in which John tried to leave the classroom and was prevented by the teacher. (These incidents led to suspensions from school.)

John described the first incident as one in which he was feeling "mad" (he used the word to describe feelings of agitation leading to loss of control) and needed to get out of school before he did something bad. The teacher stopped him in the corridor and shouted at him to get back to class. He said he told him he had to leave but the teacher grabbed him to prevent him going. He pushed the teacher, who fell over and he walked over him to get away. The other incident John described as one in which the teacher asked him to read in class and he refused (he still had significant reading problems). He tried to explain to the teacher but started stuttering. The teacher started to mimic his stutter which made him angry. He decided to leave before he lost his temper, but the teacher prevented him and he punched him so that he could escape.

Set 3—Fights in other contexts

This proved more difficult as the year head had only third party accounts. However, John volunteered a number of incidents in which he described attacking other gangs, and causing grievous injuries to them. He stated that this is what you had to do in a gang and that you couldn't let others beat you, because then you would lose face and be at risk of getting beaten senseless yourself. You had to keep your reputation. He identified a downside to this in that others could gain status by beating him in a fight and consequently he was challenged more than he would have liked. He stated with some pride that while he taken beatings when jumped by a gang while on his own he had never lost in a one to one fight, or with his gang. He described his pleasure at having someone down, beaten, and begging for mercy. His year head identified these stories as exemplars of his concern and as behaviour he found very disturbing.

One central concern was shared between them. The year head was clear that further incidents would lead to permanent exclusion and John was anxious to stay in school. They agreed that they shared a concern to ensure that John's behaviour enabled him to stay in school. It was not clear to them what the behaviour pattern that would enable him to stay in school looked like but they did agree on the need to identify it. (Their motivations were different but there was enough overlap in the concern to use it as an area for further exploration. They recognised the performance discrepancy, current behaviour in school led to consequences they both preferred to avoid, and they felt alternatives were available. This is not how it should be and it could be different. The exception was the gang fights which disturbed the teacher but not John.)

The other areas of concern proved surprising easy to define. They both agreed on the behaviours that constituted working co-operatively, and on the contexts for its occurrence, that is with teachers who were generally seen as fair and tried hard to help children with learning difficulties. John and the year head could both describe examples of John being depressed although John had many more examples. They agreed that he was better behaved in situations of caring control and both felt that he needed to be controlled otherwise matters would get out of hand.

On the basis of these areas of shared concern they agreed that we should define their contradictory hypotheses of causation and attempt to test them and to define the behaviours that would enable him to stay in school. This agreement *was put to the other parties who accepted it. However, some teachers insisted on the proviso that, psychological intervention notwithstanding, any further incident would result in suspension. Without that agreement they wanted immediate suspension. Further discussion resulted in that proviso being accepted on condition that if John felt the need to leave a situation he could do so unchallenged during the interim period while the assessment took place. However, he was not to leave the building but to report to his year head or secretary's office. She would ring the guidance centre and request that he be allowed to visit us. No party was entirely happy with the agreement but the various interests were sufficiently served for it to hold. The issue of control preoccupied everyone.*

The reader may wonder what would happen if an agreement were not reached. In these circumstances phase one continues seeking further examples, through setting up agreed observations, tests, critical incident analysis, diaries, checklists, etc., until the parties can agree that certain behaviours are occurring. The fact that we deconstruct the stories to separate definitions of the behaviours of concern from explanations of why they occur usually ensures that it is possible to agree that at least some of the behaviours happen. We proceed to phase two on the agreed items and agree to stay at phase one on the unagreed items.

On rare occasions no agreement on anything is possible. Psychotherapy, therefore, ceases to be a valid tool, and the school would adopt management control techniques to address their own concerns, and the child may possibly adopt more deviant activities to address his or hers. The negative consequences escalate for both (although the child usually comes off the worst) until they cease to work together and leave the situation through suspension or choice. This same pattern applies in other situations. If parties cannot find even a minimal area of shared concern psychotherapy gives way to attempts at social control. At some future point the child, adolescent or even the then adult does (or does not) reassess their situation and seek changes. At some future point the school or other agencies does (or does not) reassess continuing failures with some children and decides to review their approach.

As therapists we have to accept that we intervene in systems for limited periods and cannot change everything. We have to focus on objectives that generate sufficient change to improve the life chances of clients. As environmental/social change agents we can use our analytical tools to assist broader systems to change but we should not confuse the roles. Psychologists and counsellors are actively and successfully involved in the broader agenda (Stern *et al.*, 1994).

2. *What factors must be taken into account?* The exploration phase.

The research data suggests that the exploration phase may have to consider the existence of constitutional and historical factors which have shaped the behaviour of the child. These predisposing factors are part of the child's past. There is little to be gained by considering them unless they impact on the present—and in John's case there is a suggestion that they might. For example, whereas in this case there has been a history of problems between a child and a teacher, the beliefs that they hold, based on that history, influence the present. Knowing the history can help to construct a framework for change. The child's personal style of action (personality) will influence preferred behavioural styles for responding to events. Knowing those patterns has the potential to improve programme design. Individual differences will, therefore, have to be taken into account in any change programme.

The patterns of support within the school and the community/family were found to be implicated in the research data, and appear to be so in John's case so may have to be included. So some predisposing events will need to be explored, if their impact in the present can be demonstrated.

It was, however, current events that were found to most powerfully alter the balance for the child, the reinforcement available for change, and the beliefs of the participants. The meaning attached to the behaviour must be understood. The data indicated that the day to day learning experiences of the child in school were important and could be altered, resulting in beneficial effects. Events which precipitate and maintain current behaviours must feature strongly in any analysis.

Although group comparisons have been drawn in the research, the particular combinations of events for each child, happening day by day, will be unique. Global assumptions about causation are unlikely to be helpful. The research provides possible suggestions but should not drive the therapy itself. What is needed is a careful process in which hypotheses of cause are generated and tested until those that determine current outcomes and that help or hinder efforts at change are uncovered. Thus each case is an individual process of experiment with behaviour.

The task at this stage is to observe problematic behaviours in context so that we can gather data to build an explanatory model "formulation" that can be tested in the real world of the subsequent intervention plan. It is important to recognise that a formulation is just an explanatory model, not the real world. You are hoping that the model will provide an adequate explanation that when tested will generate gains (desirable and feasible changes).

Step 4. We generate hypotheses that enable us to test the various explanations of the problem that each of the partners presents.

Two key questions provide the starting point.

1. Is the problem specific to a given situation or does it occur more generally?
2. When did the problem first occur? Is it something new or have similar problems occurred in the past?

If the problem is specific to the here and now, exploration will focus on current events. However, if it represents part of an ongoing or repeating pattern an exploration of the history may be necessary. At this stage we are creating hypotheses to be tested. The distinction between past and general and present and specific helps to choose methods of analysis.

Beyond these two questions, the attributions of cause that the participants hold provide the starting point for formally defining the hypotheses. What do they think is the likely cause of the behaviour. Once we have identified the existing hypotheses, alternative possible explanations of cause relevant to the context can be discussed.

Step 5. We select the methods we are going to use to test the hypotheses.

Hypotheses are likely to have been generated in two main areas:

1. *Predispositions acquired constitutionally or experientially.* This covers developmental features of the child, and historical analysis of the noteworthy behaviour in particular how it was acquired in the first place, model exposure, and contexts for its appearance. Dispositions that can be predicated as features of the behaviour will also be explored. The contexts for occurrence will also be the subject of an organisational analysis, to identify features that make the occurrence more or less likely.
2. *Precipitating and maintaining factors.* This covers the settings in which the behaviour currently occurs, and those where it does not, and specific events that precipitate or maintain each occurrence of the behaviour. A variety of behavioural cognitive and ecological models provide useful hypotheses. Following on from that analysis, the alternative behaviours that could be appropriate to the setting are explored, along with the conditions that make their occurrence more likely. Exploration covers both what does and could occur.

The exploration process is undertaken by looking at the explanatory ideas that each of the parties (ourselves included) have formed as to why the problems occur. We agree that those explanations represent hypotheses of causation capable of test. We agree on methods to test them that are consistent with the explanatory theories. We undertake to consider the outcome of the testing process. No one has to commit to accepting the outcome, only to participating in the experimental process and then reviewing the evidence.

Step 6. We obtain observation data to test the hypotheses.

Each of the hypotheses is subjected to experimental test. The participants are themselves co-researchers undertaking the analysis, so must understand principles governing such analysis. The tests must be reliable and valid, ethical, accessible to use by the participants, economical, and easy to obtain given the constraints of the context.

John—In discussion the initial two questions were explored. It was evident that the various behaviour sets were not specific to one setting but occurred more generally. The initial discussion had caused John and his teacher to realise that maybe the variety was generated by teacher response to him. It was also apparent that the behaviour had developed over a period of time, becoming more frequent, but that the emergence of violence corresponded with his move from Junior to Secondary School. In the first instance it was decided to clarify the contexts in which problems did or did not occur, and to track the history of John's difficulties with teachers.

John was asked create a record of teachers with whom he had and did not have problems. His year head created a list of teachers with whom he predicated that John would have more or less problems, and a list was sent to all his teachers asking them to identify the problems they had or did not have with John. John's list correlated well with his teachers' lists. They all agreed where the problems occurred. We were able to establish the contexts in which problems were more or less likely to occur.

On the basis of the data John was asked to generate hypotheses as to why he had more problems in one context or the other. His year head asked a sub-set of other teachers to generate their own hypotheses. This produced a variety of hypotheses (24 in total) and those that had a degree of shared support were selected for consideration. His social worker also offered some ideas.

The initial set for which there was shared support consisted of the following:

1. *John will work for those teachers he believes like him but not the others. (This was based on the social worker's idea that he split good and bad feelings.)*
2. *John will seek confrontations in settings where he can challenge authority figures because this raises his status with his peers. (This emerged from those teachers who thought he was on a power trip.)*
3. *John will work with teachers who take specific action to assist him with his learning difficulties, but find it more difficult in classes were no specific help is offered. (This emerged from three of his more positive teachers.)*
4. *John will work when he is not teased or mimicked by his teachers. (This was John's hypothesis.)*

5. *John will get into trouble when he is put under stress (can't do the work, is teased, etc.) and cannot find a way to escape from it. (This was a joint hypothesis from John and his year head.)*
6. *John likes hurting people. (This emerged from both negative teachers and John and hence the need for control.)*

In addition to these hypotheses it was agreed that the guidance centre staff, would look through all his old school records to identify when the difficulties first emerged and then discuss with him and any teachers who were involved their recollections of what changed. Additionally, the issue of possible neurological involvement would be explored by reference to previous psychologists. A personality assessment was also undertaken (Junior Eysenck Personality Questionnaire) as a start in exploring the issue of John liking to hurt people.

A questionnaire, structured classroom observations by John and certain teachers, and discussion of critical incidents enabled the hypotheses to be tested.

The data collected revealed a more detailed account of the circumstances giving rise to difficulties. It particular it was possible to identify antecedents and consequences that appeared to reinforce his patterns. Teasing, humiliation, feeling unable to cope, mimicking, sarcasm, and bullying made him feel that he was not in control and he would not know how to deal with the situation. His stress level rose and only by leaving the situation immediately (flight) or by striking out to remove the threat (fight) could he reduce his anxiety. Both flight and fight became negatively reinforcing. The historical analysis indicated that while he had always had learning and speech problems, these seemed to him to be much worse on transfer to secondary school. Data was sought to examine the idea that the contexts in which stress was apparent had increased during secondary school, and the sources of support decreased.

A complex analysis and intervention followed. In brief, it identified certain key elements.

1. *Both his father and some male teachers provided models of aggressive behaviour. John disliked them but saw them as powerful models. He valued the compassion he was shown but saw it as weakness. His mother was compassionate, and he felt loved but she was powerless against his father.*
2. *He greatly valued being in school, as least that part of it which gave him some sense of success. He feared the prospect of further suspension.*
3. *His speech difficulty and lack of social skills prevented his expressing/ asserting himself effectively. When confronted, he found that hitting out worked: children did not tease you if you terrorised them, and being unpredictable made teachers uncertain about confronting you. Violence worked; reason did not.*

4. *The school did not have a consistent policy, and conflicts were apparent between staff dealing with these issues and this pupil and he found that events were unpredictable for him.*
5. *Secondary school initially provided no support, but he then found a number of teachers he liked (the remedial class, and others) and began to feel that if he was in a secure place he could be in control or controlled. He worked for those teachers. However, he had more recently been removed from his remedial class and the timetable gave him more time with negative teachers, hence he was getting worse, that is resorting to fight and flight as a means of control of his anxiety. His year head provided a temporary relief in that he liked him and saw him as powerful (even though he was not a violent person) but it was rumoured that the school was changing its system and he would no longer have the support of that teacher.*

In discussion of the data between John, his year head some other teachers, and the Guidance Centre it was decided to seek both proof and disproof for one central hypothesis. (It should be noted that the other behaviour sets, such as depression, have not been forgotten, they are on hold.) The initial hypotheses explored linked the idea of stress to violence as follows.

When faced with a confrontational situation, John's level of stress (anxiety) is increased. As a result, his speech difficulty becomes worse, he has difficulty expressing himself, and he flees or fights—which reduces his anxiety. The various components in this sequence can be tested. The situations in which confrontations occur can be listed, the levels of stress he feels can be established on a scale on which he rates the level (say 1–10). Speech fluency could be checked, and the occasions on which he hits out could be recorded. Specific "Attribution" or "ABC" techniques could be used to provide a fine-grain analysis of the contexts in which violent outcomes were observed (see Lane, 1990, for discussion of the techniques).

In addition he was asked to identify contexts (and events) in which he felt depressed and to record both how he felt, any thoughts that occurred to him and what he did in response. What was depression about? It occurred in a variety of contexts but they had in common denied access to reinforcement (remedial class) because of behaviour he thought he could not change and therefore was stuck with feelings of helplessness. Also he expressed a sense of hopelessness about his past (I have always been bad), his future (I am going to be kicked out of school), and the world in general. He felt alive only when he was hyper-aroused (in fights), but at the same time felt out of control and possibly mad or going mad. His sense of this was compared to teacher reports.

Advice was sought on the possibility of a scan and neurological involvement in the loss of control. The specialist who was consulted rejected the idea and did not see John and the previous psychological reports gave no indicative features. With hindsight I feel that we should have pushed harder for these issues to have been explored. It would have helped John whether the findings were negative or positive.

3. What is it like for us? A formulation phase

Each child's, teacher's, school's, family's unique view of the events which matter must be understood. This must be backed by careful experimental data collected in the context in which the problem is defined. Thus for each event, a formulation which explains what factors control the occurrence of the behaviour in context must be provided. If what is happening is understood, changing what is happening becomes possible.

The hypotheses have been generated, and experiments designed to test them. Some have been found wanting, others have proved useful. A statement of the problem has now been obtained, objectives agreed, roles assigned, and predisposing, precipitating and maintaining factors identified. A great deal is already known. This information must now be integrated into an explanation of why the problem behaviour occurs—the formulation. Ideas for intervention arise out of the formulation and are a test of its validity. The formulation is a model of the problem in context. It represents the participants' agreed and tested view of the world. It has to be stated in a way that the various parties can agree:

"Yes, that's it, we do understand what is causing this and can see a way forward".

The formulation is a model of the world, it is not presented as fact. It is a way of seeing that enables the parties to co-operate to re-establish complementary relationships. The necessary steps to this phase are:

Step 7. We check the adequacy of the hypotheses.

The hypotheses are rigorously reviewed at this stage to answer the question:

"Does the data obtained really help to explain the responses seen in the current situation?"

If the explanation seems adequate it is further checked by identifying alternative explanations, and specifically seeking items to disprove the hypotheses. If the data stills holds up as an adequate model a formulation is attempted.

Step 8. We create a formulation of the problem in context and generate intervention hypotheses that arise from it.

The formulation is a model of the world that can explain the occurrence of the behaviours in question in the context in which they occur. It attempts to be a useful tool that gives rise to ideas for intervention. It enables interventions to be ruled out as not fitting the model. The intervention hypotheses at this stage remain hypotheses. They outline the areas in which change is possible, not the precise specification of that change.

Step 9. We discuss the formulation with the participants and the redefine their objectives and roles.

The proposed model is now discussed between the participants, covering the formulation itself, the intervention options it generates, and the consequences that follow from viewing the world in this way. The desirability and feasibility of change is tested by comparing the formulation model against real world issues. The suspension of reality that accompanies modelling is now discarded in favour of reality checks. The differences between the model and the real world generates the discussion about the aspects of the real world that could be changed. The formulation provides a possible map. This comparison is a vital step, often missed by practitioners devoted to diagnostic systems. The jump from the diagnosis to the intervention plan misses the reconstruction of ways of seeing (stories about the world) that is the necessary prerequisite to a successful intervention. The parties have to agree to act in the world as if the formulation is an adequate account for the purpose of testing the account by experimenting with new behaviours and experiencing the consequences of doing so.

John—This analysis was undertaken by reviewing the hypotheses using all the contexts in which flight and fight behaviour occurred. By looking at each context it was possible to demonstrate the limits to the hypotheses. This process of observation led to the realisation that there were in fact at least four different patterns.

1. *Cognitive justification. In some settings when faced with stress, John became angry, told himself that it was wrong that he was treated that way and chose to hit out. It was a deliberate decision to do so.*
2. *Stress management/skills deficit. In some settings he would become anxious, be unable to talk his way out because of his stutter, and hit others in frustration. There was no deliberation.*
3. *Just world. In some settings where he saw someone acting unjustly he would "punish" the offender by hitting them. This was cold, calculated retribution.*
4. *Sheer pleasure. Certain settings, involving gangs, were ones in which he sought out fights for the pleasure involved. He became hyper-aroused in these situations and gained immense peer approval for his actions.*

Given these very different patterns, the hypothesis that stress leads to violence cannot be sustained. It might do, but the circumstances in which it did were very specific. In the light of all the data the following formulation was offered as a possible story (model of the world).

Formulation

The shared concern—John is a fifteen year old boy at risk of permanent exclusion from school following alleged assaults on teachers and pupils, acts of vandalism to school property, and failure to comply with teacher requests. Key teachers in his school, John and his mother share a concern to keep him at school as long as co-operative behaviour can be re-established between themselves.

Historically—John found junior school life difficult in part because of his learning problems, and a broken school experience due to extended periods of therapeutic support. The normal school setting he found bewildering and had few opportunities to make consistent friendships. However, a number of teachers and his mother were seen as supportive, and limited demands were placed upon him because of his difficulties. The environment was in part adjusted to meet his needs. He was afraid of a violent father and found school a place of security and safety. He formed good relationships with a number of teachers whom he liked and within the limits of his ability from whom he received reinforcement as a likeable boy. He was offered a secure framework and a way of making sense of the demands upon him. He did not learn how to interact with his peers, and had little confidence in his own abilities. When faced with situations he could not control he tended to withdraw from them (flee).

On transfer to the secondary school there was a sudden increase in the demands upon him, and he was confronted with larger boys who teased him unmercifully. Whereas in junior school he felt well supported by his teachers, he did not at secondary school. He mixed with other boys but had few friends and had little idea of what was going on in lessons. His previous pattern of withdrawal (flight) proved less effective as other boys simply pursued him and it gradually gave way to violently hitting out as he discovered that children did not tease you if they were afraid of you. As he was smaller than the older boys he discovered that only if he was extreme in his violent response (if he went mad) would they choose to leave him alone. (He was seen as a "nutter".) The pattern of violent response therefore started as a way to control teasing about his speech problems from other boys. He began to realise that other violent adults, such as his father and some teachers (violence was defined by him as hitting, shouting, humiliating, and sarcasm), were also controlling people, who were not confronted by other children. He began to see them as role models as powerful people whom no-one confronts. He moved from violence as something of which to be afraid (his father), that controls you, to violence as a means of controlling bad feelings in yourself or controlling bad events or bad people. The fight response became generalised.

The formulation—John is pre-occupied with control. He believes the world should operate in a way that is just and predictable and has learnt a number of different ways to control events around him to ensure that it does conform to his beliefs (world view). He has had a limited degree of success in using violence to control events but when he cannot do so will flee the situation. In situations (e.g., positive teachers) that are controlled in a way he sees as just he can predict events and seeks to work co-operatively (e.g., with his teachers.) He finds these situations highly reinforcing. In situations that are not controlled in ways he finds just and in which events are not predictable he will if confronted with stressors that he cannot manage either seek to stop the event (by fighting, threatening, bullying) or if he cannot he will leave the situation. If prevented from leaving he will take whatever action he can to secure his escape. If confronted with an act he feels is unjust he will punish the offender.

He sees himself in a world that is difficult to predict or control and in which he is a failure. The existing sources of reinforcement (at school) open to him are under threat of withdrawal as a result of impending permanent exclusion. His competence to deal with his current situation is limited as he using one set of behaviours (co-operation) only with teachers who want to keep him in school while alienating others by using fight and flight responses.

He is depressed by his situation, his future and his sense of himself. That depression is relieved by the hyper-arousal he feels in gang fights and that pattern of excessive violence is reinforced by peer approval.

He cannot see a way out of the situation but believes that if teachers placed him in a secure (predictable and just) setting he would be able to co-operate.

A formulation is a model of the world, not the truth. Its value as a model is based on its utility in creating predictions that can themselves be tested in the real world. The formulation enables us to identify contexts in which one rather than an alternative behaviour is likely to occur. It predicts the events that will precipitate behaviours and reinforce them.

We can compare the model with the real world and ask if any changes in the real world context are desirable and feasible. The model is shared by the participants, who ask not whether it is true, but whether it generates useful ideas for change, and this process continues the partnership of creating shared concerns. The desired and feasible changes then become the intervention hypotheses that give rise to a programme. They remain hypotheses that are tested by the intervention itself.

The formulation was discussed with the respective partners and there was general agreement that it could be used to generate ideas for change. In a sense all of the teachers, John, his social worker and mother could see part of their world view in the model.

Intervention hypotheses

(a) To increase co-operative working by structuring the timetable so that John continues in lessons in which problems do not occur and attends the guidance centre for the other times. (That is, temporarily, to make the world predictable and just.)

(b) For John's year head to agree with John those situations that they both agree are unfair and to accept responsibility for talking to relevant parties and agreeing contracts of co-operation.

(c) To ask John to record the patterns of behaviour used by teachers whom he sees as powerful but not violent (for these to be used as possible models).

(d) To teach John how to stop and think about the consequences of his behaviour, to research alternatives and to act on the option most likely to generate co-operative working (at the guidance centre).

(e) For John to learn alternatives ways to manage stressors (at the guidance centre, followed by practice in school).

(f) For John to learn social skills to manage confrontations non-violently.

(g) For John's year head to create a hierarchy of teachers prepared to co-operate in a planned integration of John into his full curriculum supported by remedial help from school and the guidance centre. Step by step to enable John increasingly to test his new skills in unjust and unpredictable situations.

The hypotheses relate to security and control, leading first to the re-establishment of co-operative working relationships to reduce incidents, then to teach John methods to deal with loss of control. Agreed unjust actions will be tackled while teaching John how to tolerate grey areas. These skills will be tried in phased steps (hierarchy) while retaining support followed by subsequent gradual withdrawal of that support.

Again it must be stressed that the hypotheses must arise out of the formulation and be agreed as desirable and feasible changes. They may not cover all aspects of the formulation (as indeed these do not) but it must be possible to predict that they will generate the desired change and as such test the model.

4. *What must we do to change? A planned intervention phase.*

If it is to take account of key factors and potentially involve several change agents, the change process is going to be complex. Without a step by step plan, based closely on the formulation, the process is going to become muddled. No one will be accountable, and the child will lose. Each person's responsibility for the change will have to be determined. The detail of what they are expected to do will have to be known. The outcome (performance) against which success is going to be measured must be specified. In this way the complexity might be successfully managed. However, our research data suggested that long term change might have to be managed, in addition to short term interventions. An evaluation and follow up process, to ensure that gains are not lost and new problems are tackled, will have to be included.

An understanding has now been achieved and desirable and feasible changes identified. A plan to bring about those changes is now designed.

Step 10. The behaviours that each of the parties are agreeing to change are specified and the procedures to be used to assist them are devised.

Our discussion at this point is concerned as much with how we learn as with what we need to learn. The aim is to learn new ways of responding to generate mutually satisfying patterns of behaviour. We are attempting the enactment of a new story (reconstruction) of the world, one that we believe will be reinforcing for the participants. It is useful to focus on the question:

"What has been learned in the process of generating the formulation?"

This will give rise to ideas for change that incorporate not just the behaviours to be attempted, but the ways in which each party learns best. There are likely to be three areas for change. Some behaviours will be occurring too infrequently, at too low a level of intensity, or on the wrong occasion. In these circumstances the aim will be to increase the appropriate behaviour. Other behaviours will be occurring too frequently, too intensely or on the wrong occasion. The aim will be to decrease the inappropriate behaviour. Other appropriate behaviours may not be occurring at all, and the aim is too instil these new behaviours in the participants' repertoire.

It is important to emphasise that it is not being stated that these behaviours are the right or wrong way to behave. We are agreeing the specification of behaviours that will be used to experiment in the world and record the outcome of those experiments. The results will link behaviours with outcomes (consequences) so that participants can then make decisions about the use, or not, of those behaviours on other occasions. Choice is being increased, through enabling the participants to re-construct their view of the world, and have the competence to act differently.

Step 11. A contract for change is agreed between the parties.

Once the behaviours and methods for assisting change have been agreed, the parties negotiate a contract for change. There is considerable confusion about the use of contracts in therapeutic interventions. Too often contracts are devices used by the powerful to impose behavioural change on the less powerful. Social workers may put a parent on a contract to carry out set changes, or else their child will be removed. The government in the UK is currently insisting that parents sign contracts with their child's school to carry out agreed tasks. Some behavioural practitioners in the early days used contingency contracts to modify behaviours of children with the child's teacher as the primary beneficiary. These are not contracts in either the legal sense (freely entered into, and on reasonable terms), nor in the sense meant here. For us, using the concept of exchange theory, a contract provides an agreed basis for a mutual exchange of benefits between participants (reciprocity). The concept of mutuality is central, and without it, the negotiated exchanges that have been at the centre of this process become meaningless manipulations. Contracts are such powerful tools that we constantly warn practitioners not to use them unless they fully endorse the social exchange philosophy that informs them.

Step 12. The change programme is enacted.

The programme agreed in the contract is now enacted and monitored. The enactment is itself part of the continuing process of hypothesis testing. Each component of the intervention plan has been included because it was predicted by the formulation. The intervention should bring about desired changes. It should work, that is be feasible, in the real world context in which it operates. It is an experiment with behaviour.

There were a number of adolescents who presented problems related to the issues raised by John and we had been discussing these with various colleagues. We had a complex set of stimulus situations to manage, which seemed beyond simple contingency management (although in fact this worked well within the centre but was less effective in the wider, less predictable, environment) Fortunately, Don Michenbaum and Ira Turk had sent us some unpublished material they were developing on anger management, which we were able to use. This was linked with our own stress management material that had originally been developed by us for use with drug abusers (Lane, 1975). Irwin Sarason, in some very helpful letters to us, also suggested the use of scripted social skills, which proved highly successful and powerful tools in their own right. (We had earlier developed a set of stories of problematic situations which we asked children to analyse and to generate alternatives, but Sarason's scripts were more effective.) Edward De Bono had discussed with us his thinking lessons as a way to provide problem solving skills. We also used material originally developed for learning difficulties based on self-talk, and found that by combining the elements in a programme including reinforcement (stop, think for one minute) we could get the child to stop and think, evaluate responses, try out scripts for new behaviours, evaluate the consequences, use effective analytical skills, and continually self-monitor. By adding behavioural contracting in the school situation to extend the experiments with behaviour into real settings, we had a complete set of tools the client could use or adapt, to manage stressful situations. (There was an enormous generosity of spirit in the sharing of ideas between the emerging behavioural and cognitive therapists at that time.)

John—A programme was introduced to teach John mechanisms to deal with stress situations and to develop his social skills (by observing real events in school, practising scripted alternatives, observing the relationships between behaviour and consequence and thinking though alternatives, based on lateral thinking). A review of the models in his environment took place, to help him to identify power as legitimate assertion rather than aggression. A contracted set of relationships was established with teachers, covering their behaviour towards him and his towards them so that events were rendered predictable, with defined consequences. It was made clear that any incident of bullying would be followed by a suspension, but that the issue of provocation by others would also be tackled, that is, he saw it as fair (just world). Work was undertaken in terms of his peer groups to ensure matters arising were dealt with by the school and he worked on group relationship skills with peers. In accordance with the agreement no changes were attempted at home. Neither parent was prepared to act until they saw change at school and John now felt sufficiently in control that further violence from his father was unlikely. It was agreed that this would be monitored with intervention by social services if necessary. The monitoring was agreed. Over a nine-month period, the programme took effect with only two minor incidents being reported that the school did not feel warranted suspension. The school and John created a new set of stories to describe the world as they now saw it and used those to evaluate changes that had taken place. They were both happy with the new constructions.

5. *What must we do to ensure success? An evaluation phase.*

We know that long-term outcome depends on the events that happen subsequently to the child. We also know that change in behaviour may not be related to an evaluation of change by key agents. An agreed basis must be established to measure change for each programme. Once a predetermined performance target has been reached, the new situation must be addressed. It was established that, faced with success, new demands may emerge which are difficult for the child to manage. A long term support strategy may be needed, until the child has developed the skills to meet new challenges, and not just solve the existing difficulties. A careful evaluation and follow up process is required.

Programme monitoring takes place during the intervention phase. Evaluation in this model serves a number of functions beyond programme monitoring.

Step 13. The effectiveness of the formulation as a model based on the success of the intervention plan is evaluated.

Evaluation is a continuous process throughout all phases. In the same way that the design of the programme was the result of experimental testing of hypotheses, the intervention itself is a test of the validity of the formulation as an adequate model. Failure to respond is not taken as a failing in the child or other partners, but as a shortcoming in the model. Failure is a test of the model and it is re-evaluated in the light of the "experiment with behaviour" that was the intervention.

Step 14. Gains made are maintained and the programme reviewed to optimise its value.

It was often the case for those for whom change involved a complex set of adjustments that they felt somewhat lost in the new world of opportunity presented. If they chose to continue to use the new behaviours learnt, they moved from the world they knew, its consequences, friendships and their sense of self (being) within it to a new world with uncertainties and sometimes a sense of loss. A specific process to help participants cross the abyss was needed. The generalisation and maintenance of gains had to planned. This was helped by also considering what had been learned during the intervention phase. What helped and what hindered change? Were there aspects of the intervention that added more value than other parts? This consideration helped to optimise the change process.

Step 15. The whole process is re-evaluated to ensure that all lessons are learnt.

A follow up period after the end of the formal intervention is necessary and of benefit to all the participants. The reflection on learning that it involves enables adjustments to be made for the future. It is a sad feature of much psychotherapeutic intervention that this process is skimped or omitted altogether in many programmes. How can we know that our endeavours have long term value unless we find out what happened and compare once again our models of the world with what is happening to us?

John—No violence was reported in his final year at school or in the community. He left without qualifications but did eventually obtain employment. He reported to us on the use of his skills in managing conflicts in the workplace.

The one area not covered in the original programme was the "sheer pleasure", he experienced through his involvement with a violent football gang. He had stayed out of trouble during the period of the programme and the follow up. It worried us that specific attempts to deal with this aspect of his behaviour had not been included in the programme. and it is not surprising, to discover on follow up, that no change had occurred in that area. Two years later, he was involved in an incident with others (his old gang). He self-referred at this time to the Islington Centre and re-visited his stories about this aspect of his self as someone powerful. Following this re-evaluation and a period of probation and good social work support, he stayed out of further trouble. Five years on he was working, developing an ongoing relationship and feeling positive about himself and the depressive behaviours had disappeared.

THE CENTRAL QUESTION—WHY DO SOME CHILDREN NOT IMPROVE?

This final section of the chapter will attempt to draw together some of the major points as to why, in spite of the fact that behavioural labels did predict outcomes, the variance within our research data made individual case analysis essential in the creation of effective programmes of intervention.

"What do we need to consider if we are to understand the process by which some children who present behaviour problems improve (remit) and others do not?"

Remission is, at least, simple to define. It is a process by which individuals identified as having difficulties considered noteworthy by someone in a position of power later come to be considered as no longer a cause for concern.

What Factors Correlate with Remission from Difficulties?

Our study, involving three thousand children and ten years of follow up, examined features of the child, family, education, prior interventions, current interventions and the process of labelling. It combined psychometric, biographical, and observational data and used case study, correlational and experimental methods of analysis. The relevant data for this current purpose is one of the factor analytic studies we undertook of 100 children fitting the impossible label (Lane, 1983). It confirmed the findings of other research, namely that:

1. Continuation of disorder was more likely in individuals suffering more, rather than less, adversity in their life experience.

2. Behaviour now did predict future behaviour patterns.
3. Certain features of personality (dispositions) were predictive of the occurrence and continuation of difficulties.

Although these findings might point to the value of a diagnostic system a more subtle examination was necessary to unravel the picture. For example, one child (not untypically) had multiple conduct problems in school, previous specific difficulties (bedwetting, a phobia, and specific learning difficulties), and was now involved in group delinquency. He was the victim of scapegoating within the family and by key teachers within the school. The long list of diagnostic categories that applied even when structured in terms of seriousness helped little in devising an appropriate intervention, since it had resulted in the past in his being placed in programmes that dealt with single issue treatments. He received help based on the categories, one by one, but not in terms of the multiplicity of issues that overwhelmed him. It was common in the research data to find the children progressing through a series of clinical and educational interventions over a period of years, each making little real difference to their life chances. As Newson (1992) has pointed out, many of the children she saw in her clinic had multiple problems and "were coping with life scenarios which any of us as competent adults would have experienced as problems of paralysing magnitude".

The category of "conduct disorder" was found to be too imprecise in our analysis and the behaviours within it were found to split into two orthogonal factors. There was continuity of negative behaviour rating by teachers from the first to the final years of secondary school and their subsequent delinquent career extends their conflict with others, from a period stretching in some cases from five to twenty years of age. (Our forthcoming follow up study stretches this to their forties, Lane, 1998). Yet for most there were periods when they did not present problems and teachers and other professionals with whom they had no difficulties.

One of the most important differences to emerge corresponds, in part, to the concept of "fortuitous events" influencing outcome. It was apparent that pupils showing less change long term were also the subject of negative life experiences, both as individuals and in terms of their school careers.

The detailed material from the case study data pointed to a range of factors of importance, but particularly so was their good fortune (or not) in meeting professionals who believed that change was possible. The view held by the child and key others, particularly teachers, had a major impact. The beliefs about change generated (or failed to generate) change. The extent to which professionals, teachers and social workers, for example, were able to assist children and parents to act effectively on their environment significantly affected outcomes. Some professionals said the right things about disabling systems but the more effective changed the system. The impossible child generated particular stresses at "sore spots" in social systems, resulting in their rejection not because they were unresponsive but because they made powerful system players feel uncomfortable. They challenged the professional status quo in ways that would not be tolerated. The wide range of behaviours exhibited by each child, the variation in their behaviours from context to context, and the equally wide range of techniques used to work with them indicates that individual analysis is necessary. A packaged set of approaches based on either a common category, on even one using a list of categories within which an individual child might be placed, is unlikely to meet the complexity of each situation.

What Then do we Need to Do?

It is apparent that the process of remission involves more than a change in behaviour. To some extent, it appeared in the data that the behaviour of the child and a rating as improved were independent variables. In reality the belief system of the key change agents (primarily teachers) is part of the overall pattern. If they do not believe in the possibility of change, they will not see it even when the behavioural evidence exists. As argued elsewhere, perhaps we can only see what we believe (Lane, 1989). The relationship between final ratings, life events and personality features points to some children *being less likely than others to be offered whatever help is available even when the need has been established.* In parallel with the adult psychiatric literature, black children were more likely to find themselves placed in units out of school (social control models) while white children were more likely to be offered clinic based psychotherapy (expert referral models).

Understanding remission requires a detailed knowledge of the behaviour itself and the way it is viewed by key agents. It is apparent that simply changing behaviour is not enough; one must act also to change the way the child is viewed, and to deal with the significant negative life events the child experiences. To this extent, professional attempts to promote remission require a multimodel input, focusing on the behaviour and the significant agents and events in the child's life. An effective short term therapeutic intervention, however good it might be, would need to be supported by longer term action in the child's community. The primary focus would seem to be the school.

To achieve change we must:

1. Act to change the behaviour itself.
2. Act to change the action of the school towards the child.
3. Assist the child (sometimes repeatedly) through individual crisis periods, rather than rejecting him or her because of a difficult personality. (The child most difficult to like is also the most in need of support.)
4. Act to teach the child skills to survive in or leave the environment in which they live, while they and we find ways to enhance life chances.

Some of these actions lie outside of the traditional role played by psychotherapists. The solution lies in fostering a network of partnerships who act to generate change.

Such partnerships must involve the school in providing ongoing support, and also the range of other agencies, the community and professionals involved at different stages in the life of the child and family. Psychotherapy does have a role to play and is effective but not if it treats all professional intervention as either neutral or helpful. The school, and the professionals who work with it to decide the way children are labelled and the response offered, are part of the situation of concern. Ongoing action within the community of the child, and principally to change schools, is needed.

This is not an easy task, but our long term follow up data, and that of others using versions of the model, does point to significant changes that are maintained. If we are prepared to go beyond diagnosis, complex cases need not appear so impossible.

REFERENCES

Adams, F. (1986) *Special Education*. Harlow: Longman.

Callias, M., Miller, A., Lane, D.A. & Lanyado, M. (1992) Child and adolescent therapy; a changing agenda. In Lane, D.A. and Miller, A. (1992) *Child and Adolescent Therapy: A Handbook*. Buckingham: Open University Press.

Carkhuff, R.R. & Berenson, B.G. (1967) *Beyond Counselling and Therapy*. New York: Holt Reinhart & Winston.

Clarizio, H. (1968) Stability of deviant behaviour through time. *Mental Hygiene*. **52**, 288–293.

Cohen, R. (1982) *Whose File is it Anyway?* London: National Council For Civil Liberties.

Colby, K.M. (1964) Psychotherapeutic processes. In Farnsworthy, P. McNemer, O. and McNemer, C. *Annual Review of Psychology*, **15**, 347–370.

Coser, L.A. & Rosenberg, B. (1969) *Sociological Theory*, London: Macmillian.

Cunningham, C. & Davies, H. (1985) *Partnership with Patients*. Milton Keynes: Open University Press.

EGC (1975) The Educational Guidance Centre. *Introduction to Services*. London: IEGC.

Eysenck, H.J. (1952) The effects of psychotherapy—an evaluation. *Journal of Consulting Psychology*, **16**, 319–324.

Ford, J., Mongon, D. & Whelan, M. (1982) *Special Education and Social Control; Invisible Disasters*. London: Routledge and Kegan Paul.

Galloway, D., Ball, T., Bloomfield, D. & Seyd, R. (1982) *Schools and Disruptive Pupils*. London: Longman.

Goldstein, A.P. (1971) *Psychotherapeutic Attraction*. New York: Pergamon.

Gray, P., Miller, A. & Noakes, J. (1994) *Challenging Behaviour in Schools*. London: Routledge.

Herrick, M.J. (1971) *Chicago Schools: a Social and Political History*. Beverly Hills: Sage.

Jackson, C.G. (1977) The emerging of a black perspective in counselling. *Journal of Negro Education*, **46**, 230–253.

Jones, R.L. (1972) *Black Psychology*. New York: Harper Row.

Keise, C., Kelly, E., King, O. & Lane, D.A. (1993) Culture and child Services. In Miller, A. and Lane, D.A. (1993) *Silent Conspiracies*. Stoke on Trent: Trentham Books.

Kings Fund (1975) *The Educational Guidance Centre; A New Approach to Children's Problems*. London: Kings Fund Centre.

Lane, D.A. (1969) Functional Analysis and Classroom Management. Unpublished report.

Lane, D.A. (1972) *Contract Therapy*. London: IEGC.

Lane, D.A. (1974) *Behavioural Analysis of Complex Cases*. London: IEGC.

Lane, D.A. (1975). *Drug Dependence: Prevention and Education*. DDDG/Kings Fund: London.

Lane, D.A. (1978) *The Impossible Child*, Vols 1 and 2. London: ILEA.

Lane, D.A. (1983) *Whatever Happened to the Impossible Child?* London: ILEA.

Lane, D.A. (1987) Psychological evidence in the juvenile court. In Gudjonsson, G. and Drinkwater, J. *Psychological Evidence in Court*. Leicester: British Psychological Society.

Lane, D.A. (1989) *Attributions, Beliefs and Constructs in Counselling Psychology*. Leicester: British Psychological Society.

Lane, D.A. (1990) *The Impossible Child*. Stoke on Trent: Trentham Books.

Lane, D.A. (1996) What Works. *Forensic Update*, **44**, 30–32.

Lane, D.A. (1998) *Behaviour Support Systems; Papers of the Windsor Group*. London: Professional Development Foundation.

Lane, D.A. & Green, F. (1990) Partnerships with pupils. In Scherer, M. Gersch, I. and Fry, L. (1990) *Meeting Disruptive Behaviour*. London: Macmillan.

Lane, D.A. & Miller, A (1992) *Child and Adolescent Handbook*. Buckingham: Open University Press.

Lawrence, J. (1973) *The Problem Child*. Aims of Education an interdisciplinary inquiry. London: Institute of Education.

Miller, A. & Lane, D.A. (1993) *Silent Conspiracies*. London: Fulton Books.

Mortimore, P (1988) *School Matters; The Junior Years*. London: Open Books.

Newson, E (1992) The barefoot play therapist; adapting skills for a time of need. In Lane, D.A. and Miller, A. *Child and Adolescent Handbook*. Buckingham: Open University Press.

Rachman, S. (1971) *The Effects of Psychotherapy*. Oxford: Pergamon.

Rogers, C.R. (1963) Psychotherapy today—or where do we go from here? *American Journal of Psychotherapy*. **17**, 15–16.

Rutter, M., Maughan, B., Mortimore, P. & Ouston, J. (1979) *Fifteen Thousand Hours*. London: Open Books.

Scheff, T. (1966) *Being Mentally Ill; A Sociological Theory*. Chicago: Aldine.

Scheff, T. & Sundstorm, E. (1970) The stability of deviant behaviour over time; a reassessment. *Journal of Health and Social Behaviour*. **11**, 37–43.

Scherer, M. (1992) The residential community as a therapeutic environment. In Lane, D.A. and Miller, A. (1992) *Child and Adolescent Handbook*. Buckingham: Open University Press.

Scherer, M. (1993) Ethical perspectives; who decides? In Miller, A. and Lane, D.A. *Silent Conspiracies*. Stoke on Trent: Trentham Books.

Shearer, A.C. (1983) *Integration: A New Partnership*. London: ACE.

Stern, E., Lane, D.A. & McDevitt, C. (1994) *Europe in Change. The Contribution of Counselling*. Rugby: European Association for Counselling.

Stott, D.H. (1975) *British Social Adjustment Guides*. London: University of London Press.

Tizard, J. (1973) Maladjusted children and the child guidance services. *London Educational Review*, **2.2**, 22–37.

Topping, K.J. (1983) *Educational Systems for Disruptive Adolescents*. London: Croom Helm.

Ullmann, L.P. & Krasner, L. (1975) *A Psychological Approach to Abnormal Behaviour*. Englewood Cliffs, NJ: Prentice Hall.

Warnock Report (1978) *Children with Special Needs*. London: HMSO.

West, A., Davies, J. & Varlaam, A. (1986) The management of behaviour problems; a local authority response. In Tattum, D. P. *Management of Disruptive Pupil Behaviour in Schools*. Wiley: New York.

Widlake, P. (1993) Parents as partners. In Miller, A. and Lane, D.A. *Silent Conspiracies*. Stoke on Trent: Trentham Books.

CHAPTER 7 Managing the therapeutic relationship in behavior therapy: the need for a case formulation

Peter G. AuBuchon and
Victor J. Malatesta

INTRODUCTION

> You will get further with a patient with a good therapeutic relationship and
> lousy techniques, than you will with good techniques and a lousy relationship.
> Victor Meyer (personal communication, October, 1984)

Although provocative, Dr Meyer's quotation alerts us to the importance of the therapeutic relationship in behavior therapy . This has been emphasized by prominent clinicians throughout the history of behavior therapy (e.g., Beck *et al.*, 1979; Brady, 1980; Burns, 1994; Goldfried, 1983; Linehan, 1988; Meyer & Gelder, 1963; Wolpe & Lazarus, 1966). In addition, a range of studies has examined aspects of the therapeutic relationship, including therapist characteristics, and the relationship's effect on treatment compliance and outcome (e.g., Brunink & Schroeder, 1979; Rabavillas, Boulougouris, & Perissaki, 1979). Despite these developments, there remains an absence of an empirically supported methodology which both incorporates basic principles of behavior therapy and also provides specific guidelines for the effective use of this relationship. In this chapter, we will attempt to address these problems.

The purpose of the present chapter is to describe a methodology for managing the therapeutic relationship which is based upon, and guided

Beyond Diagnosis: Case Formulation Approaches in CBT.
Edited by Michael Bruch and Frank W. Bond.
© 1998 John Wiley & Sons Ltd.

by, the case formulation. It will discuss how the formulation itself is consistent with two keystones of behavior therapy, namely the experimental method and individualized treatment. In addition, it will present two data-based case studies which not only illustrate this method, but also provide initial empirical support for the approach.

The chapter is organized as follows. First, a brief critical review of the existing literature on the therapeutic relationship in behavior therapy is presented. Second, the case formulation approach to behavior therapy is reviewed. Third, a relationship intervention based upon the formulation, the *therapist style*, is introduced and operationally defined. Fourth, the aforementioned case studies are presented which illustrate how the formulation was used to develop and guide the therapeutic relationship. Finally, a summary is presented which includes a discussion of the case studies and the advantages of the case formulation approach to the therapeutic relationship.

REVIEW OF THE LITERATURE

The therapeutic relationship in behavior therapy has been studied in several ways. First, there are studies which have compared behavior therapists to those of different orientation on a variety of characteristics. Behavior therapists were found to be at least as warm, empathic, genuine, and caring as therapists from other orientations (e.g., Brunink & Schroeder, 1979; Fischer *et al.*, 1975; Sloan *et al.*, 1975). Behavior therapists were also found to be more active, and to demonstrate more initiative, support, and direction than therapists from other orientations (e.g., Greenwald *et al.*, 1981; Sloan *et al.*, 1977). While these studies are important in disproving the early criticisms of behavior therapists as "cold or mechanistic", they offered little in the way of recommendations for how behavior therapists may approach the relationship with their patients.

A second group of writings has examined how the therapist–patient relationship may improve the efficacy of behavior therapy. For example, the role of the therapist as a nonfearful model, reassuring stimulus, safety signal, or "reciprocal inhibitor" has been addressed (e.g., AuBuchon & Calhoun, 1990; Bandura & Menlove, 1968; Meyer, 1957; Rachman, 1983; Wolpe, 1980). In addition, Linehan (1988) and Rosenfarb (1992) have written clinically useful analyses of the therapeutic relationship within the practice of behavior therapy. These authors discuss the relationship both as a vehicle for therapy, and as a therapeutic agent (e.g., through modeling and social reinforcement). More recently, Wright and Davis (1994) have offered strategies for modifying therapist behaviors based upon assessment of the patient's expectations of the therapy and/or therapist. Taken together, with the exception of AuBuchon & Calhoun (1990), these studies have a common shortcoming—a lack of empirical data to support their theoretical positions. In addition, the Rosenfarb (1992) and Wright & Davis (1994) papers limit their examinations of relationship behavior to single sets of determinants (e.g., operants; expectations).

Third, studies have demonstrated that certain types of therapist behaviors are more effective with various clinical populations. These behaviors include acceptance, limit setting, and validation with borderline personality disordered patients (e.g., Linehan, 1993; Shearin & Linehan, 1992); focusing, challenge, encouragement, and praise with anxiety disordered patients (e.g., Grayson, Foa, & Steketee, 1982; Gustavson et al., 1985; Rabavilas, Boulougouris & Perissaki, 1979; Williams & Chambless, 1990); lenient and flexible behaviors with anorexic patients (Touyz, Beumont, & Dunn, 1987); and initiative, support, and direction with depressed patients (e.g., Greenwald et al., 1981). Although useful, these findings do not indicate how to interact idiographically with any patient who may be presenting with any disorder, or combination of disorders.

THE CASE FORMULATION APPROACH

Related to the strategy of utilizing certain therapist behaviors with particular clinical populations is the case formulation approach to the therapeutic relationship (e.g., Persons, 1989; Turkat and Brantley, 1981). In this approach, various therapist behaviors are idiographically and systematically demonstrated with each patient, as determined by the therapist's formulation of the patient and his or her difficulties.

Meyer and Turkat (1979) defined formulation as "an hypothesis which (1) relates all the clients' complaints to one another, (2) explains why the individual developed these difficulties, and (3) provides predictions concerning the client's behavior given any stimulus conditions" (pp.261–262). The case formulation approach is rooted in the genesis of behavior therapy as a clinical science (e.g., Shapiro, 1957; Wolpe, 1958), and has been demonstrated empirically to be effective with a range of disorders including schizophrenia (Adams et al., 1981), chronic pain (AuBuchon, Haber, & Adams, 1985), complex phobia (AuBuchon, 1993), complicated obsessive compulsive disorder and personality disorders (AuBuchon & Malatesta, 1994; Malatesta, 1995; Turkat & Carlson, 1984), and tic disorders (Malatesta, 1990). The case formulation also has utility in managing the therapeutic relationship. First, it offers a framework within which the patient's behavior towards the therapist can be understood (e.g., lateness, mistrust, hostility). It does this because generating a case formulation most often involves gathering developmental data, and in doing so, helps the therapist understand how these problematic interpersonal behaviors were learned. By relying on basic learning principles, the formulation can then be used to predict and explain why a particular patient may have certain reactions to various behaviors and characteristics of the therapist. For example, a patient whose father ridiculed him whenever the patient demonstrated anxiety, or disclosed a concern, may be particularly reluctant to disclose and discuss difficulties when faced with an older male therapist.

Second, the formulation can be valuable in guiding the therapist's interactions with the patient. In the above example, therapist behaviors such as appropriate self-disclosure of the therapist's own anxieties can reduce the patient's anxiety about doing the same (e.g., through vicarious deconditioning or participant modeling). These therapist behaviors also help to normalize the patient's experience, and teach the patient unguarded and self-disclosive behaviors. How a therapist interacts with a particular patient can be labeled as *therapist style*.

THERAPIST STYLE

Therapist style can be defined as follows. It is a collection of purposeful interpersonal behaviors exhibited by the therapist when in contact with the patient. While these behaviors are genuine for the therapist, they are also primarily determined by the therapist's formulation of the patient's difficulties.

It is useful to compare and contrast the therapist style of formulation-based behavior therapists with those of clinicians from other orientations. A therapist style based on the case formulation has commonalities with that of clinicians from other orientations. For example, the therapist behaviors of accurate empathy, interest, respect, and instilling the expectation for change are common across orientations and have been identified to be necessary for the establishment of a productive therapeutic alliance (e.g., Frank, 1984; Strupp, 1984).

In contrast, behavior therapists' style will show greater variability across patients than the styles of other therapists. First, because behavior therapists rely less on transference as a clinical tool than do therapists from a psychoanalytic orientation, they do not have to behave in a "technically neutral" manner. Compared to the behavior therapists' style, the technically neutral style is less directive, offers less praise, has sessions located in an office for a standard period of time, and rarely uses self-disclosure.

Second, among behavior therapists, the relationship alone is not viewed as a sufficient intervention for therapeutic change. For client-centered therapists, the primary therapist behaviors demonstrated are unconditional positive regard, empathic understanding, and reflective statements. These, along with a few other relationship factors, *are viewed* as necessary and sufficient conditions for therapeutic change (Rogers, 1957). Therefore, for client-centered therapists there is no need to vary their style across patients. It follows, then, that therapist behaviors such as direction, limit setting, and constructive criticism are not likely to be demonstrated.

Table 7.1 presents two sets of therapist behaviors. Those under the heading *Constant* are considered to be necessary for the establishment of a productive therapeutic alliance and will be demonstrated with all behavior therapy patients. Those listed under the heading *Systematically varied* will be employed on a case-by-case basis, according to the formulation. These therapist behaviors are hypothesized to be valuable in (1) strengthening the therapeutic alliance, (2) improving the likelihood that the patient will benefit from implementation of specific therapeutic techniques, and (3) helping patients modify interpersonal anxieties and skill deficits likely to be demonstrated in interactions with the therapist.

The therapist's formulation and style for a particular patient are developed not only from interview data, but also from clinical

Table 7.1   Two sets of therapist behaviors

I. *Constant* Will be demonstrated with nearly all patients	II. *Systematically varied* Will be varied according to the therapist's formulation of the patient and clinical experimentation. These will vary in *amount* and *type*.	
A. Respect B. Trustworthiness C. Interest D. Caring E. Understanding F. Acceptance G. Accurate empathy H. Appears competent I. Instills the expectation for change J. Genuineness	A. Nurturing provided B. Structure in session C. Self-disclosure D. Directiveness E. Criticism F. Praise / social reinforcement G. Encouragement H. Play I. Humor J. Control K. Therapist availability L. Length of sessions	M. Frequency of sessions N. Modeling / admitting shortcomings O. Sharing notes and / or formulation P. Limit setting Q. Confronting maladaptive behaviors R. Validating the patient's feelings and experiences

experimentation, and sometimes from what the patient will "allow" the therapist to do. For example, a patient with a hypothesized fear of relinquishing control may behave in a controlling fashion early in therapy (e.g., insisting on a certain chair or session agenda). In this situation, the therapist may agree initially to such requests. Then, the therapist may help the patient to gradually relinquish excessive control by first discussing with the patient the hypothesis that some of her interpersonal difficulties could be determined by this fear of relinquishing control; second, by judicious limit-setting; third, by having the patient systematically allow the therapist to exercise increasing control over the format of sessions; and fourth, by helping the patient generalize improvement by gradually relinquishing control in interpersonal situations which do not involve her therapist.

What follows is the presentation of two data-based case studies. Both were difficult and complex cases with considerable amounts of previous treatment. With each of these patients, special attention was paid to the style in which the behavior therapist managed the therapeutic relationship. Without this attention, therapeutic alliances may not have been strong enough for the patient to work on difficult problems with the therapist. In addition, the patients may have terminated therapy prematurely, thus losing the opportunity to benefit from specific behavioral techniques. Finally, the individualized therapist styles may have helped the patients decrease their interpersonal difficulties, which in turn helped them to benefit from the work of other professionals involved in their treatment.

CASE STUDY I

Identification and Reason for Referral

Sally (a pseudonym) was a 47-year old married, former executive with an advanced degree who was referred to the behavior therapy service after several months of inpatient psychiatric treatment. She presented with diagnoses of major depression and obsessive compulsive disorder (OCD). Referral data also suggested borderline personality disorder with "narcissistic features". However, the accuracy of this diagnosis was questionable because she did not meet criteria for this disorder (e.g., absence of suicidality and identity disturbance, the presence of stable, long-term relationships, and the absence of chronic feelings of emptiness). Instead, she appeared to meet criteria for a personality disorder not otherwise specified (borderline, narcissistic, and paranoid features).

A structured clinical interview for DSM-III-R–Patient Version (SCID-P; Spitzer *et al.*, 1990) also indicated simple phobia (germs), generalized anxiety disorder, and hypochondriasis. Medical history was positive for irritable bowel syndrome and a hysterectomy. Finally, she presented with a 20-year psychiatric history, including one previous hospitalization, and multiple trials of medication and/or psychotherapy.

Behavior therapy consultation was requested because of two major problem areas: (1) "noncompliance and treatment resistance," and (2) "germ phobia and compulsive rituals."

The Initial Interview

Sally presented as a very articulate, formal, and highly assertive individual who was moderately overweight. Early in the interview, she revealed herself as an anxious, angry, and highly vigilant individual who exhibited exquisite social graces and who was highly inquisitive regarding my (VJM) credentials, my experience and success with OCD, and my initial impressions about her psychiatric history. It seemed very important to her that her questions be responded to directly and completely.

Since this interview represented my initial contact with this patient, and since I had been informed earlier about her "angry reactions," I decided to respond to her questions directly in an open manner, and to forego the more standard interview procedure. In other words, she appeared to need to "control" the interview. I hypothesized that if I attempted instead to exert control in this first session (e.g., by performing a more structured interview), this stance would result in her feeling more anxious and perhaps result in anger and noncompliance. I decided instead to share control with her by allowing her to set the focus and pace of the session. The goal of this initial intervention was to begin to develop a collaborative therapeutic relationship, and to respect her need for control.

In response to this intervention, Sally appeared to relax and to allow a more balanced dialogue during this first interview session. Her response also provided some confirmation regarding a "control issue" hypothesis.

As the interview progressed, Sally described a range of contamination fears, including fears of contracting various diseases through contact with others' body fluids. As a consequence, she reportedly experienced severe anxiety and marked difficulty in having contact with other patients during mealtimes (e.g., "I can't use the salad bar or eat family style unless I'm first"), milieu therapeutic activities, and during more informal social encounters. As a consequence, she received her meal-trays privately in her room (specifically covered in plastic), and she spent the majority of her time alone or with her husband who visited frequently.

Sally described ongoing difficulty with her nondirective psychotherapy and her psychiatrist ("I don't know how to read him . . . I don't know what he's thinking . . . He won't answer my questions . . . I get angry with him . . . I don't know what's occurring"). The patient's view was corroborated later by her psychiatrist who indicated that the patient was "extremely resistive to the therapeutic process," and she often "stormed out" of his office—thus abruptly terminating a particular session.

Initial Hypothesis

Based upon this information, I continued to hypothesize that the patient was struggling with issues of control. More specifically, in situations where control could not be established by the patient, she tended to react with increased anxiety, anger, and/or interpersonal avoidance through obsessive compulsive (OC) rituals. In contrast, based upon the interview, seeking specific information and having her questions answered directly seemed to help her exercise a level of control, thereby decreasing her anxiety level and the likelihood of an angry outburst.

Problem List

Behavioral assessment identified five problem areas:

(1) *Difficulties with nondirective psychotherapy.* Described above.
(2) *Obsessive compulsive disorder.* Described above.
(3) *Interpersonal difficulties.* The patient demonstrated an excessive use of controlling interpersonal behaviors, excessively entitled attitudes and behaviors, and deficient self-perception skills. Finally, she displayed interpersonal problem-solving deficits which reflected dichotomous reasoning, overgeneralization, drawing conclusions from limited data, and personalization.
(4) *Explosive anger episodes.* Described above.
(5) *Chronic depression.* Reflecting low self-esteem, pessimism, cynicism, and hopelessness.

Behavioral Formulation

Developmentally, two sets of factors appeared to predispose the patient to these problems. First, born as the oldest of three children to a wealthy European family, Sally described her father as an "extremely critical", perfectionistic, and "withholding" individual (1) who seemed dissatisfied with the fact that his oldest child was born a girl, and (2) who "orchestrated" a variety of "family secrets" that repeatedly would "end up pitting" the patient against her mother and younger sister in a "quest" for her father's approval and love. Besides feeling mistrustful, vigilant and isolated from her mother and sister, the patient reported that "blowing up with anger" represented one way to remove herself from these stressful situations.

A second set of predisposing factors pertained to her childhood physical appearance and peer relationships. The patient indicated that "I always saw myself as bad . . . ugly." She reported that she was always overweight and received a rhinoplasty at age 12. Sally recalled frequent "teasing" by her peers, feeling "left out" of social activities, and spending much of her time alone. In this regard, Sally's major strength was her intellect, and she received a measure of recognition and self-esteem for achievements in this area.

The patient's onset of OCD was associated with three precipitating (traumatizing) events. First, although describing her family of origin as extremely conscientious and "germ phobic to begin with," the patient reported the onset of marked phobic avoidance and OC rituals following the death of her "favorite" aunt to cancer two years prior. Caring for her at her bedside over a 9-month period prior to her death, the patient complained of feeling "powerless and out of control." After she died, she refused to return to her home and refused possession of a number of her valuable and cherished belongings—not because of emotional avoidance *per se*—but because of fears that the house and its belongings were contaminated.

The other traumatizing events were related to recent medical problems which highlighted the patient's fear of contamination and loss of control. First, she developed a severe myofacial infection secondary to root canal treatment, and second, she developed endometriosis which required a hysterectomy. Following these events, contamination fears, phobic avoidances and compulsive rituals generalized rapidly, even though she received a number of different psychotropic medications and ongoing psychotherapy throughout this period. It was notable that her husband remarked that "my wife's OCD gives her a special tool," apparently allowing her to avoid painful emotions and situations, while also permitting her to control her contact with people.

Based upon these data, *all five problem areas were formulated as manifestations of a fear of not being in control of interpersonal situations, particularly those where information is withheld.* Because of her family and peer experiences, the patient developed low self-esteem, mistrust, and feelings of inadequacy which were moderated somewhat by her formal, but distant interpersonal style. In social situations where she could not establish control, she experienced increased anxiety which, developmentally, she learned to manage through anger. The OCD symptoms appeared to provide her with both a measure of control over her interpersonal environment and with a way of avoiding anxiety and uncertainty associated with most initial interpersonal encounters. Her pattern of anger outbursts seemed to function similarly by allowing her, first, to exert control over her interpersonal environment, and then to remove herself from a stressful social situation.

Clinical Experimentation: A Test of the Formulation

Given the case formulation, the following was predicted.

(1) Anxiety level will be highest when the patient is exposed to an interpersonal situation where information is withheld (e.g., nondisclosive therapist).
(2) Anxiety level will be lowest when information and feedback are readily provided (disclosive therapist).

To test these hypotheses, a controlled single subject design was used. An event sampling procedure was employed during portions of two different therapy sessions. During these periods, the patient's questions were responded to within one of the two conditions (i.e., disclosive vs. nondisclosive therapist). In the disclosive condition, all questions posed by the patient were responded to in an open and direct manner. In the nondisclosive condition, questions were responded to in a nondirective manner. Each condition was presented twice, such that the experimental design can be conceptualized as follows: ABAB, with A representing the disclosive condition and B representing the nondisclosive condition. The dependent variable, anxiety level, was measured by the patient's responses to the State-Trait Anxiety Inventory (FormY-1: Spielberger et al., 1983).

Independent Review and Informed Consent

In order to maintain the highest ethical standards involving this clinical experimentation, the test of the case formulation and the proposed treatment plan were reviewed and approved by two independent reviewers. Written and verbal informed consent was obtained from the patient at our institution. Moreover, all clinical and experimental actions were supervised by the attending psychiatrist on our clinical medical staff. Following the clinical experiment, the patient was thoroughly debriefed. It should also be noted that the patient found the information to be extremely helpful as well as useful, and she suffered no adverse consequences.

Results

Results are shown in Figure 7.1 where each data point represents the patient's score on the STAI. Confirming prediction 1, the patient displayed the highest levels of state anxiety when exposed to an interpersonal situation where information was withheld (nondisclosive condition). Prediction 2 was also confirmed showing that provision of information produced the lowest rates of state anxiety. Anecdotally, the patient indicated that the nondisclosive condition was also associated with feelings of irritability, anger, and expectations of harm. Taken together, these findings lend support to the case formulation involving a fear of not being in control of interpersonal situations where information is withheld or not available.

Treatment Interventions and Response

Based upon this case formulation, a behavioral treatment plan was designed with special attention directed at establishing a working

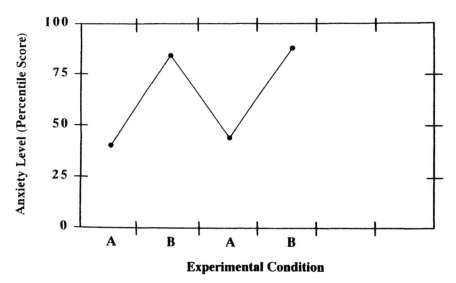

Figure 7.1 State anxiety level as a function of experimental condition. A, baseline/disclosive condition; B, nondisclosive condition

relationship with the patient—the initial goal of which was to treat her OCD symptoms. The first intervention involved a complete sharing of the case formulation with the patient, including a discussion of predisposing and precipitating causes, as well as maintaining factors related to OCD. Emphasis was placed upon the anxiety-inhibiting role of information, and the special challenge posed by interpersonal situations where such information is not readily available. In this regard, the patient agreed with the case formulation and was very appreciative of my open discussion regarding her difficulties. Her response helped to enhance our working relationship and to prepare her for active treatment.

Second, the patient was provided with a folder containing copious reading materials related to the behavioral treatment procedures to be employed. A gradual, self-directed response prevention and exposure program was proposed which permitted the patient to exercise maximum control of the procedure in a slowly graded manner (Turner & Beidel, 1988). The provided reading materials explained in an explicit manner her role in the treatment, duration of treatment and exposures, documented effectiveness, etc. In this manner, the perceived withholding of information was not an issue in treatment. Similarly, by providing the patient with maximum control of the treatment procedure, the issue of control within the context of the therapeutic relationship was also avoided.

Sessions were scheduled two or three times weekly on an inpatient basis to help moderate the intensity of the relationship, and my initial approach was to be completely noncritical, supportive, and openly responsive to her questions during the early stages of therapy. The eventual goal, however, was to expose the patient to normal criticism, feedback, and withholding of information in a graded, hierarchical fashion. Finally, a contamination hierarchy designed with the patient included a range of interpersonal exposures at the top of the list.

Since the patient's OCD represented a maladaptive coping response to anxiety and interpersonal situations, the patient participated concurrently in a program of coping skills training and interpersonal skills training. The rationale was shared completely with the patient and reading materials were provided. Coping skills training utilized progressive relaxation training and self-instructional training with emphasis placed upon Novaco's (1975) anger management program. (*Note:* Linehan's Dialectical Behavior Therapy had not been published when this case was treated.) Describing the various "functions" of anger (e.g., preventing rejection by others by rejecting first), the program utilized a cognitive–behavioral model to help the patient analyze and select the best interpersonal option, given a particular social situation.

Interpersonal skills training emphasized emotional regulatory skills, her impact on others, and cognitive–behavioral methods to cope with interpersonal situations where sufficient information is not readily available. For example, using a self-instructional model, the patient developed a written list of questions to manage various social situations.

Don't react until the following questions are asked:

(1) Why is information being withheld?
(2) Is the material being withheld important?
(3) Is it worth reacting to in a personalized or emotional manner?
(4) If I do, will it alter anything? What difference does it make?
(5) How do I want to respond to this situation? What are my options?

Treatment was conducted over a 10-week inpatient period. As shown in Figures 7.2 and 7.3, the patient experienced significant improvement in OCD symptoms, frequency of milieu activities, and frequency of anger episodes, as measured by daily patient ratings of OCD severity and by a frequency count of documented anger episodes in nursing staff progress notes. At one year follow-up, the patient maintained her gains regarding OCD symptoms, and reported ongoing success with anger management and interpersonal involvement. She had returned to part-time work, and she continued in outpatient psychotherapy. Finally, because of changes in

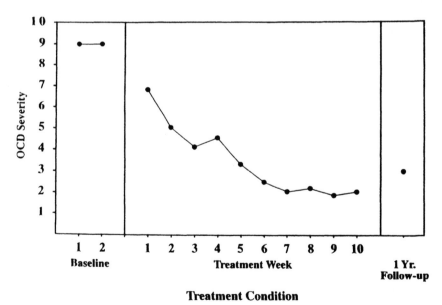

Figure 7.2 Mean patient ratings of OCD severity level as a function of treatment conditions

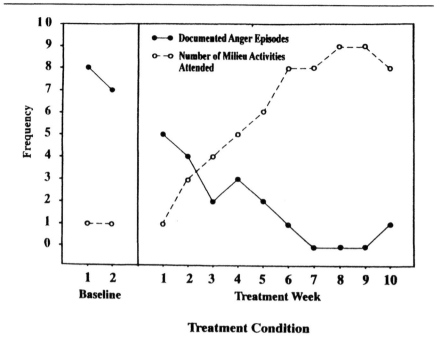

Figure 7.3 Patient chart-derived frequency counts of documented anger episodes and mileau activity attendance as a function of treatment condition

her relationship with her husband, the patient had recently begun marital therapy.

It should be noted that prior to discharge, I met on two occasions with her outpatient treating psychiatrist, along with the patient, in order to model the therapist style that had been effective during inpatient treatment. He was also provided with a copy of my treatment plan and case summary, along with the names of skilled behavior therapists in their area if such services became necessary.

CASE STUDY II

Identification and Reason for Referral

Philip was a 14-year-old Hispanic male who was referred to the BTS after four months of inpatient treatment at a private psychiatric hospital (see Malatesta & AuBuchon, 1992). This was the patient's second psychiatric admission. He was referred because of continued disruptive behavior, and inadequate response to intensive psychotherapy and milieu-based contingency plans.

Problem List

Initial behavioral assessment included interviews with Philip, his parents, and staff. In addition, nursing staff systematically observed and recorded the patient's behavior in order to develop and refine functional analyses of the patient's difficulties. Two major problem areas were identified.

(1) *Conduct disorder behavior.* Philip had a six-year history of these behaviors. Those exhibited on the adolescent unit included: (1) refusal to attend the hospital school; (2) self-injurious behaviors (e.g., hitting walls or window screens with his hands); (3) dangerous behaviors (e.g., throwing and breaking furniture); and (4) rude and vulgar verbal behavior. An important consequence of much of this behavior appeared to be social reinforcement in the form of attention, approval, and special status from his peers when such behaviors were demonstrated. In addition, Philip demonstrated a lack of concern for the negative consequences of inappropriate behaviors, and stated that "sooner or later I'll be 'let-off-the-hook' " by an authority figure administering appropriate punishment.

(2) *Interpersonal difficulties.* While the patient was often quite charming, he also had tendencies to be deceitful and manipulative. In addition, Philip often engaged in stereotypical masculine behaviors (e.g., *macho*). Finally, it appeared that the patient had difficulties trusting others, especially older males. For example, while Philip often made initial attempts to gain acceptance and approval from older males, he then withdrew from these men by becoming guarded in conversations, and resistant to spending time with them.

Behavioral Formulation

Philip's difficulties were understood as follows. First, it was hypothesized that the patient longed for attention and nurturing from older males, yet mistrusted such individuals. Second, the patient's interpersonal difficulties and conduct disordered behaviors were hypothesized to be well ingrained, yet socially learned, behaviors.

Data which supported these hypotheses included the following. The patient's biological father was an extremely sporadic presence in Philip's life from infancy through adolescence. Insufficient attention and nurturing from older males also characterized the patient's relationship with his stepfather (e.g., the stepfather worked two jobs; he "gave up trying to spend time" with Philip because of the patient's resistance, and the tendency of Philip's mother to undermine the stepfather's discipline with the patient). More recently, the patient and his older male psychiatrist had failed to establish a therapeutic alliance, and the patient did not have productive relationships with the male staff on the adolescent unit.

The modeling of antisocial, manipulative, and *macho* behaviors by the patient's biological father appeared to be influential in the patient's acquiring these behaviors for his own interpersonal style. Social reinforcement from peers strengthened these behaviors.

A history of inconsistent disciplining within the home, and Philip's success at manipulating his mother to excuse him from appropriate punishments at home or school, reinforced the patient's charming and manipulative interpersonal skills. These factors also reinforced the patient's expectations of being able to escape appropriate punishments, and his apparent lack of concern for negative consequences of his conduct disordered behavior.

Treatment Interventions and Response

Interventions designed to modify the patient's problematic behaviors were implemented in the milieu and in individual sessions. Some of these interventions were established behavior therapy techniques (e.g., contingency plans, social skills training). More important was the use of an individualized therapist style with Philip. Based on the case formulation, it was hypothesized that therapist behaviors of *availability, nurturance,* and *consistency* were critical if behavior therapy with this treatment-refractory young man was going to work.

As soon as this hypothesis was generated, the behavior therapist (PGA) set up a *consistent* schedule of sessions with the patient (e.g., 5:30 p.m., three days a week). These appointment times were also selected because early evening was a time when staff members tended to be less *available* due to dinner breaks, and during which Philip demonstrated an increase in conduct disordered behavior. *Availability* of the behavior therapist was demonstrated by providing the patient with the behavior therapist's office telephone number which Philip "could call at any time", and by letting the patient know that if his Monday, Tuesday, and Thursday behavior therapy sessions were productive, the behavior therapist would be available on Friday for an "extra" session.

Nurturance and *play* were also included in the therapist style. Treating the patient to a soda *en route* to a session, offering bits of heterosocial advice during the course of the assessment, and conducting some of the initial interviews while playing pool with the patient, were all examples of therapist behaviors purposefully demonstrated in accordance with the case formulation.

Figure 7.4 depicts the effects of various interventions on the frequency of Philip's problem behaviors. Self-injurious behaviors, and those which could cause harm to others, were collapsed under the variable of "Dangerous Behaviors". Baseline data were easy to obtain from nursing staff records since these problematic behaviors were readily observable and required a documented intervention (e.g., giving time-outs for vulgar verbal behavior; scraping his knuckles against a window screen required a medical intervention). The effects of the individualized therapist style can be seen as early as the assessment phase. After approximately two weeks with three sessions per week with the behavior therapist, there was a decrease in each of Philip's problem behaviors.

After the first two weeks of assessment, a new contingency plan for use in the milieu was developed. In this plan, Philip was given opportunities for enjoyable and positive interactions with male staff members (e.g., listening to music, playing catch). In addition, specific negative consequences were administered when Philip demonstrated a problem behavior. These consequences involved the loss of some reinforcer. If staff needed to provide medical attention for a self-injurious behavior, they were to do so

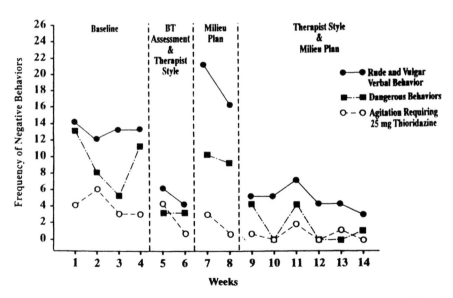

Figure 7.4 Patient chart-derived frequency counts of documented episodes of rude verbal behavior, physically dangerous behaviors, and agitation severe enough to require a dose of a major tranquilizer

with a minimal amount of attention, demonstrated emotion, and conversation. *Consistency* of staff responses to Philip's positive and negative behaviors was emphasized. Finally, if Philip's behavior improved to a point where he had earned the next-to-highest unit privilege level, then he became eligible for trips off hospital grounds with his behavior therapist as a reward and as an opportunity for *in vivo* social skills training.

Philip's initial response to being told about the milieu plan was to destroy his copy of the plan in front of the treatment team. He also demonstrated an escalation of problem behaviors (see week 7 on Figure 7.4), and began a total boycott of behavior therapy sessions.

Consistency with the milieu plan eventually resulted in steady decreases of several problem behaviors. Despite this improvement, Philip still refused to meet with the behavior therapist.

As per the case formulation, the behavior therapist continued to *consistently* appear for sessions at the regular time. These attempts to get sessions going were kept brief, however, so as to minimize any peer reinforcement the patient might receive for refusing an authority figure's request. In addition, knowing of the patient's interest in drawing, *nurturance* was demonstrated by privately giving Philip a "Learn to Draw Animals" book (beginning of Week 9). Immediately after receiving this gift, Philip met productively with the behavior therapist for every session.

The remainder of the interventions employed in individual sessions included sex education, social skills training, anger management training (e.g., Feindler & Ecton, 1988). Because Philip's parents lived in a nearby state, treatment included telephone family sessions directed at communication skills training and discharge planning.

Figure 7.5 depicts increase in positive behaviors exhibited by Philip in response to behavior therapy. These positive behaviors were measured by taking a frequency count of positive comments in nursing staff progress notes (e.g., "ate his dinner without making rude comments"; "attained [an advanced] privilege level for the first time"). Figure 7.5 also depicts the increase in the patient's school attendance.

As demonstrated in Figures 7.4 and 7.5, Philip's behavior improved considerably during the 10 week behavior therapy intervention. It appeared that the therapist style employed in the patient's treatment had beneficial effects in the assessment phase, enabled Philip to overcome a therapeutic impasse, and resume his attendance of behavior therapy sessions—thereby allowing himself to benefit from the more technical behavioral interventions (e.g., anger management and social skills training).[1]

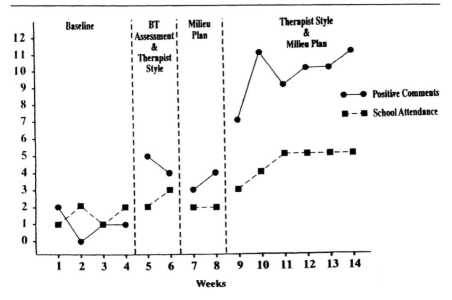

Figure 7.5 Patient chart-derived frequency counts of documented positive comments by nursing staff and of attendance at on-grounds school

Two follow-up telephone sessions with Philip and his parents at one month post-discharge yielded reports of continued good behavior on Philip's part (e.g., better communication in the family, Philip respecting his parents' discipline, adaptive peer relations, and no conduct disordered behavior). An eight month follow-up call was less positive. Philip's grades had dropped in school and there was some increase in problem behaviors (e.g., being disruptive in class, smoking in the lavatory). In addition, it was learned that Philip had dropped out of his outpatient therapy soon after the one-month follow-up. This premature termination was reportedly due to Philip "not liking (his) new therapist", and it sounded as though a sound therapeutic alliance had not been established. In addition, the patient's mother reported that the "[therapist of this case study] was the only therapist who really got through to Philip". These clinical data appear consistent with the need for the formulated-based therapist style employed in this case study.

SUMMARY

In this chapter we have described the case formulation approach to managing the therapeutic relationship in behavior therapy, presented two case studies which illustrate and provide initial empirical support for this approach, and have critically reviewed the current literature on the therapeutic relationship in behavior therapy. In the literature review, several important limitations of the previous research were identified. Most notable was the absence of a comprehensive methodology for utilizing the therapeutic relationship with any patient who might be presenting with any combination of difficulties. When an approach has been suggested, it has relied upon limited determinants of relationship behavior and/or has not been accompanied by empirical data (e.g., Rosenfarb, 1992; Wright & Davis, 1994).

We hypothesized that the case formulation approach may provide a more effective means of utilizing the therapeutic relationship. The case formulation approach is based on two keystones of behavior therapy: the experimental method and utilization of an idiographic approach to treatment. The approach has also received considerable support through the writings of prominent behavioral clinicians (e.g., Meyer & Turkat, 1979; Shapiro, 1957; Turkat, 1985; Wolpe, 1986), and through the empirical data presented in several case studies, and at least one group study (e.g., AuBuchon, 1993; AuBuchon & Malatesta, 1994; Malatesta, 1990, 1995; Turkat & Carlson, 1984). In this chapter, we have also described a specific relationship intervention based upon the case formulation, e.g., the *therapist style*, and provided guidelines for utilizing this intervention with a range of patients.

The case studies illustrate several important points. First, they illustrate how the therapeutic relationship can be conceptualized and managed according to the case formulation. In the first case study, therapist behaviors such as providing copious amounts of information, answering all questions directly, and sharing control were frequently and systematically demonstrated in accordance with an experimentally validated case formulation. In the second case study, the therapist behaviors of consistency, availability, nurturance, and play were demonstrated systematically in response to hypotheses about the patients' basic psychological problems, needs, and developmental stage. Clinical experimentation (e.g., giving of a gift) validated these hypotheses. In both case studies, hypotheses about the primary psychological mechanisms which determined the patient's difficulties were generated based on the patient's behavior and other clinical data. These hypotheses were tested, and specific therapist behaviors based on these formulations were incorporated into the therapists' style of relating to the patient. The case formulations also guided the use of other therapeutic interventions.

Second, the preceding case studies not only illustrate a methodology for managing the therapeutic relationship, they also provide some initial empirical support for this approach. With the exception of a few group studies which have examined specific behaviors with certain diagnostic groups (e.g., Leitenberg *et al.*, 1975; Linehan, 1993; Touyz, Beumont & Dunn, 1987), there has not been a study that has both described a methodology for managing the therapeutic relationship, and provided empirical data on the validity of the approach. The most recent example appears to be Wright and Davis (1994) who offered strategies for assessing the patient's expectations of the therapist and for modifying therapist behaviors. However, they presented only anecdotal data in their report.

Third, the case studies illustrate several advantages of the case formulation approach to the therapeutic relationship. The first is that this approach appears more consistent with important principles of behavior therapy, namely, reliance on the experimental method, and use of an individualized approach to treatment (see Earleywine's interview of Davison, 1994). In this approach, hypotheses are generated and tested, and an operationally defined set of therapist behaviors are implemented. In this way, the therapist style can be thought of as an independent variable in an experimental approach to difficult psychiatric cases. For example, in the second case study several improvements were observable during the assessment phase when the only intervention employed was the therapist style. The nurturing aspect of this style also appeared to help the patient attend behavior therapy sessions later in his treatment.

A second advantage of the approach is that it helps the therapist establish a better therapeutic alliance with difficult patients. There are empirical and anecdotal data which suggest that relationship-based interventions may be more important in the treatment of complex and difficult cases (e.g., Linehan, 1993; Young, 1990). Similarly, the majority of patients referred to our service presented with severe interpersonal difficulties, years of previous treatment, comorbid personality disorder, and multiple psychiatric diagnoses (e.g., AuBuchon & Malatesta, 1994; Malatesta and AuBuchon, 1992). In our experience, a therapeutic relationship based on the case formulation has been a way to modify difficult interpersonal problems and to anticipate and reduce therapeutic noncompliance ("resistance"). The results of the case studies support these experiences.

A third advantage of the case formulation approach is that a skillfully managed therapeutic relationship can help the patient benefit from other empirically supported interventions. In the first case study, providing the patient with considerable information and sharing control enabled the patient to benefit from exposure and response prevention for her OCD, and to benefit from anger management skills training. In the second case study, a therapist style which emphasized consistency, nurturance, and availability enabled the patient to participate in social skills and anger management skills training sessions, and to better participate in the hospital's adolescent program. Increases in school attendance and positive statements in nursing notes, and decreases in tranquilizing medication are data which illustrate the patient's response to the combined interventions of therapist style and skills training.

Future research on case formulation involving the therapeutic relationship can be directed toward several areas. First, in this climate of manualized treatment there remains the need for a group study comparing manualized and case formulation based approaches. Second, future research could include the use of direct measures of strength of the therapeutic alliances and/or sequential analysis techniques to better assess how changes in therapist behaviors affect the therapeutic alliance and patient behaviors, and how changes in patient behaviors affect therapist behaviors (Alexander & Luborsky, 1984; cf. Rosenfarb, 1992).

In conclusion, this chapter has addressed the therapeutic relationship in a manner consistent with the methodologies of case formulation and the experimental approach. It has attempted to operationally define a formulation-based relationship intervention, namely the therapist style, by specifying various therapist behaviors which can be systematically employed. Finally, it has attempted to study the therapeutic relationship as a specific treatment intervention, and gather data on the effects of this intervention in a manner consistent with single case design.

ACKNOWLEDGEMENT

The authors thank Ms Susanne Kern, Ms Lorraine Amato, and Ms Karen Tierney for their help in preparing this manuscript.

NOTE

1. The slight relapse of Philip's problems in week 11 were due to a very difficult Easter Sunday. As it happened, the patient had expected a visit from his parents that day. Early that Sunday, however, Philip received a telephone call from his parents explaining that they were unable to visit.

REFERENCES

Adams, H.E., Malatesta, V.J., Brantley, P.J. & Turkat, I.D. (1981). Modification of cognitive processes: A case study of schizophrenia. *Journal of Consulting and Clinical Psychology*, **49**, 460–464.

Alexander, L. & Luborsky, L. (1984). Research on the helping alliance. In L. Greenberg & W. Pisoff (eds.), *The Psychotherapeutic Process: A Research Handbook*. New York: Guilford Press.

AuBuchon, P.G. (1993). Formulation-based treatment of a complex phobia. *Journal of Behavior Therapy and Experimental Psychiatry*, **24**, 63–71.

AuBuchon, P.G. & Calhoun, K.S. (1990). The effects of therapist presence and relaxation training on the efficacy and generalizability of *in vivo* exposure. *Behavioural Psychotherapy*, **18**, 169–185.

AuBuchon, P.G., Haber, J.D., & Adams, H.E. (1985). Can migraine headaches be modified by operant pain techniques? *Journal of Behavior Therapy and Experimental Psychiatry*, **16**, 261–263

AuBuchon, P.G. & Malatesta, V.J. (1994). Obsessive compulsive patients with comorbid personality disorder: Associated problems and response to a comprehensive behavior therapy. *Journal of Clinical Psychiatry*, **55**, 448–453.

Bandura, A. & Menlove, F.L. (1968). Factors determining vicarious extinction of avoidance behavior through symbolic modeling. *Journal of Personality and Social Psychology*, **8**, 99–108.

Beck, A.T., Rush, A.J., Shaw, B.F. & Emery, G. (1979). *Cognitive Therapy of Depression*. New York: The Guilford Press

Brady, J.P. (1980) Some views on effective principles of psychotherapy [special issue]. *Cognitive Therapy and Research*, **4**, 271–306.

Brunink, S.A. & Schroeder, H.E. (1979). Verbal therapeutic behavior of expert psychoanalytically oriented, gestalt, and behavior therapists. *Journal of Consulting and Clinical Psychology*, **47**, 567–574.

Burns, D.D. (1994, February). Therapeutic empathy and the treatment of depression. Paper presented at the meeting of the Philadelphia Behavior Therapy Association, Philadelphia, PA.

Earleywine, M. (1994). An interview with Gerald Davison. *The Behavior Therapist*, **17**, 213–217.

Feindler, E.L. & Ecton, R.B. (1988). *Adolescent Anger Control: Cognitive–Behavioral Techniques*. New York: Pergamon Press.

Fischer, J., Paveza, G.J., Kickertz, N.S., Hubbard, L.J. & Grayson, S.B. (1975). The relationship between theoretical orientation and therapists' empathy, warmth, and genuineness. *Journal of Counseling Psychology*, **22**, 399–403.

Frank, J.D. (1984). Therapeutic components shared by all psychotherapies. In J.H. Harvey & M.M. Parks (Eds.), *The Master Lecture Series: Vol. 1. Psychotherapy Research and Behavior Change* (pp.9–37). Washington, D.C.: American Psychological Association.

Goldfried, M.R. (1983). The behavior therapist in clinical practice. *The Behavior Therapist*, **6**, 45–46.

Grayson, J.B. Foa, E.B. & Steketee, G. (1982). Habituation during exposure treatment: Distraction versus attention-focusing. *Behaviour Research and Therapy*, **20**, 323–328.

Greenwald, D.P., Kornblith, S.J., Hersen, M., Bellack, A.S. & Himmelhoch, J.M. (1981). Differences between social skills therapists and psychotherapists in treating depression. *Journal of Consulting and Clinical Psychology*, **49**, 757–759.

Gustavson, B., Jansson, L., Jerremalm, A., & Ost, L.G. (1985). Therapist behavior during exposure treatment of agoraphobia. *Behavior Modification*, **9**, 491–504.

Leitenberg, H., Agras, W.S., Allen, R., Butz, R. & Edwards, J. (1975). Feedback and therapist praise during treatment of phobia. *Journal of Consulting and Clinical Psychology*, **43**, 396–404.

Linehan, M.M. (1988). Perspectives on the interpersonal relationship in behavior therapy. *Journal of Integrative and Eclectic Psychotherapy*, **7**, 278–290.

Linehan, M.M. (1993). *Cognitive–Behavior Treatment of Borderline Personality Disorder*. New York: Guilford Press.

Malatesta, V.J. (1990). Behavioral case formulation: An experimental assessment study of transient tic disorder. *Journal of Psychopathology and Behavioral Assessment*, **12**, 219–232.

Malatesta, V.J. (1995). "Technological" behavior therapy for obsessive–compulsive disorder: The need for adequate case formulation. *The Behavior Therapist*, **18**, 88–89.

Malatesta, V.J. & AuBuchon, P.G. (1992). Behavior therapy in the private psychiatric hospital: Our experiences and a model of inpatient consultation. *The Behavior Therapist*, **15**, 43–46.

Meyer, V. (1957). The treatment of two phobic patients on the basis of learning principles. *Journal of Abnormal and Social Psychology*, **55**, 261–266.

Meyer, V. & Gelder, M.G. (1963). Behavior therapy and phobic disorders. *British Journal of Psychiatry*, **109**, 19–28.

Meyer, V. & Turkat, I.D. (1979). Behavioral analysis of clinical cases. *Journal of Behavioral Assessment*, **1**, 259–270.

Novaco, R.W. (1975). *Anger control: The development and evaluation of an experimental treatment*. Lexington, MA: Lexington Books.

Persons, J. (1989). *Cognitive therapy in practice: A case formulation approach*. New York: W.W. Norton.

Rabavilas, A.D., Boulougouris, J.C. & Perissaki, C. (1979). Therapist qualities related to outcome with exposure *in vivo* in neurotic patients. *Journal of Behavior Therapy and Experimental Psychology*, **10**, 293–294.

Rachman, S. (1983). The modification of agoraphobic avoidance behavior: Some fresh possibilities. *Behaviour Research and Therapy*, **21**, 567–574.

Rogers, C.R. (1957). The necessary and sufficient conditions of therapeutic personality change. *Journal of Consulting Psychology*, **21**, 95–103.

Rosenfarb, I.S. (1992). A behavior analytic interpretation of the therapeutic relationship. *The Psychological Record*, **42**, 341–354.

Shapiro, M.B. (1957). Experimental method in the psychological description of the individual psychiatric patient. *International Journal of Social Psychiatry*, **111**, 89–102.

Shearin, E.W. & Linehan, M.M. (1992). Patient-therapist ratings and relationship to progress in dialectical behavior therapy for borderline personality disorder. *Behavior Therapy*, **23**, 730–741.

Sloan, R.B., Staples, F.R., Cristol, A.H., Yorkston, N.H. & Whipple, K. (1975). *Psychotherapy Versus Behavior Therapy*. Cambridge, MA: Harvard University Press.

Sloan, R.B., Staples, F.R., Whipple, K. & Cristol, A.H. (1977). Patients' attitudes toward behavior therapy and psychotherapy. *American Journal of Psychiatry*, **134**, 134–137.

Spielberger, C.D., Gorsuch, R.L., Lushene, R., Vagg, P.R. & Jacobs, G.A. (1983). *Manual for the State-trait Anxiety Inventory* (Form Y). Palo Alto, CA: Consulting Psychologists Press.

Spitzer, R.L., Williams, J.B., Gibbon, M. & First, M.B. (1990). *Structured Clinical Interview for DSM-III-R: Patient Edition (SCID-P, Version 1.0)*. Washington, DC: American Psychiatric Press.

Strupp, H.H. (1984). The outcome problem in psychotherapy: Contemporary perspectives. In J.H. Harvey & M.M. Parks (Eds.), *The Master Lecture Series: Vol. 1. Psychotherapy Research and Behavior Change* (pp.43–71). Washington, DC: American Psychiatric Press.

Touyz, S.W., Beumont, P.J. & Dunn, S.M. (1987). Behavior therapy in the management of patients with anorexia nervosa: A lenient flexible approach. *Psychotherapy and Psychosomatics*, **48**, 151–156.

Turkat, I.D. (Ed.) (1985). *Behavioral Case Formulation*. New York: Plenum.

Turkat, I.D. & Brantley, P. (1981). On the therapeutic relationship in behavior therapy. *The Behavior Therapist*, **4**, 16–17.

Turkat, I.D. & Carlson, C.R. (1984). Data-based versus symptomatic formulation of treatment: The case of a dependent personality. *Journal of Behavior Therapy and Experimental Psychiatry*, **15**, 153–160.

Turner, S.M. & Beidel, D.C. (1988). Treating Obsessive–Compulsive Disorder. New York: Pergamon Press.

Williams, K.E. & Chambless, D.L. (1990). The relationship between therapist characteristics and outcome of *in vivo* exposure treatment for agoraphobia. *Behavior Therapy*, **21**, 111–116.

Wolpe, J. (1958). *Psychotherapy by Reciprocal Inhibition*. Stanford, CA: Stanford University Press.

Wolpe, J. (1980). *The Practice of Behavior Therapy*, (3rd edn). New York: Pergamon Press.

Wolpe, J. (1986). Individualization: The categorical imperative of behavior therapy practice. *Journal of Behavior Therapy and Experimental Psychiatry*, **17**, 145–153.

Wolpe, J. & Lazarus, A. (1966). *Behavior therapy techniques*. New York: Pergamon Press.

Wright, J.H. & Davis, D. (1994). The therapeutic relationships in cognitive–behavioral therapy: Patient perceptions and therapist responses. *Cognitive and Behavioral Practice*, **1**, 25–45.

Young, J.E. (1990). *Cognitive therapy for personality disorders: A schema-focused approach*. Sarasota, FL: Professional Resource Exchange.

CHAPTER 8

AIDS phobia, compulsive rituals and undifferentiated somatoform disorder

Hans Reinecker

INTRODUCTION: THEORETICAL BACKGROUND AND DESCRIPTIVE PORTRAYAL OF THE PATIENT

The theoretical model presented here is closely linked with the approach of self-regulation (Karoly, 1995) and of self-management therapy (Kanfer, Reinecker & Schmelzer, 1996). Consequently behavioural therapy consists of a continuous process of change, in the course of which the patient should, with the support of the therapist, gain, in a step by step fashion, increasing control of his or her problems. During the first stages of intervention characteristics of role-structuring and of the establishment of a relationship, of clarification and specification of the patient's motivation, as well as the clarification of the therapeutic aims, play a decisive role. The notion of human nature on which self-management therapy is based (the philosophy of this approach) is conveyed to the patient continuously from the beginning of the intervention and constitutes, so to speak, the background for the way the disturbance is seen on the one hand and for the practical therapeutic intervention on the other hand.

Mrs L., a 40 year old woman, was living with her husband and her two children, aged 14 and 17, near a small university town. Her husband owned a small craft enterprise, and she worked together with him in that firm. She had always enjoyed her job, largely because she and her husband had founded and extended their enterprise, dedicating much energy and effort to it.

Beyond Diagnosis: Case Formulation Approaches in CBT.
Edited by Michael Bruch and Frank W. Bond.
© 1998 John Wiley & Sons Ltd.

Two years before she contacted our outpatient's department and asked for therapeutic support, her mother died after a long illness; Mrs L. had nursed her intensively. Taking good care of her mother had been time consuming, emotionally demanding and had absorbed her almost entirely. Two weeks after the funeral she developed a depression ("nervous breakdown") with panic attacks as a concomitant symptom. During her panic attacks she was assailed with the idea of being infected by the HIV virus. At that time the media abounded with information on AIDS. Mrs L. started worrying about the possibility of having been infected by her mother who received blood serum transfusions during the last months of her life.

Mrs L. was terribly frightened of already having been infected while nursing her mother or of being infected by contact with other persons. She increasingly started to avoid physical contact with others. At first she stopped touching people with whom she was not familiar, and later on she even avoided close physical contact with the members of her own family. She was panic-stricken that her husband or particularly her daughter (who was a nurse) might come into contact with blood or she might be infected by going to a sauna, a swimming pool or public toilets, by way of physically contacting people, as for instance by kissing or handshaking, or even by an insect bite etc.

Mrs L. consulted her physician who at first prescribed tranquillisers and then antidepressant drugs. Subsequently her general emotional condition improved, but only for a short while. Several HIV tests (which turned out to be negative) had the same reassuring effect, albeit only for a short period of time. During the following weeks her anxiety generalised and turned into a phobia concerning a wide range of situations and activities, such as touching money, eating at a restaurant, using glasses, china and cutlery which she had not cleaned herself. Even reading newspaper articles or watching TV reports on this subject triggered new attacks of phobia. Thus her scope of activity became more and more restricted. Moreover, she started to spy on her family members with regard to "dangerous contacts" (as she put it).

At this particular point of time she considered it necessary to search for psychotherapeutic help. Her problems had even affected her husband and her children. They suffered from the accompanying circumstances as well and urgently requested a change of the situation. In addition to the above described she refused to continue to take her medication. She felt that in the long run there was no positive effect and, moreover, she suffered from several side effects of the medication. For several weeks she went to see a psychologist. But neither this treatment nor relaxation techniques nor self-observation brought about an improvement of her health situation. In the course of several calls to a HIV self-help group she received the address and the telephone number of our outpatients' department and asked for help. She considered submitting to ambulatory psychotherapy because her physician had told her that the symptoms of her disease might originate from "psychological" problems.

The fact that our outpatients' department for psychotherapy is part of the university's section for clinical psychology underlines its scientific soundness and reliability and conveys a feeling of security to the patients. In a big institution they can be certain that their anonymity is guaranteed. Particularly in a small town, this seems to be very important for people.

When Mrs L. came to contact us for the first time, we tried to obtain from her some information concerning her case history and the development of her symptoms. According to our impression things had been aggravated to such a degree that this situation was no longer bearable, either for herself or for her family. She no longer was able to drive a car, consequently her husband had to bring her to the first therapy sessions.

During the first period of therapy we put emphasis on getting a distinct picture of the patient's symptoms and on role-structuring (Kanfer & Schefft, 1988). This means that it is important that the patient enters into a strong working alliance with the therapist. An essential precondition for success is that the patient recognises the therapist as a professional who is willing to give support in overcoming problems and in restructuring his or her life. In order to strengthen the patient's active collaboration in the therapy we give some "homework" from the very beginning. At first we request answers to a "life questionnaire". This provides us with detailed information on specific and essential characteristics of the patient's problem situation and the underlying process. Further complementary information is gathered by symptom-specific questionnaires (Fear Survey Schedule, FSS III, Wolpe & Lang, 1964).

ASSESSMENT AND CLASSIFICATION

The collection of relevant data is performed under the perspective of *functional analysis;* this means that we are searching for some information which provides us with the possibility to identify, to understand and to explain the patient's symptoms as a function of situational circumstances (Kanfer & Saslow, 1965). When we describe and analyse the patient's condition and its determinants, it goes without saying that we not only take into consideration the obviously discernible items, such as the patient's behaviour or the external situation, but we rather differentiate several levels. We refer to the α, β and χ level (see Kanfer & Schefft, 1988). According to our opinion in functional analysis the level of self-regulation (Karoly 1993, 1995) plays an important role as well. Self-regulation includes the patient's objectives, expectations, intentions, the way he or she assesses external stimuli as well as personal views, opinions, way of thinking, desires, beliefs etc.

Description of the Problem

Analysing Mrs L.'s problems in accordance with a functional schema provided the following information:

Mrs L. could no longer maintain a relationship to persons other than those of her family. This meant: no invitations, no social activities, no swimming or sauna, no sports. Thus her behavioural repertoire became restricted in a very peculiar way. The reason for this was her difficulty in eating and drinking together with other people. She was so afraid that someone incidentally might have exchanged his glass or cutlery with hers or that somebody's saliva might somehow get into contact with her food that she avoided joint meals altogether. Also using public toilets, touching door handles, visiting a hospital, even watching people whose outer appearance indicated that they might be sick scared her to death so that she practically couldn't leave the house any longer, not to mention travelling. Her entire thinking and her attention continuously revolved around one single topic: blood—and how to avoid coming into contact with blood or other body fluids. Even mentioning the subject or seeing a red spot ("which might be blood") left her panic-stricken. The same applied to newspaper articles or TV reports on this subject—she was literally totally absorbed by her fears.

She became utterly alarmed by any minimal physical symptom. Even tears or running of the eyes were interpreted as initial signs of an infection with the HIV-virus. The way she started to control her own activities and those of her family as well as the way she searched for relevant information was obsessive. She felt so scared that she frequently asked for reassurance by her husband or her physician. Sometimes she went to see her doctor two or three times a week.

On the cognitive level (β) she was continuously worrying about a possible contamination: on the one hand she tried to build up a resistance against her permanent worries, on the other hand she was not able to eliminate them. This mechanism is known as "rebound effect" with regard to unwanted thoughts.

On the somatic-physiological level (χ) her problems found expression in a generalised tension in all parts of her body, fatigue, headaches and several other psycho-physiological symptoms of diffuse character.

Part of the self-regulation system of Mrs L. was to characterise herself as being very sensitive to information concerning health and disease. She considered herself as being responsible not only for the well-being of herself but also for that of her family. That is why she tried to also control their activities and behaviour. For instance she accompanied her son to sports events for reasons of control. She watched over the social activities of her children obsessively, which resulted in heavy conflicts, especially when her children started to date the other sex. Her obsession also caused far-reaching and severe secondary consequences with regard to her husband and their craft enterprise—she forced him to wash his hands whenever he had welcomed a client by handshaking.

Mrs L.'s fears generalised and thus caused a wide range of difficulties. Not only was she scared of the sexual contacts of her children, she even tried to control ordinary activities such as going to a restaurant, visiting friends, going to school or work. Whenever her family members came home after having had contact with the "dirty" environment, she insisted in excessive cleaning rituals in order to avoid a possible contamination of their "clean" household.

Functional Analysis

As the predisposing background it has to be mentioned that Mrs L. was, in the time period before her mother died, highly stressed by the task of nursing her. This emotional burden has to be considered as particularly problematic, because the patient characterises herself as having always been very apprehensive of diseases, cleanness etc. Additionally it has to be mentioned that she felt unable to give expression to her resentment against other family members who barely cared about nursing her mother.

Moreover, the fact that the patient had massive feelings of guilt has to be seen as an important releasing situation: persuaded by her husband, Mrs L. allowed herself some days' rest from nursing her mother. So it happened that she was absent when her mother died, and she blamed herself bitterly for not being present right then.

The linkage of her fears and emotions to a possible HIV-infection has to be seen against the background of her above-mentioned anxiety, the meaning of blood, disease and the death of her mother as well as the coincidental (?) linkage to several personal contacts (the kiss of a colleague; information in the media etc.). In a functional respect her anxiety problem constituted a "way out" from a situation of massive stress, whereby the contents of her fears were linked with a special personal meaning.

Mrs L.'s core problem seemed to be her extreme fear of being infected by the HIV-virus and consequently developing AIDS. This anxiety syndrome also included her family members for whom she felt responsible. She tried to protect and control them by exaggerated cleaning rituals. More and more stimuli triggered her fears, so that the extent of her cleaning and controlling rituals increased. With regard to the psychological dimension a generalisation took place. The only way to alleviate her fear was to steer clear of social contacts whenever possible and to exert extensive cleaning rituals in all cases when they could not be avoided and a possible infection with the virus might thus have happened. The only way she could stabilise herself resulted in a negative reinforcement. Table 8.1 provides a schematic view of this functional perspective.

Mrs L.'s strategies of self-control had already resulted in an aggravation of her problem situation: in trying to avoid a wide range of situations aiming at alleviating her fears she restricted herself to staying at home and thus set the vicious circle in motion. Also other attempts at helping herself did not result in a substantial alleviation. One of these attempts was to carefully watch and control herself for the slightest physical symptoms which might indicate an infection with the HIV-virus and to consult many different physicians who could only provide her with an unspecified reassurance after an extensive and time-consuming physical

Table 8.1 Functional analysis of Mrs L.'s problems

Situation	Self-regulation system	Reaction	Consequences
External cues such as blood, handshaking, sauna, TV-reports, etc. And also: thinking of those situations	Special form of processing information Automatic thoughts (inflated responsibility) Somatic reactivity	Avoiding rituals Checking, cleaning Somatic complaints Thoughts about danger of special situations	Negative reinforcement by reduction of anxiety ($\mathcal{C}$-) Support by family members (C+) Long-term: Reduction of activity level etc. (C-)

C+: positive reinforcement
C-: negative consequence
$\mathcal{C}$-: negative reinforcement

examination. All these attempts to regain a feeling of security resulted at best in a temporary reassurance.

With regard to the "health beliefs model" we found out that her explanations were not very precise. The source or the origin of her problems, so she assumed, had been the severe emotional stress in the course of caring for her mother over a long period of time. Her present helplessness was aggravated by the fact that neither her family doctor nor any of the medical specialists nor the psychologist whom she had consulted in the past nor a non-medical practitioner could provide her with any substantial support.

Classification According to DSM IV Criteria

The diagnostic classification according to the criteria of DSM IV (American Psychiatric Association 1994) has the following purposes: The first is to enable the respective specialists to easily communicate with each other. Classification is the common practice to communicate problems on several levels without the necessity or claim to create a new diagnostic entity. DSM IV is, other than its earlier editions, no longer burdened with theories on different causes of symptoms and remains in its descriptions and definitions on the observational level. The second purpose of a diagnostic classification according to DSM IV is the provision of therapeutic objectives for alleviating the patient's problems. To achieve this goal the classification has to be on the highest possible level of accuracy, objectivity and concreteness.

It seems to be justified to classify Mrs L.'s problem situation according to axis I (= clinical syndrome) as follows:

(1) AIDS-Phobia (as a special form of Specific Phobia)
     criterion s. DSM IV: (300.29), see Table 8.2.
(2) Obsessive–Compulsive controlling and cleaning rituals
     criterion s. DSM IV: (300.3), see Table 8.3.
(3) Undifferentiated Somatoform Disorder
     criterion s. DSM IV. (300.81), see Table 8.4.
     Special form of direction of perception /
     direction of attention /
     valuation and interpretation of minimal physical symptoms.

CLARIFICATION OF TREATMENT TARGETS

It seems necessary to establish a specific and precise clarification of treatment goals, because not even a precise functional analysis provides the

Table 8.2 DSM-IV diagnostic criteria for 300.29 specific phobia

A. Marked and persistent fear that is excessive or unreasonable, cued by the presence or anticipation of a specific object or situation.

B. Exposure to the phobic stimulus almost invariably provokes an immediate anxiety response which may take the form of a situationally bound or situationally predisposed panic attack.

C. The person recognises that the fear is excessive or unreasonable.

D. The phobic situation is avoided or else is endured with intensive anxiety or distress.

E. The avoidance, anxious anticipation, or distress in the feared situation interferes significantly with the person's normal routine, occupational (or academic) functioning, or social activities or relationships, or there is marked distress about having the phobia.

Table 8.3 DSM-IV diagnostic criteria for 300.30 obsessive–compulsive disorder

A. Either obsessions or compulsions:

Obsessions as defined by (1), (2), (3) and (4):

(1) recurrent and persistent thoughts, impulses, or images that are experienced, at some time during the disturbance, as intrusive and inappropriate and that cause marked anxiety or distress
(2) the thoughts, impulses or images are not simply excessive worries about real-life problems
(3) the person attempts to ignore or suppress such thoughts, impulses, or images, or to neutralise them with some other thought or action
(4) the person recognises that the obsessional thoughts, impulses, or images are a product of his or her own mind.

Compulsions as defined by (1) and (2):

(1) repetitive behaviours (e.g., hand washing, ordering, checking) or mental acts (e.g., praying, counting, repeating words silently) that the person feels driven to perform in response to an obsession, or according to rules that must be applied rigidly
(2) the behaviours or mental acts are aimed at preventing or reducing distress or preventing some dreaded event or situation; however, these behaviours or mental acts either are not connected in a realistic way with what they are designed to neutralise or prevent or are clearly excessive

B. At some point during the course of the disorder, the person has recognised that the obsessions or compulsions are excessive or unreasonable.

C. The obsessions or compulsions cause marked distress, are time consuming (take more than 1 hour a day), or significantly interfere with the person's normal routine, occupational (or academic) functioning, or usual social activities or relationships.

Table 8.4   DSM-IV diagnostic criteria for 300.81 Undifferentiated Somatoform Disorder

A. One or more physical complaints (e.g., fatigue, loss of appetite, gastrointestinal or urinary complaints).

B. Either (1) or (2):
   (1) after appropriate investigation, the symptoms cannot be fully explained by a known general medical condition or the direct effects of a substance
   (2) when there is a related general medical condition, the physical complaints or resulting social or occupational impairment is in excess of what would be expected from the history, physical examination, or laboratory findings.

C. The symptoms cause clinically significant distress or impairment in social, occupational, or other important areas of functioning.

D. The duration of the disturbance is at least 6 months.

E. The disturbance is not better be accounted for by another mental disorder.

F. The symptom is not intentionally produced or feigned.

direction of an intervention. In the process of laying down specific targets of the intervention we have to take into consideration *normative* aspects of a patient's life. This means that we have to adjust to the general ideas and notions as to how patients want to live, should they be able to free themselves of their problems.

Social and Situational Aspects of Mrs L.'s Life

In spite of her obsessive behaviour like trying to control every move of a family member, it was possible to keep up a generally good relationship with her husband and her two children. In contrast to this she experienced a lot of resentment towards her two brothers and her sister while her mother was in need of being nursed. They didn't care about her or her mother's needs. But Mrs L. was unable to express her anger. So an emotional conflict arose. On the one hand she felt obliged to nurse her mother, on the other hand there were her unsatisfied desires to have her own personal life, to leave the house and have a social life. Since these wishes remained unsatisfied she developed a lot of resentment and aggression which she did not dare to express.

When Mrs L. became ill herself she experienced a lot of support from her husband and her children. The fact that this support had been comprehensive and had not been confined to a few single activities hindered her efforts to find a solution by her own. This set a vicious circle in motion: while her family helped with the housekeeping, did the shopping etc. in order to diminish stressful chores, her activities were further reduced and her helplessness and dependence increased. This means that their support induced a secondary helplessness and a further restriction of her scope of activities.

Goal Clarification

The symptoms of her disease made Mrs L. suffer severely, especially since her scope of activity as well as her social and personal life became more and more restricted. This resulted in a form of negative motivation with regard to changing the problematic situation.

Already in the first sessions of therapy Mrs L. described as the predominant target her desire to reduce and overcome her anxiety. She clearly expressed her wish to take up swimming again as well as going to the sauna and to consult an ophthalmologist, which was currently impossible due to her fear of tears, and, moreover, to participate in social events and to eat and drink together with other people, to shake hands and have physical contact with other people without being scared to death. One of her very important objectives was to leave the house for a longer period of time; for example to go on a holiday, where it would be unavoidable go out for eating and to use public toilets. She was particularly scared by being far away from home since no medical support and reassurance and no immediate help in case of emergency would be available.

From the therapist's viewpoint it seemed to be the most important goal to change and restructure her core assumptions of her risk of becoming infected with the HIV virus. Her imaginations and false perceptions of the possibility of being infected appeared to be the central determinant of her problem. This part of her self-regulation system was obviously the central determinant, rather than her behaviour as such.

Even though Mrs L. was obviously not aware of the importance of this central determinant and only rated the effectiveness of the therapy in terms of a clearly perceptible change of her and her family's problem situation, this issue—e.g. her core assumption—had to be subject to a critical consideration. Her expectations concerning the success of psychotherapy were of a somewhat medical character, in so far as she expected to remain passive while someone else—a medical or psychological professional—would eliminate her problems. That is why it was of particular importance, in the first stage of her therapy, to motivate Mrs L. to actively participate in therapeutic methods, measures and steps to overcome her problems.

TREATMENT PLANNING

The general principle of therapy was the mastery of the patient's anxiety and the conveyance of a corresponding scope of action (see self-management therapy). The objective of the intervention could not be limited to a reduction of her anxiety and her avoidance strategies. It was also a central intent to develop together with the patient practical objectives as to how her living situation (concerning her family and her professional life) could be improved and to initiate strategies for the implementation of these objectives.

On the basis of a functional analysis and a goal clarification it was quite easy to set up a treatment plan in cooperation with Mrs L. The situations she feared the most were classified according to a hierarchical system ranking from 0 to 100. This hierarchy implied the degree of fear she experienced in the respective situation. Part of the ranking was done by Mrs L. at home in absence of a therapist. Table 8.5 illustrates the list and the ranking of those situations.

In the course of the entire treatment Mrs L. had been fully informed on the theoretical background regarding the possible origin of her problems (plausible explanation) as well as on the respective steps of the treatment. A very important aspect of her treatment was that she not only learned to overcome her fears of special situations and to interpret somatic symptoms differently but that she also acquired general active coping strategies to prepare for her anxieties. An analysis of her already existing skills and of positive aspects of her life was made for this reason—aiming at enhancing the agreeable and enjoyable things in her life as a means of therapy.

Several aspects of treatment planning were *standardised* elements, as they are part of every cognitive–behavioural treatment, such as the necessity to confront the patient with the situations he is particularly scared of. But these standardised elements have to be adapted to the problems of the respective patient and to the individual situation, the individual pace of change (pacing of therapy) and motivational aspects. The latter seems to be of special importance, because the best motivation for a change is a rapid effect clearly perceptible in everyday life, which means within days or weeks of the beginning of the therapy.

Thus it was necessary to adapt the respective stages of therapy to the current needs of Mrs L. Whenever one of the situations (see Table 8.5) was likely to happen the following days, as for instance a social event like an invitation, then we choose the expected activity and the resulting fears as the topic for the next session. We prepared Mrs L. for the situation by

Table 8.5   Hierarchy of feared situations (the figures indicate the weighting of subjective units of disturbance, SUDs)

20	40	60	80	100
Contact with family members	Touching money	Embracing somebody	Dentist	Public toilets
Joint meals with family members	Magazines, newspapers	Door handles	Ophthal-mologist	Shaking hands in case of an injury
		Hotel beds	Using cutlery	Ungroomed persons
		Trying on clothes	Cats, dogs	Seeing blood, sometimes also a red spot
		Dancing (touching each others hands)	Insect bites	Hospital
		Public trans-portation	Tears	Surgery
		Massage treatment	Saliva	Injections
		Hairdresser	Sauna	Drawing blood
			Swimming pool	Somebody using her own bathroom or toilet

training her to cope with the situation during the therapeutic session and in motivating her to try to face and cope with the situation in her real life as well. Since this experience in turn provided her with a perceptible and definite progress, a motivation to tackle the other difficult items on her list as well was further increased.

So we planned and prepared an intensive phase of training in presence of the therapist which was accompanied by his active support. The new stages of progress had to be completed by exercises which Mrs L. had to carry through in the meantime at home between the therapy sessions. In the long run, every patient should be able to transfer and employ the therapeutic targets in everyday life situations and activities.

PROGRESS IN THERAPY: ADVANCING FROM THE PLANNING STAGE TO PRACTICAL APPLICATION

Appointments for therapy were made once a week on a regular basis; sometimes it proved to be necessary to arrange a second date, especially so during the intensive phase of the therapy.

With regard to the duration of a session we did not adhere to a strict schedule. Sometimes it lasted for 1 hour, sometimes for 2 to 4 hours in cases when an intended exposure to a phobic stimulus was carried through (prolonged exposure). As far as the therapist is concerned great flexibility is needed to employ this method successfully.

The therapist, aged 44, who carried through Mrs L.'s therapy, had a special training in cognitive–behavioural therapy; he is very experienced with regard to the treatment of anxiety disorders.

The Implementation of the Treatment

The therapeutic interventions started in the course of the first session. Mrs L. had been motivated to consider the therapy as *her own process of change*, a process which provides her with the opportunity to improve her situation decisively. The principle of self-management in therapy results in a procedure, in which every step of diagnosis and therapy is planned and implemented with the perspective to help the client to be his or her own therapist in the long run (self-management therapy). Keeping this perspective in mind Mrs L. was motivated to carefully observe and analyse her physiological symptoms, while she was exposed to a phobic stimulus (self-observation and self-monitoring). This was a way to let her experience that her anxiety was not an "all-or-nothing" phenomenon: on the one hand there sometimes have been longer spans of time during which she felt no anxiety at all, on the other hand she learned to differentiate between various degrees of anxiety.

As it is the case in every therapeutic treatment of a specific phobia, Mrs L. had to be exposed to the fear-evoking situations. She had to clearly experience that the degree of her anxiety at first increased sharply and then decreased again gradually (see Figure 8.1).

Progress in therapy can best be achieved if the patient is able to withstand the desire to escape from those situations which usually evoke panic attacks. When the patient is exposed to these situations, deliberately for therapeutic reasons, he has to remain in the situation if at all possible, until the degree of his anxiety decreases or even disappears entirely. In

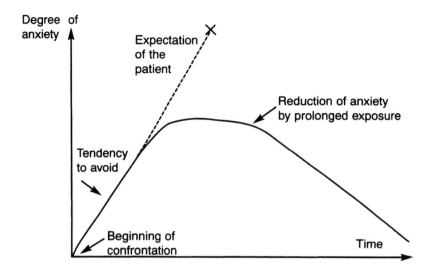

Figure 8.1 Schematic view of confrontation: In the beginning, anxiety and the tendency to avoid become stronger, as the patient expects a quasi-linear augmentation of anxiety. If the patient remains in the situation for a longer period of time, this will result in a reduction of anxiety and in a change of expectations

this case progress can be observed in the therapeutic process. But if the patient tries to avoid to really feel the panic—for instance by cognitive rituals or by distraction—then the "emotional processing" (Foa & Kozak, 1986) cannot take place. This means that any progress in therapy inevitably requires that the patient experiences and perceives the full intensity of the anxiety while exposed to the frightening situation. Thus it is learned by practical experience that after a while anxiety reduces itself. Sometimes it can be helpful to demonstrate to the patient this procedure and the respective theoretical dimensions by a simple diagram.

Special Problems in the Treatment of an AIDS Phobia and the Resulting Disease

When treating an AIDS phobia and the resulting disease some very specific problems arise which have to be taken into account. In case of other phobias concerning a different object or situation, as for instance in claustrophobia or in all kinds of social phobias, the patient is immediately (or at least after several hours) able to experience and realise that his anxiety is irrational. But in the case of a patient suffering from AIDS phobia, the exposure situation does not immediately bring a realisation that the anxiety is unreasonable. The patient can still assume that infection has occurred but will only be detected some months later. So the reduction of anxiety may only set in when an HIV test turns out to be negative.

In the case of Mrs L. it was difficult to obtain her willingness to expose herself to a possibly "dangerous" situation. She was terribly afraid to become infected and she could not experience a reduction of her panic fear in the short run. The fact that she did not immediately experience a relief made her therapy not an easy task to perform. She constantly tried to escape from the exposure to the frightening situations, especially since the degree of anxiety she felt was almost unbearable. So the efforts she made to avoid the fear-evoking situations were quite understandable. But there is no alternative to enduring the anxiety, no matter how strong it may be. Only a prolonged exposure and a response prevention (see Marks, 1987) can in the long run be successful.

Since in many cases the patient has, during the period of illness, lost his ability for a reasonable assessment of a situation, it is necessary to help him or her to regain the criteria which will help to assess the dangerousness of a situation realistically. Teaching these criteria is an important therapeutic strategy which includes cognitive strategies as well as modelling.

Moreover, the therapy helps the patient to *relearn* strategies for coping with difficult situations. An important element of any cognitive–behavioural therapy is *response prevention* while the patient is exposed to a phobic stimulus. This means that the patient has to refrain from avoidance strategies such as compulsive rituals during the therapeutic session while being confronted with his or her anxiety objects. If the situation is coped with, the success as such—apart from the anxiety reducing effect—will result in a new self-confidence, in a new positive self-feeling, and the patient will be confident about mastering difficulties which will arise in future.

Mrs L.'s AIDS phobia included elements of a somatisation disorder and of hypochondria which also had to be taken into account. Mrs L. had a tendency to concentrate her attention even on minimal physical symptoms. This exaggerated vigilance increased the intensity of her perception of minor ailments like pain or nausea, and, consequently, she interpreted them as initial signs of a severe illness. Thus her nervousness and her irritation further increased. This in turn intensified her anxiety and resulted in a general aggravation of her symptoms.

Therapeutic efforts had to be directed to cognitive aspects as well as to these special aspects of physiological arousal. Mrs L. had to learn to interpret her symptoms differently. The gradual removal of avoidance behaviour, such as her exaggerated controlling and cleaning behaviour regarding her family and herself and her permanent search for reassurance (Warwick & Salkovskis, 1989), had the same purpose.

During the first therapy sessions Mrs L. could exercise and train forms of behaviour which she had avoided since the beginning of her phobia. Being under the protection of the therapist she touched the door handle and the telephone and picked up a pen from the floor without employing her usual avoidance rituals. Attended by the therapist she gradually tackled situations which were more difficult for her, such as eating in a restaurant or going to the newspaper stand in a railway station. So she could take up again more and more activities which she had avoided so far. Her success during the therapy sessions motivated her to train coping with respective situations at home as well where she could not rely on the therapist's immediate support and reassurance. Her increasing practice and growing self-confidence encouraged her to tackle even the most difficult situations.

With regard to her somatic complaints, such as emotional blush or nausea, she needed to recognise their relation to psychological processes. Another important element of therapy was to include her husband in the treatment. He participated twice in her sessions. Firstly he had to learn about the nature of his wife's problems and symptoms (plausible explanation). Secondly we had to explain to him that a much better support of his wife was to encourage her to do those things by herself which she had so far avoided (such as driving a car) instead of relieving her of those tasks.

In general the therapeutic process was not easy at all, as Mrs L. experienced several relapses. After having a first success she was quite happy and confident, but when a task seemed to be too difficult to cope with, she reacted almost depressively and she uttered: "Nobody can help me anyway." At this point her frustration tolerance seemed to be very low. Several times she could not bear the anxiety caused by the exposure to phobic stimuli and she escaped. These setbacks undermined her self-confidence and sapped her strength in general. In these cases it was the therapist's primary task to reassure her and to explain to her that such setbacks were quite normal and would not indicate a complete failure, and that no change, whatever it may be, would be a straight-line development. He had to remind her of the progress she had already achieved so far, something she neglected, as many patients do. He repeatedly had to convince her that she would only profit if she continued the therapy—even if it were only to "lose anxiety".

RESULTS

The overall duration of Mrs L.'s treatment amounted to 1½ years and included 32 therapy sessions. They sometimes lasted for 2–4 hours when she had to practise the situations mentioned in her hierarchy of phobic stimuli. At the end of the treatment the frequency of sessions was gradually reduced to one session every other week and then to one session per month.

Mrs L. was afraid that she would not be able to come to terms with the future on her own, knowing that there would be no other treatment session ("What shall I do if anxiety returns?"). We tried to encourage her and back her up by referring to her positive development, to her success and the capabilities of coping with frightening situations which she had acquired in the course of the treatment. At the end of therapy Mrs L. was able to cope with all situations which she had mentioned in her anxiety hierarchy, even with the most difficult ones which at the beginning she never expected to be able to cope with.

The process of extinction with regard to phobic fears is very complex. In cognitive–behavioural therapy at first the behavioural aspects (e.g. avoidance behaviour) have to be reduced since the treatment primarily aims at excessive anxiety responses to normal everyday life situations. The patient's autonomic responses are extinguished by gradual habituation to the feared situations and objects. In this context cognitive aspects seem to be very persistent. Mrs L. and many other patients told us that it was almost impossible to avoid "phobic thoughts" even though, in the meantime, she was able to cope with the feared situations easily. It can be concluded that these thoughts are very resistant to extinction. The reason for this may be that they are part of a "network system" (Lang, 1985) which takes a long time to be changed. The more the patient tries to actively attack or suppress those aversive thoughts, the more persistent they become; this is known as a "rebound phenomenon" concerning unwanted thoughts (Wegner, 1989).

Six months after the termination of the treatment we asked Mrs L. to come for a follow-up interview. She told us that she was content with her emotional condition and her family situation. She had taken up her work again, and even though she sometimes experienced a stressful time in her job, her situation was satisfactory in general.

With regard to the cost–benefit analysis we come to the following conclusion: on the one hand there had of course been expenses which the medical insurance system had to cover. And the patient had to invest a lot of emotional energy and staying power. On the other hand this form of brief psychotherapy prevented a further deterioration and thus the development of a chronic disease which might then have required an inpatient treatment, a long-term medication and, of course, much greater expense.

The fact that we had been successful in the treatment of Mrs L. was confirmed by the results of the follow-up interview. Her overall situation had improved significantly. Her daughter was about to leave home. A further confirmation that she was satisfied with the result of the treatment was the fact that she sent a good friend who was suffering from psychological problems to our outpatient's department.

REFERENCES

American Psychiatric Association (APA). (1994) *Diagnostic and Statistical Manual of Mental Disorders*, IVth edn (DSM IV). Washington, D.C.: American Psychiatric Press.

Foa, E.B. & Kozak, M. (1986) Emotional processing of fear: Exposure to corrective information. *Psychological Bulletin*, **99**, 20–35.

Kanfer, F.H., Reinecker, H. & Schmelzer, D. (1996) *Selbstmanagementtherapie. Ein Lehrbuch für die Klinische Praxis*. 2. *Auflage*. Berlin: Springer-Verlag.

Kanfer, F.H. & Saslow, G. (1965) Behavioral Analysis: An alternative to diagnostic classification. *Archives of General Psychiatry*, **12**, 529–538.

Kanfer, F.H. & Schefft, B.K. (1988). *Guiding the Process of Therapeutic Change*. Champaign, Ill.: Research Press.

Karoly, P. (1993) Goal systems: An organizational framework for clinical assessment and treatment planning. *Psychological Assessment*, **5**, 273–280.

Karoly, P. (1995) Self-control theory. In W. O'Donohue and L. Krasner (eds), *Theories of Behavior Therapy*. Washington, D.C.: American Psychological Association.

Lang, P.J. (1985) The cognitive psychophysiology of emotion: Fear and anxiety. In A.H. Tuma and J.D. Maser (eds), *Anxiety and the Anxiety Disorders*. Hillsdale, N.J.: L. Erlbaum.

Marks, I.M. (1987) *Fears, Phobias, and Rituals*. New York: Oxford University Press.

Warwick, H.M.C. & Salkovskis, P.M. (1989) Hypochondriasis. In J. Scott, J.M.G. Williams and A.T. Beck (eds), *Cognitive Therapy in Clinical Practice*. London: Routledge & Kegan Paul.

Wegner, D.M. (1989). *White Bears and Other Unwanted Thoughts: Suppression, Obsession and the Psychology of Mental Control*. New York: Viking Press.

Wolpe, J.D. & Lang, P.M. (1964) A fear survey schedule for use in behavior therapy. *Behaviour Research and Therapy*, **2**, 27–30.

CHAPTER 9

Utilising case formulations in manual-based treatments

Frank W. Bond

TAKE YOUR CORNERS

The authors contributing to this volume clearly endorse the principle that individualised case formulations should constitute the basis upon which psychological interventions are selected, and perhaps even developed, for clinical use. Moreover, AuBuchon and Malatesta (see Chapter 7) argue that idiographic case formulations should guide the nature and style of the therapeutic relationship itself. In contrast to the present volume of glittering endorsements for case formulations (CFs), writers, such as Wilson (1996, 1997), express doubts about the usefulness of this cornerstone of behavioural and cognitive–behavioural psychotherapy. Specifically, Wilson (1997, p. 205) maintains that not only is it "challenging" to devise a good CF, but, even with the appropriate training and competencies, it may be difficult for clinicians to formulate accurate and therapeutically efficacious case formulations. To support this suggestion, Wilson cites research in the area of social cognition, which indicates that people's judgements can be heavily biased in uncertain situations.

As an alternative to CF-based treatments, Wilson (1996, 1997) advocates employing, where they exist, empirically validated, manual-based treatments. He states that these manuals have been shown to be, by definition, effective in controlled outcome studies. In addition, because of people's cognitive biases, treatments specified by these validated manuals will probably be, on average, more effective than those predicated upon a CF.

Beyond Diagnosis: Case Formulation Approaches in CBT.
Edited by Michael Bruch and Frank W. Bond.
© 1998 John Wiley & Sons Ltd.

Wilson states that research comparing the relative effectiveness of manual-based and CF-based treatments is mixed, but that "the best controlled study to date" (Wilson, 1997, p. 206) indicates that the former is more effective than the latter, in treating people with phobias. Despite Wilson's clear preference for manual-based therapies, he does acknowledge that CF-based treatments are necessary when (1) clients are treatment resistant, or (2) there are no empirically supported protocols for a particular problem (1997).

MANUAL-BASED TREATMENTS NEED TO BE ADAPTED TO THE INDIVIDUAL

The debate on the relative merits of manual-based and CF-based treatments has been addressed by other authors (e.g., Davison & Lazarus,1995; Hickling & Blanchard, 1997; Malatesta, 1995; Wilson, 1996; 1997). It will not, therefore, be considered further in this chapter. Instead, the focus here is on the need to employ idiographic case formulations, even when utilising empirically validated, nomothetic treatments. As Wilson (1996) indicates, even when used in an outcome study, many treatment manuals call for a degree of individualised tailoring; for example, in the areas of selecting alternative techniques (e.g., Beck et al., 1979; Fairburn, Marcus, and Wilson, 1993; Linehan, 1993a,b), and in the timing of various interventions (e.g., Hayes, Strosahl, and Wilson, in press). It is maintained here, however, that employing a treatment manual often requires even more adaptation to the individual than is specified by Wilson. This personal accommodation will occur whether or not a CF is conducted, but it is thought that individualising a manual, based upon a thorough CF, will help to maximise the manual's efficacy, for reasons discussed in the following section.

REASONS FOR USING A CASE FORMULATION APPROACH TO TAILOR A MANUAL-BASED TREATMENT TO AN INDIVIDUAL

Before progressing further, I should note that the type of case formulation referred to in the present chapter incorporates at its core a functional, or causal, analysis (Cone, 1997; Skinner, 1953). This examination attempts to identify the variables that cause psychological problems. To conduct this analysis, clinicians detect (1) the stimuli that occasion (2) the client's responses, or dysfunctional behaviours. Lastly, they identify (3) the consequences that result from the responses. Turkat (1979) recommends that clinicians should detect stimuli and consequences on the cognitive, physiological, motor, and environmental levels; and, they should assess responses on the cognitive, physiological, and motor levels. Radical behaviourists insist that dysfunctional behaviours (i.e., responses) cannot be divorced from the stimuli that trigger them and the consequences that follow from them (Skinner, 1974). Thus, the complete stimuli–responses–consequences (S–R–C) event, or contingency, constitutes a problem behaviour, not just the dysfunctional responses.

As illustrated below, it is thought that treatment manuals often have to be tailored to individuals, if they are to address the specific stimuli, responses, and consequences that constitute a person's psychological disorder. Since a CF is well equipped to identify systematically this S–R–C contingency, it appears ideally suited to accommodate a manual to an individual.

A CF is also considered an ideal tool with which to tailor a manual to an individual, because its approach to assessment and treatment strongly advocates testing the validity of functional analyses through "clinical experiments" (Meyer & Turkat, 1979, p. 264). In these experiments, the clinician "manipulates" the pertinent environmental, cognitive, emotional, motor, and physiological stimuli, responses and consequences that can help test the functional analyses. This experimentation phase of a CF differs from the assessment phase (Meyer and Turkat). To elaborate, during the former, the clinician and client are actually manipulating variables, in order to test predictions made by the functional analyses. On the other hand, in the latter phase, these predictions are being established, often only through a behavioural interview and self-monitoring forms that a client employs. As can be seen, a thorough CF does not merely involve clinician hypotheses as to the S–R–C contingencies that constitute psychological disorders. For, a complete CF also requires that a clinician tests these hypotheses by creating situations in which he or she manipulates the relevant variables.

If a thorough CF is not conducted, clinicians will still construct hypotheses as to S–R–C contingencies, in order to tailor a manual to a person. These hypotheses, however, may derive from incomplete information, and/or they may not be properly tested, as just described. Unstructured and untested analyses of a person and his or her problems may result in a manual-based intervention that is not maximally efficacious; however, this proposition has not yet been tested empirically.

EMPLOYING A CF TO INDIVIDUALISE TREATMENT MANUALS FOR OBSESSIVE–COMPULSIVE DISORDER

A case example is presented below, in order to illustrate that (1) even a treatment manual for a relatively "straightforward" intervention like exposure and response prevention (Emmelkamp, Bouman, & Scholing, 1992) has to be individualised; and, (2) this tailoring process can be facilitated by employing a CF procedure that establishes and then verifies the specific S–R–C contingencies that require the manual-based intervention.

The case that is discussed below concerns a woman who fulfils the Diagnostic and Statistical Manual for Mental Disorders, Fourth Edition (American Psychiatric Association, 1994) criteria for obsessive–compulsive disorder (OCD). In accordance with a nomothetic perspective on treatment, she qualifies, therefore, for exposure and response prevention (ERP) treatment (which was originally developed by Meyer, 1966). Briefly, ERP involves exposing people to stimuli that evoke their obsessions, that is, their intrusive, anxiety provoking thoughts, images, or impulses (e.g., causing self or others great harm or even death) (American Psychiatric Association, 1994). Whilst exposed to these stimuli, people are strongly encouraged not to engage in their compulsions; that is, in their repetitive behaviours, including mental behaviours, that function to (1) prevent or reduce the distress caused by the obsessions, and/or (2) thwart the occurrence of unwanted events that the obsessions specify (American Psychatric Association, 1994). Research has demonstrated that ERP is a highly effective psychological intervention for OCD (for reviews of outcome studies see Foa, Steketee, and Ozarow, 1985; Rachman and Hodgson, 1980), and it does appear to be the "treatment of choice" for this disorder.

Manuals for ERP (e.g., Emmelkamp, Bourman & Scholing, 1992; Riggs and Foa, 1993) place considerable emphasis on detailing clients' obsessive–compulsive behaviours, and the stimuli that occasion them. To this end, these manuals recommend obtaining substantial information on how OCD operates in a particular person. Interestingly, gathering this type of individualised information is also a primary goal of the functional analysis part of a CF. It appears, then, that a CF-based approach to treating OCD requires the same type of personalised data as does an (ERP) manual-based approach. Despite this similarity, however, nomothetic and idiographic approaches to OCD, and every other type of psychological problem, employ personalised information to different ends. Specifically, manual-based approaches use this information to tailor to a person a pre-packaged treatment that has already been selected, based upon (probably) a DSM diagnosis. In contrast, a CF-based approach uses the personalised information that it has generated, in order to select amongst or even create (e.g., Bruch, Chapter 2 of this volume) interventions.

Even though nomothetic and idiographic approaches to treatment employ personalised information differently, it does not then follow that they have to obtain it via distinct procedures. Indeed, as noted above, this chapter emphasises that clinicians who use manual-based interventions would do well to tailor these treatments to individuals, using a CF approach. To accomplish this tailoring process, consider the following case example in which a clinician accommodates an ERP to an individual.

USING A CF TO TAILOR AN ERP MANUAL TO AN INDIVIDUAL: A CASE EXAMPLE

Mary (a fictitious name) was referred to the Cognitive Behavioural Psychotherapy Unit, University College London (UCL) by her general practitioner. She was a fifty-year old, married, freelance journalist who had been experiencing "obsessive–compulsive problems" for the past five years. She reported that, over the past year, they had become particularly debilitating. Through questioning and Mary's own description of her current difficulties, it appeared that she fulfilled the DSM-IV criteria for OCD.

During the initial interview, Mary stated that her obsessions and compulsions occurred in four areas of her life, and that each of these domains required therapeutic attention. The four problem areas were: (1) overwashing her hands, food, cooking utensils, and cutlery; (2) an inability to discard rubbish without checking and cleaning it; and over-checking her (3) articles, letters, (4) home appliances, and items in the supermarket.

For clients like Mary, who present with more than one OC complaint, the clinician and client must decide whether to employ ERP on all problem areas at once or sequentially. Mary, who had to work, could not afford to take the hiatus that was necessary, in order to apply ERP to each of her four problem areas at once. She and I (the therapist) decided, therefore, first to employ ERP on the complaint that, for her, was most problematic. Having to take this important decision provides one example as to how a manual-based treatment needs to be tailored to an individual. If the clinician and client take this decision together, it can facilitate a collaborative relationship and the client's commitment to the therapeutic process.

After obtaining a client's list of problems, the CF approach used at UCL (see Meyer and Turkat, 1979; and Chapters 2 and 5 of this volume) has therapists and clients work collaboratively to generate a list of therapeutic goals. For Mary, generating this list provided an opportunity for her to decide which of her four problem areas she wanted first to address. By taking this and the previous, related decision, Mary was certainly tailoring a nomothetic treatment to her own needs. More importantly, however, she was beginning to take charge of her own problems, which hopefully provided her with some motivation for the ERP.

Of course, clinicians do not need to employ a CF approach, in order to allow their clients a voice in determining a treatment plan. By using one, however, clinicians may be reminded of the importance of tailoring a manual to an individual and collaboratively establishing a treatment contract. Such a reminder may not go amiss. For, when reading an ERP treatment protocol such as Riggs and Foa's (1993), one may not get the impression that clinicians base treatment planning on individual circumstances or a co-operative effort.

At the initial interview, Mary and I tentatively agreed that she might wish to work towards the following treatment goals, in turn, and in the order listed: (1) discard rubbish in a timely manner, without having to check it or clean its contents; (2) refrain from over-washing her food, cooking utensils, and cutlery; and not check too many times her (3) articles, letters, (4) home appliances and items in the supermarket. (Mary and I waited to finalise these goals until after the "testing session", described below. After this session, however, we did not alter the above list.) Mary wished to accomplish these therapeutic goals so she could achieve her current life goals of: spending more time listening to music, reading, being with her husband, lunching with friends in restaurants, watching television, investigating stories and publishing them quickly.

In accordance with the case formulation approach employed at UCL, I conducted a functional analysis for each of Mary's four problem areas. For space considerations, however, I will only present the first two analyses.

Functional Analysis of Checking and Discarding Rubbish

From interviewing Mary, it appeared that, for each of her four problem areas, the following rule (or verbal stimulus that specifies a contingency) occasioned her OC behaviours: when I think that I may be responsible for irreparably harming myself or others, I must do everything that I can to prevent such harm from occurring; and, if I do not, then I will be responsible for any disaster that ensues. In accordance with contemporary, radical behavioural accounts of rule-governed (or cognitively controlled) behaviour (e.g., Catania, Matthews & Shimoff, 1990; Catania, Shimoff & Matthews, 1989; Hayes & Hayes, 1989), it was hypothesised that Mary's rule was elicited when she was exposed to stimuli that she perceived as potentially harmful to herself or others. (Cognitive–behavioural therapists who do not subscribe to radical behaviourism can, throughout this chapter, substitute the word "belief" for the word "rule"; because, for the purposes of this chapter, the terms are interchangeable.) The harmful stimuli that concern discarding rubbish are presented now in the following functional analysis. This analysis, of course, also provides detailed information regarding the responses occasioned by exposure to the "rubbish" stimuli, the consequences that these responses produce, and the relationship between the S–R–C components.

Stimuli

When Mary had to throw away rubbish or place the bin liner outside to be collected by the dustmen, her rule was elicited, which was, as noted: when I think that I may be responsible for irreparably harming myself or others, I must do everything that I can to prevent such harm from occurring; and, if I do not, then I will be responsible for any disaster that ensues. Upon contact with her rule and having to discard rubbish or put the bin liner outside, Mary engaged in behaviour that was consistent with her rule; that is, she attempted to prevent harm from occurring.

Responses

Mary's responses are divided into three categories: cognitive, autonomic, and motor:

(1) *Cognitive responses.* Mary had thoughts that included: "chemical containers should be clean, because, when they are burned, they may poison the atmosphere", "glass may cut rubbish collectors", and "the contents of jam jars may poison people when they are exposed to the air".

(2) *Autonomic responses.* Mary became tense in her arms and neck and experienced a sensation that she labelled as "agitated", which appeared to be slight shaking in the presence of the just mentioned cognitions.

(3) *Motor responses.* Mary first ensured that all containers (e.g., liquid soap bottles or jam jars) were cleaned thoroughly of their contents before she placed them in the bin; and, when discarding items, she was very careful to safeguard that nothing broke in the process. Immediately before she placed a bin liner outside for the dustmen, Mary went through the bin and removed any metal items that could possibly harm someone. She then gave these to her husband to discard (because, by so doing, she reported that she was then not responsible for any harm to others that could result from these items being

thrown-away). After removing any metal items, Mary then looked into the rubbish bin from several different angles to ensure that the contents were actually rubbish. Once she was satisfied that they were (after approximately three minutes), she placed the bin liner very carefully into the outside bin. After discarding an item or placing a bin liner outside, Mary washed her hands for approximately two minutes.

Consequences

Mary reported that her responses to the rubbish stimuli had the immediate effect of eliminating her tension, "agitation", and negative thoughts. Mary stated that the longer term effects of her responses were "humiliation" and sadness.

Functional Analysis for Over-washing Food, Cooking Utensils, and Cutlery

Stimuli

The stimuli that set the occasion for Mary to over-wash food, cooking utensils, and cutlery were those that surrounded the process of cooking and eating. Specific stimuli included: touching the refrigerator, unwrapping food products, touching food, preparing to use cooking utensils (e.g., pots and pans), and preparing to use cutlery and plates. Being in contact with these stimuli elicited Mary's rule: when I think that I may be responsible for irreparably harming myself or others, I must do everything that I can to prevent such harm from occurring; and, if I do not, then I will be responsible for any disaster that ensues. Upon contact with her rule and any of these above stimuli, Mary then followed her rule (i.e. she engaged in "rule-governed behaviour") and responded in ways that she thought would prevent harm from occurring.

Responses

Mary's responses are divided into three categories: cognitive, autonomic, and motor:

(1) *Cognitive responses.* "I may poison myself and people who eat the food".
(2) *Autonomic responses.* Tension all through her body.
(3) *Motor responses.* (It should be noted that, unless otherwise indicated, the term "hand washing" specifies that Mary washed her hands once

for approximately thirty seconds.) Before she began to prepare any meal, Mary washed her hands and cleaned all kitchen surfaces. She then washed each cooking utensil she was going to use. After this, Mary gathered all of the food that she was going to prepare, and upon doing this, she washed her hands. Mary then rinsed a fruit or a vegetable that was to be eaten, and, if necessary, she peeled it. If she did peel anything, she would then wash her hands, before chopping it. After chopping it, she rinsed the fruit or vegetable again, and then ended this procedure by washing her hands. Any other fruits or vegetables that were to be eaten were prepared in this same manner.

When preparing meat, Mary washed her hands, rinsed the grill, opened the meat packet, washed her hands, rinsed the meat under running water, put the meat on the, as yet, unheated grill, threw away the meat packet, washed her hands, washed the sink and taps, and then washed her hands again. Mary then put spices or dried herbs on the meat, turned on the grill, and then washed her hands. Whenever Mary checked the meat on the grill, or turned it over, she washed her hands. She never used the same fork twice to turn over or check the meat.

Just before eating the meal, Mary prepared to set the table. This process always began by Mary checking each plate and item of cutlery, which potentially would be used, for any noticeable dust. If she noticed dust on a plate or an item of cutlery, then she considered it dirty and did not use it for dinner that evening. Mary placed all approved items by the sink and then washed her hands before rinsing each of the plates and pieces of cutlery that she selected for dinner. Mary then set the table by placing the cutlery on the plates but never on the table next to the plates.

Consequences

Mary reported that her responses had the immediate effect of eliminating her tension and negative thoughts, but she stated that the longer term effects of her responses were "humiliation" and sadness.

With this detailed information that is provided by the functional analyses, I could tailor an ERP programme so that it addressed all of the stimuli, responses, and consequences that constituted Mary's various OC behaviours. With regard to these behaviours, I offered an hypothesis, in the above two analyses, as to the rule that occasioned them. Aware of this rule, I employed an intervention (discussed below) that was designed to weaken the control that the rule had on Mary's OC responses. As can be seen, this CF revealed the S–R–C contingencies that constituted Mary's OC behaviours, and the rule that triggered them. With this crucial information, I was able to mould a manual-based ERP intervention to the unique contours of this individual's OCD. Before shaping this intervention to Mary's problem behaviours, however, I had to test the data that were to guide this casting process.

Mary and I tested the validity of the functional analyses by conducting a "home meeting". During this home session, I asked Mary to expose herself to situations that would trigger her OC behaviours. By testing the functional analyses *in vivo*, I did not have to rely on Mary's own report of her behaviours, which occurred at very anxious moments for her. In addition, the *in vivo* tests allowed me to manipulate stimuli and her responses so as to verify (and perhaps establish more) behaviours and controlling variables that required targeting. To provide an example of how these functional analyses were tested, I will now describe how I examined Mary's "rubbish" analysis. It should be noted that I tested all of the functional analyses on the same day, and it took five hours to verify and modify them. In particular, the rubbish analysis took approximately twenty minutes to test.

When examining the rubbish analysis, I first asked Mary to discard various bathroom-related items. During the initial interview, Mary had not mentioned any problems regarding throwing away rubbish in her bathroom bins, and when I asked about such problems, she denied having them. During the "bathroom test", Mary was able to discard tissues used to blow her nose, and cotton wool with astringent on it. She was not able to discard, however, sanitary towels that she pretended were used, shampoo bottles, and liquid soap containers. Mary noted that she left the shampoo and soap containers for her husband to place in the outside bin. She then showed me how she dispensed of her used sanitary towels: a process that involved wrapping them in heavy paper, placing duct tape around the paper, and then, with difficulty, placing them in the bin. Mary stated that she went through this procedure, in order to ensure that no one could accidentally get a disease such as HIV or hepatitis from her. She did not *think* that she had these diseases, but as she said, "Who can ever really know?". By conducting this test, I was able to identify therapeutically relevant stimuli and responses that Mary had not specified during the initial interview.

I asked Mary why, when trying to discard items into the bathroom bins, she left the soap and shampoo containers for her husband to throw away. She said that, by having him dispose of the containers, she was not responsible for any harm that might result from them. This statement, and similar ones that she made when the "testing process" moved to the kitchen bin, appeared to support the rule (noted above) that was collaboratively developed, during the initial interview. Whilst at the kitchen bin (the most "terrifying" one in the house), I noticed further motor and physiological responses that Mary did not realise she made. For example, Mary did not know how slowly and haltingly she moved, when discarding a "harmful" item. In addition, she did not realise that her arm shook when she threw away items that she thought could inflict damage.

This "testing session", which is a crucial component of the CF approach employed at UCL, certainly confirmed important elements of Mary's functional analyses. Furthermore, it provided new information that I needed to integrate into these analyses, if the ERP programme was to be properly individualised and thus made maximally effective. To elaborate, without conducting this testing session, it is conceivable that I may not have identified Mary's OC rubbish responses in the bathroom. In addition, it is very likely that neither Mary nor I would have known of the motor and physiological responses that she made when discarding rubbish in the kitchen. Without being aware of these "new" bathroom and kitchen OC behaviours, it would obviously have been difficult to prevent them during ERP.

As has been emphasised, it is not necessary to conduct a CF, in order to establish and test (*in vivo*) hypotheses as to the stimuli, responses, and consequences that constitute a psychological problem. However, without the structure of a CF approach, it is questionable as to whether or not clinicians would actually spend the time that such hypothesis generating and testing require (see Wilson, 1996).

Developmental History of Mary's Four Problem Areas

As will be seen, Mary's case demonstrates that, when tailoring a manual-based treatment to an individual, understanding the developmental history of his or her psychological problem(s) can be very useful. In addition, Mary's case will show that further assistance in this tailoring process can be obtained by including, in this history, information on any previous treatment for the target problem.

Mary stated that she grew up in North London with a father who had strict rules, "hated emotional expressions and illness" and was "obsessed by cleanliness and order". Mary recalled that her father always became very critical of her when she was not neat and orderly. For example, she remembered constantly being terrified about spilling a drop of tea on the dining room table, because he would become angry at this type of accident. Despite her father's critical and demanding behaviours, Mary stated that she had "great admiration" for him, because he had great charisma and was respected by many people, due to his success as a classical musician. Mary reported that her admiration for him waned when, at age twenty-one, she discovered that her father had always been homosexual.

During her childhood and adolescence, Mary said that she had a very strong relationship with her mother. She reported that her mother was very protective of her and "extremely domineering". For instance, Mary stated that her important decisions (e.g., whom to date) were often made by her mother, despite Mary wanting to make them herself. Mary reported that her mother was a "very anxious person" who entertained many superstitious ideas. For example, she told Mary, repeatedly, that she was not to touch dogs, because she would contract an (unspecified) disease. At this time in her life, Mary maintained that she was not bothered by any of the problems with which she presented in therapy.

From the ages of twenty-one to thirty-nine, Mary reported that she was "a rather casual person", and that she was free of the problems that she presented with at this unit. She stated that she obtained a degree in journalism at age twenty-one, worked as a civil servant for fourteen years, and then left this job at age thirty-five, in order to become a freelance journalist. Mary reported that she "loved" working as a journalist and succeeded in the occupation almost immediately.

At the age of thirty-nine, Mary married and wished to have children. She stated that, whilst pregnant, she took medication that her doctor wrongly prescribed, and it deformed the foetus that she was carrying. Mary said that, two weeks after learning of these deformities, she miscarried. Since that miscarriage, Mary reported being hypersensitive to anything that could potentially harm a baby. She stated that, from the time she was forty, she began avoiding any medication or chemicals and found it "hard to believe doctors". In addition, Mary reported that her food preparation problems began at this time. She could not indicate why these problems began when they did.

From ages forty-one to forty-five, Mary reported that she had four miscarriages and two abortions, due to severe abnormalities in the developing foetuses. Mary stated that, during this period, she developed fears of being contaminated by a wide variety of stimuli. Once again, Mary could not state why these problems began when they did, but she said that she coped with these fears by performing the washing behaviours that were described above. In addition, Mary stated that she began over-washing her hands during this time. Furthermore, she reported that her checking behaviours also began at this time. Mary stated that these washing and checking behaviours became fairly incapacitating during this four-year period, although she was able to work. (Mary was not experiencing at this time problems concerning: (1) discarding the rubbish, and (2) checking her articles and letters.)

From ages forty-five to forty-nine, Mary maintained that her problematic behaviours became even more debilitating, and, at age forty-nine, she sought the help of a psychologist. Mary reported that her therapy (which appeared to be ERP) was very successful at treating her hand washing problem. Nevertheless, she stated that her checking behaviours and food preparation behaviours were still problematic several months after beginning therapy. Mary said that she stopped therapy "early", because her psychologist "ignored the thoughts flying around [her] head".

At age fifty, Mary reported that she won several awards for an article that she wrote for a newspaper. She said that during this year of her life, her checking behaviours and food preparation behaviours were very debilitating. In addition, Mary reported that she began experiencing new problematic behaviours, which were: (1) an inability to discard rubbish, and over-checking her (2) letters and (3) articles. When questioned, Mary stated that these three problematic behaviours developed gradually and became even worse during her fifty-first year. At age fifty-one, she found it very difficult to work, due to her OC behaviours, and went to her general practitioner so that he could refer her for psychotherapy (and he referred her to UCL). Mary reported that he wanted to give her medication as well, but, she refused, because "doctors are incompetent . . . I mean, really, God knows what those tablets would have done to me".

As may be evident, these historical details of Mary's problems and health care experiences revealed three very important implications for therapy and how the ERP programme should be tailored to her. Firstly, her above account indicated that she greatly distrusted "so-called professionals", which suggested that I needed to establish an extremely collaborative relationship with her. I hypothesised that, if I were not collaborative and transparent in my interactions with her, Mary would be very untrusting of me and perhaps even leave therapy prematurely.

Secondly, Mary's misgivings about professionals and therapy indicated that it was wise to have her document, very carefully, any important changes that occurred, as a result of the ERP programme. For, if she did not have concrete evidence that she was (hopefully) improving, she might "minimise" her progress and become rather more pessimistic about her chances of overcoming her OC behaviours. Finally, Mary's past experience with ERP suggested that she might not comply with this form of treatment, if her thinking was once again "ignored"; thus, when adapting

ERP to her, I thought it was necessary to address her cognitions directly (and how I did this is discussed below).

As can be seen, by understanding the history surrounding a person's problems, which is strongly recommended from a CF approach, a clinician can better accommodate a manual-based treatment, such as ERP, to a client's individual requirements. Such close tailoring, it is hypothesised, can increase not only the efficacy of treatment, but, in cases like Mary's, the probability that the person even remains in treatment.

To end this discussion on the benefits of obtaining an historical development of problems, I should note that, in my view, understanding how a problem developed (including how it has been previously addressed by health care professionals) is different from knowing how a person acquired a problem. To elaborate, information about problem development is knowledge about how the client (and perhaps a partner or a family member) views the progress of his or her presenting difficulties (e.g., "It became worse after my husband left me"). Whereas, information about problem acquisition is knowledge about how a problem started, in the first place (e.g., a biological vulnerability and a consistently deprecating family). Of course, in obtaining a developmental history of a disorder, clients may offer opinions as to why a problem began. Their explanations, however, whilst needed to be noted and respected, may not necessarily be correct or complete. Likewise, it is probable that a clinician's hypotheses as to how a person acquired a problem are, if not inaccurate, then at least functionally false; that is, the hypotheses "are a very small part of the picture and they are based on a great deal of ignorance" (Hayes, 1995, p.62). Thus, unlike Meyer & Turkat (1979) and Bruch & Meyer (1993), who developed the CF approach employed at UCL, I do not think that historical material can be usefully used to construct valid hypotheses as to how a person acquired his or her problem.

To demonstrate the difficulties of using historical material to speculate on how a person acquired a problem, consider Mary's case. Specifically, in order to understand how Mary's OC behaviours began, it is necessary to hypothesise as to: (1) whether or not there is a biological predisposition to OCD and if there is, whether she has it; (2) how the particular stimuli involved in her four problem areas became heralds of harm; and, (3) how her rule came to exist. Unfortunately, hypotheses regarding the first point cannot yet be verified, nor can they even be generated from interviewing a client. Assumptions concerning the second two points are unfalsifiable. In addition, they are based upon historical information that may be of questionable validity (Poppen, 1989), and this information is, in any event, critically incomplete, as noted above (Hayes, 1989).

As Mary's case demonstrates, speculation as to how people acquired problematic behaviours produces unverifiable and unscientific hypotheses, which could be, of course, incorrect and misleading. Furthermore, it is not thought that historical material concerning problem acquisition is necessary to have, in order either to adapt a manual-based intervention to a person, or to develop an intervention from a CF (Poppen, 1989). For, much to everyone's chagrin no doubt, variables that caused current, psychological problems cannot be changed, because they occurred in the unalterable past. (However, the present variables that maintain these problems can be modified, and this is, of course, the goal of psychotherapy.) It is thought that problem development, not problem acquisition, is the better focus for forays into a person's past; because, as noted above, information connected with the former can be employed usefully to tailor a manual-based treatment to an individual, and such accommodation may increase a therapy's efficacy. How details of Mary's problem development were used to tailor an ERP programme to her is considered below.

Behavioural Formulation

As noted above, by obtaining functional analyses, I knew (1) the S–R–C contingencies that constituted Mary's OC behaviours, and (2) the rule that occasioned these behaviours. In the case formulation approach employed at UCL, this information is summarised in what is called the "behavioural formulation" (Meyer & Turkat, 1979). Furthermore, in this formulation, a clinician should hypothesise as to how the rule and the responses described in the three-term contingencies are maintained. These hypotheses are important, because the ERP programme (or any other manual-based treatment) should be tailored to address not only the individual's specific S–R–C contingencies, but the variables that purportedly maintain these contingencies as well. How this accommodation process occurs in this case example is discussed, after presenting the following behavioural formulation:

Mary's primary problems were: (1) over-washing her hands, food, cooking utensils, and cutlery; (2) an inability to discard rubbish without checking and cleaning it; and over-checking her (3) articles, letters, (4) home appliances, and items in the supermarket. It appeared that these four problem areas related to one another in that each involved stimuli that indicated to Mary that profound harm to herself or others was very likely. It was hypothesised that when Mary encountered these stimuli, a rule was elicited that specified how she should respond to the potentially harmful event. Mary's rule that occasioned her responses was: when I think that I may be responsible for irreparably harming myself or others, I must do everything that I can to prevent such harm from occurring; and, if I do not, then I will be responsible for any disaster that ensues. In accordance with operant behavioural accounts of rule-governed behaviour (e.g. Catania, Matthews & Shimoff, 1990; Catania, Shimoff & Matthews, 1989; and Hayes & Hayes, 1989), it was hypothesised that this rule maintained Mary's unhelpful responses, some of which were outlined in the above, functional analyses. Furthermore, it was posited that Mary's rule was maintained, because her rule-governed responses resulted in a cessation of her unpleasant bodily tension and negative thoughts. It was hypothesised that this cessation provided negative reinforcement for Mary's unhelpful rule.

Treatment Rationale

In Mary's behavioural formulation, I hypothesised that her unhelpful rule maintained her OC responses. Therefore, the rationale of Mary's treatment was to encourage her to act against her dysfunctional responses (via an ERP programme). By not engaging in her OC behaviours, Mary would then have the time to begin accomplishing her therapeutic and current life goals (noted above). I thought that experiencing such accomplishment would probably provide her with more positive contingencies of reinforcement. Based on Catania (1995; Catania, Matthews & Shimoff, 1990; Catania, Shimoff & Matthews, 1989), I hypothesised that if Mary could experience more positive contingencies, she might develop a rule that could lead to non-OC behaviours, when she encountered "harmful" stimuli.

Using the CF to Adapt the ERP Programme to Mary: Some Examples

Consistent with the treatment rationale, Mary agreed to go through an ERP programme that took place at her home, amongst the actual stimuli that triggered her OC behaviours. I do not discuss here the ERP treatment protocol that I employed, because Emmelkamp, Bouman & Scholing (1992) have already detailed it. Instead, I shall describe some ways in which I employed Mary's CF to adapt the ERP intervention to her requirements.

Firstly, consistent with the therapeutic goals (noted above), Mary's four problem areas were addressed sequentially, beginning with her rubbish behaviours. As noted above, Mary and I established, through collaboration, these goals and almost every detail of the tailoring process (e.g., issues concerning the case formulation, goals of therapy, and scheduling of the ERP). In fact, even the decision to use a very collaborative approach was established by consensus between her and me, at the first session. Specifically, I asked Mary if she would find it difficult to be "prescribed" treatment for her OC behaviours. Consistent with the information that I obtained from the developmental history of her problems, she stated that it would be difficult to accept what doctors of any kind told her to do, because of having been prescribed medication that "killed" her developing baby. Based upon these comments, we decided that Mary would not be "prescribed" anything; instead, we would both consider alternatives and, together, reach a decision as to how we should proceed with each step in the therapeutic process. Mary appeared to be very comforted by this collaborative approach.

Establishing mutually agreed treatment goals and deciding to work together in carrying out the intervention are two examples of how the ERP programme was tailored to Mary. I thought that if this initial accommodation process had not occurred, Mary would have left treatment early. Of course, this initial tailoring process happened, in the first place, because of information obtained from Mary's CF.

As stated above, the functional analyses and behavioural formulation of Mary's OC behaviours were crucial templates that were used to accommodate the ERP to her. This tailoring process involved, firstly, the stimuli, detailed in the S–R–C contingencies, that signalled harm. Specifically, for each of her four problem areas, all stimuli involved in the relevant functional analysis were placed on a "hierarchy of horrors" (from 0 to 10). She was then exposed to each point on the hierarchy, in ascending order. As described above, it was hypothesised that contact with any stimulus that was listed in her functional analyses triggered a rule, which was: when I think that I may be responsible for irreparably harming myself or others, I must do everything that I can to prevent such harm from occurring; and, if I do not, then I will be responsible for any disaster that ensues. Whilst exposing herself to the "harmful" stimuli listed on the hierarchy, Mary was asked to concentrate on her rule, and especially the parts pertaining to responsibility for harm and perfection (the latter of which represented to her the part of the rule that stated, "I must do everything that I can to prevent such harm from occurring"). As can be seen, the functional analysis provided specific and thorough information as to the exact stimuli (both external and internal) that needed to be elicited during the ERP programme.

Of course, Mary's S–R–C contingencies also provided detailed information regarding her OC responses. During her ERP sessions, therefore, I was very clear as to what responses constituted Mary's OC behaviours, and I diligently targeted these for change. For example, based upon the home meeting that tested her functional analyses, we concluded that Mary's very slow movements were compulsive behaviours. Thus, during the ERP sessions, she was encouraged to "prevent" herself from moving slowly, by performing tasks (e.g., discarding items and unwrapping meat) more quickly. As indicated above, it is possible that, without the home meeting required by our CF approach, I would not have known about Mary's "slow motion" responses and, thus, would not have been able to have prevented them during the ERP sessions.

In the behavioural formulation, I hypothesised that Mary's OC behaviours had the almost immediate consequence of stopping her negative affect, and this consequence served to maintain her rule, via negative reinforcement. To shape a more helpful rule that could maintain more helpful behaviours, I added an additional technique to the ERP programme. I saw this technique as necessary, due not only to the behavioural formulation, but also due to the comment that Mary made whilst I obtained the developmental history of her problems. Specifically, as may be recalled, Mary stated that she was unhappy that her previous psychologist had "ignored" her thoughts. The technique that was employed to address Mary's behavioural formulation and her "ignoring my thoughts" comment is not specified in any known ERP manual; therefore, if any such manuals were being employed in a psychotherapy outcome study, this technique could not be used. Most clinicians, most of the time, however, are probably not engaged in outcome studies, and when they are not, it is possible to add on CF-consistent techniques to the manual-based treatment. Obviously, the contribution of any add-ons should be assessed, ideally by using a single case experimental design (Barlow and Hersen, 1984). However, it is unlikely that the additional technique will diminish the efficacy of the manual-based treatment. The add-on technique that was employed in Mary's case is now discussed.

A pleasant side-effect of the ERP programme was that Mary had more time to accomplish her current life goals that she had specified at the beginning of the initial interview (and which were noted above). The ERP freed up more time for Mary, because it prevented her from spending literally hours checking and cleaning. To demonstrate this pleasant consequence of response prevention to her, each ERP session ended by having Mary engage in a life goal (e.g., watching television, planning a story, or lunching with friends). I also asked her to engage in such goal-directed behaviour, after doing an ERP homework assignment, which she did alone or with her husband. I hoped that the positive reinforcement that she received from goal-directed behaviours would begin to shape a new rule that would trigger more helpful behaviours. Also, I hoped that this new rule could often "override" the OC rule that served to maintain her compulsive responses.

To facilitate the shaping of a new rule, Mary performed the following exercise. After participating in an ERP session and a goal-directed behaviour, she wrote down "what happened when [she] did not do her compulsive behaviours". Mary wrote down these consequences each day, and, once a week, she summarised them in a written statement. At the end of each month, she wrote down a summation of the four or five weekly statements, and, at the end of the therapy, she abstracted the monthly summaries. This very last summary was: "If I don't do my compulsive behaviours, I don't know if harm will occur, but I do know that I'll get to live my life as I want to." This summary was consistent with most of the other ones that she wrote. By having Mary focus on and write down the consequences of not performing her OC behaviours, I hoped that a new rule could be shaped (e.g., Catania, Matthews, and Shimoff, 1982) that would occasion helpful responses to "harmful" stimuli.

As can be seen, the CF informed me as to Mary's current life goals, and this information was used to develop positive reinforcement that could undermine the negative reinforcement that was hypothesised to maintain her unhelpful rule (which was, in turn, thought to maintain her OC behaviours). This example and the two previous ones in this section hopefully demonstrate how the rich data that are obtained from a CF can be used to mould a manual-based treatment to the particulars of an individual, and, thus, hopefully, increase the efficacy of a treatment.

USING STRATEGIES FROM MANUALS IN CF-BASED TREATMENTS

This chapter has maintained that manual-based treatments need to be tailored to individuals, and that CFs are ideally suited to guide this accommodation process. Thus, the focus of this chapter has been on how the latter therapeutic approach can be helpful to the former one. Although not the aim of this chapter, I should also mention briefly that treatment manuals can, perhaps, assist interventions that stem from a CF. Specifically, it is possible that techniques from empirically validated, manual-based treatments can improve the efficacy of CF-based treatments. For example, Linehan (1993a,b) has carefully described an empirically validated treatment manual for people who suffer from borderline personality disorder (BPD). After conducting a thorough CF, a clinician, who is treating a person with BPD, may find it advantageous to employ techniques from Linehan's protocol which are consistent with the CF. For, by doing so the clinician is implementing strategies that come from an empirically validated manual.

Alternatively, manuals such as Linehan's (1993a,b) can inform a clinician about techniques of which he or she was unaware. Thus, even if a clinician prefers to implement a specific set of techniques, he or she is still made cognisant of alternatives that can be used, if his or her "favourite" ones prove unsuccessful with some clients. In these two BPD examples, it is important to realise that the CF still guides the therapeutic process, but strategies that are consistent with the CF can be imported from treatment manuals.

I should stress that, just because particular therapeutic strategies are part of an empirically validated treatment manual, it does not then follow that these components are agents of helpful change. It could be that they are therapeutically inert and should be excluded from the manual. Nevertheless, if a clinician is employing a CF thoroughly, he or she will be monitoring, with valid and reliable measures, the client's progress (or lack thereof). Therefore, the clinician will be able to establish whether or not any manual-based technique, or set of techniques, is promoting desirable change. Hopefully, this section makes clear the hypothesis that techniques from empirically validated, manual-based treatments can improve the efficacy of CF-based treatments. Regrettably, there has been no empirical examination of this proposition.

SUMMARY

Since the empirical evidence regarding the relative efficacy of manual-based and CF-based treatments is equivocal, it appears too early to claim assuredly that one approach is more effective than the other one in treating psychological disorders. The goal of this chapter has not been to advocate for any one side in this on-going debate: research findings, themselves, will eventually be the best promoter for one the approaches, or some combination of the two. Rather, this chapter has sought to emphasise the utility of conducting case formulations, when employing manual-based treatments. It was argued that all nomothetic treatments must be accommodated, at least somewhat, to an individual client, and a CF provides a guide that can be used to obtain information that can facilitate this tailoring process. In fact, it was posited that, due to its emphasis on structured data collection and hypothesis testing, a CF is a tool that can best tailor a manual-based treatment to an individual. An empirical exploration of this hypothesis is hopefully forthcoming. Finally, this chapter suggested that techniques from empirically validated, manual-based treatments can improve the efficacy of CF-based treatments. This hypothesis, also, will hopefully soon receive empirical attention.

REFERENCES

American Psychiatric Association. (1994) *Diagnostic and Statistical Manual of Mental Disorders* (4th edn). Washington, DC: American Psychiatric Association.

Barlow, D.H. & Hersen, M. (1984) *Single Case Experimental Designs: Strategies for Studying Behavior Change* (2nd edn). New York: Pergamon.

Beck, A.T., Rush, J., Shaw, B. & Emery, G. (1979) *Cognitive Therapy of Depression*. New York: Guilford Press.

Bruch, M.H. & Meyer, V. (1993) The behavioural interview. *Psychopathologia*, **11**(3), 167–186.

Catania, A.C. (1995) Higher-order behavior classes: Contingencies, beliefs, and verbal behavior. *Journal of Behaviour Therapy and Experimental Psychology*, **26**(3), 191–200.

Catania, A.C., Matthews, B.A. & Shimoff, E. (1990) Properties of rule-governed behavior and their implications. In D.E. Blackman and H. Lejeune (Eds.), *Behaviour Analysis in Theory and Practice: Contributions and Controversies*. Hove: Lawrence Erlbaum Associates.

Catania, A.C., Shimoff, E. & Matthews, B.A. (1982) Instructed versus shaped human verbal behavior: Interactions with nonverbal responding. *Journal of the Experimental Analysis of Behavior*, **38**, 233–248.

Catania, A.C., Shimoff, E. & Matthews, B.A. (1989) An experimental analysis of rule-governed behavior. In S.C. Hayes (Ed.), *Rule-governed Behavior*. Nevada: Context Press.

Cone, J.D. (1997) Issues in functional analysis in behavioral assessment. *Behaviour Research and Therapy*, **35**(3), 259–275.

Davison, G.C. & Lazarus, A.A. (1995) The dialectics of science and practice. In S.C. Hayes, V.M. Follette, R.M. Dawes, and K.E. Grady (Eds.), *Scientific Standards of Psychological Practice: Issues and Recommendations*. Reno, NV: Context Press.

Emmelkamp, P.M.G., Bouman, T.K. & Scholing, A. (1992) *Anxiety Disorders: A Practitioner's Guide*. Chichester: John Wiley & Sons.

Fairburn, C.G., Marcus, M.D. & Wilson, G.T. (1993) Cognitive behaviour therapy for binge eating and bulimia nervosa: A comprehensive treatment manual. In C.G. Fairburn & G.T. Wilson (Eds.), *Binge Eating: Nature, Assessment and Treatment*. New York: The Guilford Press.

Foa, E.B., Steketee, G.S. & Ozarow, B. (1985) Behavior therapy with obsessive–compulsives: From theory to treatment. In M. Mavissakalin (Ed.). *Obsessive–Compulsive Disorder: Psychological and Pharmacological Treatment*. New York: Plenum Press.

Hayes, S.C. (1989) *Rule-governed Behavior*. Nevada: Context Press.

Hayes, S.C. (1995) *Acceptance and commitment therapy: A working manual*. Unpublished manual.

Hayes, S.C. & Hayes, L.J. (1989) The verbal action of the listener as the basis for rule-governance. In S.C. Hayes (Ed.), *Rule-governed Behavior*. Nevada: Context Press.

Hickling, E.J. & Blanchard, E.B. (1997) The private practice psychologist and manual-based treatments: A case study in the treatment of post-traumatic stress disorder secondary to motor vehicle accidents. *Behaviour Research and Therapy*, **27**, 191–203.

Linehan, M.M. (1993a) *Cognitive–Behavioral Treatment of Borderline Personality Disorder*. New York: The Guilford Press.

Linehan, M.M. (1993b) *Skills Training Manual for Treating Borderline Personality Disorder*. New York: The Guilford Press.

Malatesta, V.J. (1995) Technological behavior therapy for obsessive compulsive disorder: the need for adequate case formulation. *The Behavior Therapist*, **May**, 88–89.

Meyer, V. (1966). Modification of expectations in cases with obsessional rituals. *Behaviour Research and Therapy*, **4**, 273–280.

Meyer, V. & Turkat, I.D. (1979) Behavioural analysis of clinical cases. *Journal of Behavioural Assessment*, **1**, 259–269.

Poppen, R.L. (1989) Some clinical implications for rule-governed behavior. In S.C. Hayes (Ed.), *Rule-governed Behavior*. Nevada: Context Press.

Rachman, S. & Hodgson, R. (1980) *Obsessions and Compulsions*. Englewood Cliffs, NJ: Prentice-Hall.

Riggs, D.S. & Foa, E.B. (1993) Obsessive compulsive disorder. In D.H. Barlow (Ed.). *Clinical Handbook of Psychological Disorders* (2nd edn). New York: The Guilford Press.

Skinner, B.F. (1953) *Science and Human Behavior*. New York: The Free Press.

Skinner, B.F. (1974) *About Behaviorism*. London: Penguin Books.

Spielberger, C.D. (1983) State-trait Anxiety Inventory. Palo Alto, Ca: Mind Garden.

Turkat, I.D. (1979) The behaviour analysis matrix. *Scandinavian Journal of Behaviour Therapy*, **8**, 187–189.

Wilson, G.T. (1996) Manual-based treatments: The clinical application of research findings. *Behaviour Research and Therapy*, **34**, 295–315.

Wilson, G.T. (1997). Treatment manuals in clinical practice. *Behaviour Research and Therapy*, **15**(3), 205–210.

AUTHOR INDEX

SUBJECT INDEX

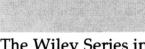

The Wiley Series in

CLINICAL PSYCHOLOGY

Ian H. Gotlib and Constance L. Hammen	Psychological Aspects of Depression: Toward a Cognitive-Interpersonal Integration
Max Birchwood and Nicholas Tarrier (Editors)	Innovations in the Psychological Management of Schizophrenia: Assessment, Treatment and Services
Robert J. Edelmann	Anxiety: Theory, Research and Intervention in Clinical and Health Psychology
Alastair Agar (Editor)	Microcomputers and Clinical Psychology: Issues, Applications and Future Developments
Bob Remington (Editor)	The Challenge of Severe Mental Handicap: A Behaviour Analytic Approach
Colin A. Espie	The Psychological Treatment of Insomnia
David Peck and C.M. Shapiro (Editors)	Measuring Human Problems: A Practical Guide
Roger Baker (Editor) (Editor)	Panic Disorder: Theory, Research and Therapy
Friedrich Fösterling	Attribution Theory in Clinical Psychology
Anthony Lavender and Frank Holloway (Editors)	Community Care in Practice: Services for the Continuing Care Client
John Clements	Severe Learning Disability and Psychological Handicap

Related titles of interest...

Outcome and Innovation in Psychological Management of Schizophrenia

Edited by Til Wykes, Nicholas Tarrier and Shôn Lewis

Provides an overview of the current innovative treatments: cognitive behaviour therapy, compliance therapy, family therapy and cognitive deficits remediation.

0-471-97659-8 304pp 1998 Hardback
0-471-97842-6 304pp 1998 Paperback

Cognitive Analytic Therapy for Borderline Personality Disorder

Anthony Ryle

The interventions illustrated here have been used to treat outpatients for 15 years. Results indicate that treatments can achieve clinically significant changes in the course of 16-24 sessions in a substantial proportion of patients.

0-471-97617-2 206pp 1997 Hardback
0-471-97618-0 206pp 1997 Paperback

Multiple Selves, Multiple Voices

Working with Trauma, Violation and Dissociation

Phil Mollon

Provides a clinically-based conceptal model and account of the therapeutic process with patients whose personalities are structured around trauma and pretence.

0-471-95292-3 228pp 1996 Hardback
0-471-96330-5 228pp 1996 Paperback

Cognitive Therapy for Delusions, Voices and Paranoia

Paul Chadwick, Max Birchwood and Peter Trower

Guides professionals towards a better practice by treating the individual symptoms of delusions, voices and paranoia, rather than by the categorization of schizophrenia.

0-471-93888-2 230pp 1996 Hardback
0-471-96173-6 230pp 1996 Paperback